The seventh volume of letters writ by a Turkish Spy, who lived five and forty years undiscovered at Paris:… The twenty-fourth edition. Volume 7 of 8

Giovanni Paolo Marana

PRINT EDITIONS

The seventh volume of letters writ by a Turkish Spy, who lived five and forty years undiscovered at Paris:... The twenty-fourth edition. Volume 7 of 8

Marana, Giovanni Paolo

ESTCID: T091591

Reproduction from British Library

V.1 is a translation of 'L'Esploratore turco .. ' by G.P. Marana originally published in Paris in 1684; subsequent volumes have been variously attributed, but were probably edited by Robert Midgley from William Bradshaw's translation of the original Itali

Dublin : printed for G. and A. Ewing, W. Smith, G. Faulkner, and R. James, 1754.

8v.,plate ; 12°

Eighteenth Century
Collections Online
Print Editions

Gale ECCO Print Editions

Relive history with *Eighteenth Century Collections Online*, now available in print for the independent historian and collector. This series includes the most significant English-language and foreign-language works printed in Great Britain during the eighteenth century, and is organized in seven different subject areas including literature and language; medicine, science, and technology; and religion and philosophy. The collection also includes thousands of important works from the Americas.

The eighteenth century has been called "The Age of Enlightenment." It was a period of rapid advance in print culture and publishing, in world exploration, and in the rapid growth of science and technology – all of which had a profound impact on the political and cultural landscape. At the end of the century the American Revolution, French Revolution and Industrial Revolution, perhaps three of the most significant events in modern history, set in motion developments that eventually dominated world political, economic, and social life.

In a groundbreaking effort, Gale initiated a revolution of its own: digitization of epic proportions to preserve these invaluable works in the largest online archive of its kind. Contributions from major world libraries constitute over 175,000 original printed works. Scanned images of the actual pages, rather than transcriptions, recreate the works *as they first appeared.*

Now for the first time, these high-quality digital scans of original works are available via print-on-demand, making them readily accessible to libraries, students, independent scholars, and readers of all ages.

For our initial release we have created seven robust collections to form one the world's most comprehensive catalogs of 18th century works.

Initial Gale ECCO Print Editions collections include:

History and Geography

Rich in titles on English life and social history, this collection spans the world as it was known to eighteenth-century historians and explorers. Titles include a wealth of travel accounts and diaries, histories of nations from throughout the world, and maps and charts of a world that was still being discovered. Students of the War of American Independence will find fascinating accounts from the British side of conflict.

Social Science

Delve into what it was like to live during the eighteenth century by reading the first-hand accounts of everyday people, including city dwellers and farmers, businessmen and bankers, artisans and merchants, artists and their patrons, politicians and their constituents. Original texts make the American, French, and Industrial revolutions vividly contemporary.

Medicine, Science and Technology

Medical theory and practice of the 1700s developed rapidly, as is evidenced by the extensive collection, which includes descriptions of diseases, their conditions, and treatments. Books on science and technology, agriculture, military technology, natural philosophy, even cookbooks, are all contained here.

Literature and Language

Western literary study flows out of eighteenth-century works by Alexander Pope, Daniel Defoe, Henry Fielding, Frances Burney, Denis Diderot, Johann Gottfried Herder, Johann Wolfgang von Goethe, and others. Experience the birth of the modern novel, or compare the development of language using dictionaries and grammar discourses.

Religion and Philosophy

The Age of Enlightenment profoundly enriched religious and philosophical understanding and continues to influence present-day thinking. Works collected here include masterpieces by David Hume, Immanuel Kant, and Jean-Jacques Rousseau, as well as religious sermons and moral debates on the issues of the day, such as the slave trade. The Age of Reason saw conflict between Protestantism and Catholicism transformed into one between faith and logic -- a debate that continues in the twenty-first century.

Law and Reference

This collection reveals the history of English common law and Empire law in a vastly changing world of British expansion. Dominating the legal field is the *Commentaries of the Law of England* by Sir William Blackstone, which first appeared in 1765. Reference works such as almanacs and catalogues continue to educate us by revealing the day-to-day workings of society.

Fine Arts

The eighteenth-century fascination with Greek and Roman antiquity followed the systematic excavation of the ruins at Pompeii and Herculaneum in southern Italy; and after 1750 a neoclassical style dominated all artistic fields. The titles here trace developments in mostly English-language works on painting, sculpture, architecture, music, theater, and other disciplines. Instructional works on musical instruments, catalogs of art objects, comic operas, and more are also included.

The BiblioLife Network

This project was made possible in part by the BiblioLife Network (BLN), a project aimed at addressing some of the huge challenges facing book preservationists around the world. The BLN includes libraries, library networks, archives, subject matter experts, online communities and library service providers. We believe every book ever published should be available as a high-quality print reproduction; printed on-demand anywhere in the world. This insures the ongoing accessibility of the content and helps generate sustainable revenue for the libraries and organizations that work to preserve these important materials.

The following book is in the "public domain" and represents an authentic reproduction of the text as printed by the original publisher. While we have attempted to accurately maintain the integrity of the original work, there are sometimes problems with the original work or the micro-film from which the books were digitized. This can result in minor errors in reproduction. Possible imperfections include missing and blurred pages, poor pictures, markings and other reproduction issues beyond our control. Because this work is culturally important, we have made it available as part of our commitment to protecting, preserving, and promoting the world's literature.

GUIDE TO FOLD-OUTS MAPS and OVERSIZED IMAGES

The book you are reading was digitized from microfilm captured over the past thirty to forty years. Years after the creation of the original microfilm, the book was converted to digital files and made available in an online database.

In an online database, page images do not need to conform to the size restrictions found in a printed book. When converting these images back into a printed bound book, the page sizes are standardized in ways that maintain the detail of the original. For large images, such as fold-out maps, the original page image is split into two or more pages

Guidelines used to determine how to split the page image follows:

• Some images are split vertically; large images require vertical and horizontal splits.
• For horizontal splits, the content is split left to right.
• For vertical splits, the content is split from top to bottom.
• For both vertical and horizontal splits, the image is processed from top left to bottom right.

THE
SEVENTH VOLUME
OF
LETTERS

Writ by a

Turkish Spy,

Who lived Five and Forty YEARS
undiscovered at

PARIS:

Giving an impartial ACCOUNT to the *Divan* at
Constantinople of the most remarkable Transactions of
Europe: And discovering several *Intrigues* and *Secrets*
of the *Christian Courts*, (especially of that of *France*)
continued from the Year 1642, to the Year 1682

Written Originally in Arabick *Translated into* Italian,
and from thence it to English, *by the Translator of the*
First Volume

The TWENTY-FOURTH EDITION.

DUBLIN
Printed for G. and A. EWING, W. SMITH,
G. FAULKNER and R. JAMES,
M DCC LIV.

TO THE

READER.

 T is not to be expected, that the World will take it for an Excuse of the tedious Delay has been made in publishing the VIIth Volume of the *Turkish Spy*, to say, that our *Arabian* now grows Old and Decrepit, is forced to walk with a Staff or Crutch, as he himself confesses in one of the following *Letters*; and is besides worn out with Sickness and Care; so that he cannot be so expeditious in

Business

Bufinefs as he was in his Youth. It may be faid, this Apology would be more proper for the *Englifh Tranflator* to make, were he in the fame Condition. But he is in his Prime, in the Flower of his Age, Vigorous and Active; and therefore might have made more Hafte, they will fay, to oblige the World, and gratify the Expectations of thofe Gentlemen who perpetually dun the *Bookfellers* for the reft of his *Mahometan* Letters.

It were eafy to anfwer this, by only putting you in Mind, that he who undertakes to lead a flow-footed, fhort-winded, and weak Perfon by the Hand, and conduct him to his Journey's End, muft of Neceffity keep the fame Pace with his Charge, tho' he himfelf

were

were fwift as a Stag, when alone and at Liberty. Befides that, a Man is apt to attract a Contagion from the Company he keeps, and turn their ill Qualities into Habits of his own.

But all this is trifling, and our *Englifh* Tranflator is under none of thefe Circumftances. To come to the Purpofe therefore, Gentlemen, you will commend our *Tranflator's* Wifdom, for not being in fuch *Poft-Hafte* at this Juncture, when you reflect, that like a wife *Racer*, tho' he gave a Start in the Beginning, at firft fetting out, yet he foon flackened his Pace, that he might make fure of the *Goal*, remembring the Old *Englifh Proverb, The more the Hafte the worfe Speed.* Thus he fuffered three Years to flide by him,

him, before he reached the *Second*

2d *Vol.* *Stage.* And tho' he began to take up his heels more nimbly afterwards, so as to recover by Degrees his lost Time and Ground, yet still he did but moderately jog on; now springing, then halting, as Occasion offered, and as he found his Strength could hold. At length having but two *Stages* more, wonder not, that he is a little more tedious than ordinary in this: For he does it to refresh himself, and keep his *Breath* for the last Strain of all, which brings the Prize: Observing herein the *Old Adage,* *Finis coronat Opus.*

As to the *Letters* contained in this Seventh *Volume,* there is little to be said more particular than of those that have gone before. They

To the READER.

They in general contain a Miscellany of *Historical* Transactions, *Moral* and *Philosophical* Thoughts, interspersed here and there with *Mahometan Politicks* and *Divinity*.

Only you will find our *Arabian* engaged with a certain *Jew* at *Vienna*, in fomenting the *Discords* of the *German Empire*, encouraging the *Rebels* of *Hungary*, *Croatia*, and mutinous *Provinces*. You will hear of the *Deaths* of *Count Serini*, *Frangipani*, and *Nadasti*, who were all beheaded for being Ringleaders in this *Rebellion*.

The next and last *Volume* has this of singular in it, that it will present you with the Rise and Preferment of *Count Teckeley*, who has made so much Noise in the World. It relates many of his

Publick

To the READER.

Publick Actions, and not a few of his Secret Intrigues. In fine, it discovers the Train that was laid to blow up all *Europe* into the Flame of open War, and universal Hostility, which to this Day consumes the Lives and Estates of so many thousand *Christians*, impoverishes and lays waste whole Nations, and it is to be feared will end in letting in the *Turks* once more upon us to our final Ruin and Confusion; since those *Infidels* never take greater Advantage to invade and conquer the *Dominions* of *Christians*, than when they find us involved in domestick Wars one with another.

A TA-

A
TABLE
OF THE
LETTERS and MATTERS
contained in this VOLUME.

VOL. VII.

BOOK I.

LETTER I.

b   III.

The TABLE.

                                               XII. *To*

The TABLE.

The TABLE

The TABLE

BOOK II.

LETTER I.

Y.

The TABLE

Of

The TABLE.

BOOK

The TABLE

BOOK III.

LETTER I

The TABLE.

BOOK

The TABLE.

BOOK IV.

LETTER I.

The TABLE.

The TABLE.

LETTERS

LETTERS

Writ by a

SPY at *PARIS*.

VOL. VII.

BOOK I

LETTER I

Mahmut the Arabian *at* Paris, *to* Mirmado-lin, Holy Santone *of the* Vale *of* Sidon.

WHY was I made a Man to endure thefe cruel Agonies, of which no other *Species* of known *Beings* can poffibly be capable? Or why, at leaft, was I particularly formed of fuch a Conftitution, as to attract the Evils which are fcattered up and down the World, and *Piece-meal* dropped on the *Nativities* of other Mortal Men, whilft I alone am made the common fink of Human Mifery? Surely my partial *Horofcope* monopolized the moft envenom-ed afpects of the *Stars*, without partaking of the leaft benign and favourable Glance The Planets had laid up an ancient deep Referve of fatal *Influences,* which they poured out at large upon the very Moment of my Birth Nor could the careful *Midwife* with all her

Skill and Charms, defend my tender ductile, reeking Body, from the invincible *Cabals*, which flowed upon me from all the envious *Signs* and *Constellations* in *Heaven*

My whole Life has been but one continued Tragedy wherein the various Change of *Scenes* hath not relieved me from the least real Evil hid behind, but only amused my Sense with some new Pageantry, some fair *Idea* of Honour, Pleasure or Profit, When before the *ACT* was done, I found my self cajoled, overwhelmed in fresh Calamities, Misfortunes which I never dreamed of

Oh! that the *Omnipotent*, when from eternal silent Thought, he drew the *Ideas* of every *Species*, and every Individual *Being*, which he designed for actual Existence in the World, had formed me for a Tree, an Herb, a Blade of Grass, a Stone, a Mushroom, or any insensible thing, incapable of Pleasure or Pain, of Grief or Joy, or other Passions, which hourly thus torment our human Race I had been then a happy Neuter to all false Shews of Happiness, and real Sense of Misery Oh! that I had been an Oak, a Beech, a Palm, or Cypress of the Forest For then, if *Vegetables* have any feeling of their own State, I should be only touched with secret Pleasure, when the gentle Winds should play among my amorous Branches, and teach my wanton Leaves to dance the Measures of young harmless Love, or when I felt the seasonable Rain distilling on my withered Bark, and from thence sliding to my thirsty Roots, or when great *Phœbus* prints warm vigorous Kisses on my Cheeks and Neck But if this be too proud a Thought, I wish I had been only some humble Shrub, some Pigmy Plant, some vegetable Dwarf, Page unto the mighty Trees, subsisting on the Drops and Fragments of their large Banquets, meekly clinging at their Feet, whilst I stood safe and free from Storm under the Shade of their extended Boughs, in happy low, Obscurity

When I pass through the Fields, and see the harmless Sheep browzing upon their tender Grass, and hear the bleating to their wanton Lambs, I cannot chuse but er

vy them a Life so void of Care and Pain They range
and sport at large in Flowery Meadows near some
Crystal Stream, or take the Pastures of the Mountains :
whilst chearful Shepherds tune their Pipes, and sing in
Praise of *Amaryllis, Daphne, Sylvia,* or some other
Nymph , and watchful Dogs lie scouting on the Plain,
to give the Alarm, and chase away sly Wolves, and
other ravenous Beasts

After I have let my Envy fix itself a while on these,
a warbling Melody from neighbouring Groves divert-
eth my melancholy Thoughts, and turneth them to
new Objects Then I lament my Fate in that I was not
made a Nightingal, a Thrush, a Lark, or any of the
feather'd Choir, who with sweet chearful Notes salute
Aurora and the rising *Sun,* and chirp all Day the Prai-
ses of that Source of Warmth and Life who vesteth the
Earth in green Attire, who decketh the Trees with verdant Leaves, and filleth the World with Light They
chirp and fly from Tree to Tree, from Bough to Bough,
rejoicing in the Beams that dart and glide among the
moving Shades of Branches rocked by Winds Their
Thoughts are taken up in building Nests, wherein to
hatch their young, and shelter them from Injuries They
have no Plots nor Politick Tricks, to undermine each
other , but pass away their Time in innocent Security
and harmless Pleasures

Methinks the Worms and little Reptiles of the Earth
are happier far than I They crawl and creep about
in hollow Trees, in Clefts of Rocks and Crannies
of the Ground to hunt for Food and for Divertisement.
They live at Ease without being racked by supernu-
merary Cares and Fears And if some ruder Foot of
Man or Beast shall trample them by Chance to Death,
or more malicious Hand with Stone or other Weapon
shall wilfully bereave them of their Life, it is done so
suddenly that they have no Sense of Pain , Whereas my
Life is a constant Martyrdom, a long continued Series
of Torments.

I de

I do not complain of the Distempers and Maladies which afflict my *Body*, altho' those are sometimes so violent as to make me wish for Death, that so I might be at Ease But it is the fretting Anguish of my Mind, that forceth all the Sighs and Exclamations from me I am embarrassed in the World Snares compass me round about, my own good Nature has betrayed me those of my *Blood* conspire against me, they hunt me up and down like a *Partridge* in the Wood, the closely pursue my Life The Kindnesses that I have sown, spring up in my Blades of bitter Ingratitude and Perfd, My *Seminaries* bring forth *Aconite* and stinking Weeds, instead of pleasant Flowers and wholsome Fruits *Tagot* hath set his Foot in all my Works.   That sly interloping *Spirit* hateth to see any good Thing prosper, or come to Perfection He stealeth behind us in all our Ways, and as fast as we weave any Web of *Virtue*, he secretly unravelleth it, or deformeth the Work with intermixing some Threads of *Vice* I am weary of striving against the Current of my *Fate* O! that I were as though I had never been! That my Soul were drenched in *Lethe*'s forgetful Waters, where all past Things are buried in eternal Oblivion! Then would my Anguish be at an End, whereas I am now rowled about upon a Wheel of Miseries

Holy *Santone*, when thou shalt read this, pity me, and amidst thy divine Ejaculations dart up *Mohmut*'s Soul to *Paradise*, on the Point of a strong Thought, that so at least I may have a Moment's Respite from my constant Sadness.

Paris, *27th of the 2d Moon,*
  of the Year 1667

LETTER II.

To the Kaimacham.

THERE is now some Probability of a *Peace* between the *Engly* and the *Dutch* which will also reconcile this *Crown* to that of *Great-Britain* since the *King* of *France* engaged in this *War*, only on the Account of the *Dutch* his *Allies* The *Advances* towards this Accommodation, took their Rise from the *Alliance* lately concluded between the *States* of the *United Provinces*, the *King* of *D ark*, the *Duke* of *Brandenburgh*, and the *Princes* of *Brunswick* The King of *England* protesteth against the *Dutch*, as the first Aggressors, in that they had taken above two hundred of his Merchant Ships before he offered the least Act of *Hostility* Which the *States* seeming to acknowledge, desire the King to appoint some Neutral Place of *Treaty* with them and their *Allies* in Order to a *Peace*, the Security of Navigation, and the Establishment of Commerce for the future

Here is great Joy for the Birth of a young *Princess* of whom the Queen was deliver'd on the 2d of the *Moon* of *January* She is call'd *God's New Year's-Gift to France*; in regard, the first Day of that *Moon* begins the Year with the *Christians*. And it is common among them to send mutual Gifts and Presents to one another at that Time, which they call *New Year's Gifts* And so it seems, *God Almighty* has appeared very Modish and Complaisant in thus timing the Nativity of the *Royal* Babe. For which they express their Thanks in revelling, Dancing, Ballads, and a thousand other Vanities And these Divertisements continue to this Time, it being the *Nazaranes Carnival*, a Season consecrated to Sport and Mirth, to Liberty, Buffoonry and all manner of comical and ridiculous Apishness

During this Time, you shall see an infinite Variety of odd Humours, and mimical Actions in the open Streets according to every Man's particular Fancy Here you shall meet with one dressed half in the *F ench* and half in the *Span sh* Fashion On the left side of his Head hangs dangling down a long thick curled Peruke, which reaches to his Breast, while on the Right you see nothing but his own Hair croped close to his Ears A long Mustach as black as Jet, graces the Right Side of his upper Lip, whilst on the Left, he is as beardless as a Boy of seven Years old And so from Head to Foot, he wears two contrary Garbs One walks with Gloves upon his Feet, and Shoes upon his Hands Another wears his Breeches like a Mantle on his Shoulders Here comes a stately Coach, jogging along with a grave slow Pace and drawn by Six fair Horses, as if some *Prince* or *Cardinal* were in it when behold there is nothing but a silly *Ass* puts forth his giddy head with flapping Ears, half drunk with the jolting unaccustomed Motion Sometimes he brays aloud, and then the Rabble fall a laughing A thousand other Fopperies there are, not worth thy Knowledge For both the Noble and the Vulgar are all upon the Frolick at this Time, and indulge their wanton Fancies to the Height But it is a fatal Season for the poor *Cats* ; few of which escape the Multitude, whose peculiar Pastime it is to toss these Creatures in a Blanket till they are dead, or else to tye them two and two together by the Tails, and then they will bite and scratch one another to Death, The *Cocks* also are generally great Martyrs during the *Carnival* ? The Rabble have a hundred cruel Ways to murder them in Sport All their Devices are inhuman and bloody They did not learn these prophane Courses from *Jesus*, or any of the *Prophets* or *Apostles* of God But they are the Reliques of *Gentile* Vanity, in the Beginning connived at by the *Priests* the easier to retain their Proselytes in Obedience, who would rather have parted with their New *Religion*, than with their old barbarous Customs And thus the Pagan Fooleries were handed down to the Posterity of the *Primitive Christians*, and were adopted into the Family of *Church Traditions* And Men are not more zealous for the *Gospel* it self, than for these ridiculous Prophanations of it So dangerous a Thing it is for Governors, by a

criminal

crimin il Indulgence, to permit their *Subjects* any Liber-ty which interferes with the *Fundamental Principles* of the *Law* for such a Dispensation once granted passeth into a credent, which in Process of Time, becometh of equ l force with the Law it self   And by such pre-posterous Methods of winning and retaining Converts, Christianity arrived to the Height of Corruption it is now infected with

Sage *Minister*, it was for this Reason *God* raised up our *Holy Prophet* and gave him a new Law, with Power to reform and chastise the *Infidels*   He planted the *Undefiled Faith* with Scymetar in Hand, not palliating or encouraging the smallest vicious Practice, but subduing all Things by the Dint of Reason, or the keen Edge of the Sword.   *God* hasten his Return, for the Prevarica-tions of this Age require it

Paris, *27th of the 2d Moon,*
  of the Year 1667.

LETTER III.

To Dgnet Oglou.

I Believe thou hast not forgot the Observations we used to make on the *Religion* of the *Christians,* when we were Slaves together in *Sicily*   How ridiculous some of their Practices appeared to us, and yet what a Sanctity was manifest in other.? How much we approved the *Majesty* of their *publick Worship,* the *Solemnity* of their *High Mass,* the *Gravity* of their *Processions?* And yet how great was our Disgust, when we considered that all these Honours were performed to Figures and Statues of Stone, Wood, Silver, Gold, or other Materials, the *Creatures* of the *Painter* or *Carver?*

We scanned their *Doctrines* also, which we learned from their *Priests* and *Books,* and descanted variously on them, as they were more or less conform to the Truth, and to

the

the *Volume* brought down from *Heaven* In a word, we praised the Good, and censured what was Evil in their *Faith* and *Manners*, or at least what we thought to be so , for herein we followed the Dictates of our Education

But now in our riper Years, if we should call over our former Thoughts, perhaps we should be of a different Judgment and find Matter to condemn even in our own past Censures For whatever we might then think of the *Nazarenes*, upon a maturer Search, I cannot find them to be altogether such gross *Idolaters* and *Infidels*, as we and all *Mussulmans*, are apt to believe

That which gives me the greatest Scandal is, That the *Doctors* entertain some unwarrantable Speculations about *Three Substances* in *One Essence*, and are too venturous in their Thoughts concerning the *Eternal Generation* of the WORD, and *Emanation* of the BREATH, by which they say, *All Things* were *Created*, and are conserved in their *Beings* They teach a *Doctrine* repugnant to the *Alcoran*, when they say, That *God has a Companion equal to himself*

As to the *Incarnation* of *Jesus* the *Son* of *Mary*, the *Nazarenes* assert nothing, but what is suitable to the *Alcoran*, which teaches us, that he is the WORD of *God* In the *History* of his *Life*, they indeed come short of the *Mussulmans* There being not the least mention made, in the whole *Book* of the *Gospel*, of many Passages of his Infancy and tender Years, wherewith the *Alcoran*, with other *Holy Books* and *Traditions* of the *devout*, acquaint the true Believers The *Message* of *God* tells us, that *Jesus* spoke in his Cradle, resolved Doubts, cleared up Mistakes, and preached the *Unity* of the *Divine Essence* Other *Writings* also inform us, that while he was young, he formed the Figures of divers Birds and Beasts of Clay and his own *Species*, and having breathed on them they became living Creatures, and prostrated themselves at his Feet They relate also that he made a *Pigeon*, which flew up and down through divers Regions, and brought him News of whatever was done in the *Courts* of *foreign Princes*, and that from the Day

of his *Birth* to that of his *Translation*, twelve *Angels*
waited on him, and brought him down Food from *Paradise*. Of these things the *Christians* are ignorant, and
of many other Passages So that in the whole it is evident, that the *Mussulmans* have a more particular Relation of the *Life of Jesus*, than the *Christians* themselves
have, since we recount those Miracles, and other Actions of his, whereof the *Gospel* is silent

But then, on the other side, they believe Things
concerning his Death, whereof neither the *Alcoran*, nor
any other of our *Writings* or *Traditions* make any mention, unless it be to confute the Error of the *Nazarenes*
in that Point I have heard the Arguments of their
learned *Doctors*, and comparing them with our Objections, I know not well what to conclude

They insist much on the publick Signs and Wonders,
that fell out at that Time of the supposed *Crucifixion* of
the *Messiah*, the rending of Rocks opening of Graves,
Resurrection of many Dead, and the preter-natural Eclipse of the *Sun*, when the *Moon* was in sight in the
other Part of the *Horizon* at the same Moment :
Which made a great *Philosopher* then in *Egypt*, cry out,
Either the Frame of the World is dissolved, or the GOD *of
Nature suffers.*

They tell a Story also of a certain Ship, that was,
on that very Day sailing in the *Archipelago*, and that as
they passed by certain Rocks, the Mariners heard a
Voice calling *Thamus, Thamus,* very often and loud.
Now there being one of that Name on board the Vessel, he answered to his Name Upon which the Voice
said, *When thou comest to the Island of the* Palodes, *proclaim it aloud, that the* great Pan *is dead* Which he did
accordingly, and there followed a horrible Howling
and Roaring from the Shore of that Island This Passage was afterwards made known to the *Senate* of *Rome*,
who thereupon, at the Instance of some noble *Romans*,
sent to enquire in the *Provinces*, Whether any remarkable Person had died on that Day ? And they were informed, That the *Jews* had on the same Day put to
Death *Jesus* the Son of *Mary*. And *Tiberius* the Emperor,

ror, on the Credit of this Paffage, being alfo informed of the Miracles which *Jefus* wrought among
the *Jews*, conceiving an immediate Veneration for fo
divine a Perfon, caufed his *Statue* to be fet up in the
Capitol, and would have had him numbered among the
Gods, but in this he was oppofed by the *Senate*, becaufe they had before decreed, That no new *Deities*
fhould be added to the *Kalendar*

In thefe things I rely on the Account which the *Chriftians* give of the *Death* of *Jefus* though they bring Au-
thorities alfo and Teftimonies of their very Enemies,
and inveterate Perfecutors, the *Gentiles*, who therefore,
one would think, cannot be fufpected of Partiality In
a word, I know not what to think of thefe Things For
if it be true that *Jefus* died on the *Crofs* for the *Sins* of
the *World*, as the *Chriftians* believe, and that there is
no other Way to be faved but by believing this, then
in what a fad Condition are all the *Jews* and *Mufulmans*, the one glorying in having murdered the *Saviour*
of the *World*, and the other not believing that he was
murdered ? The firft feem to merit moft of Men, fince
tho' the Act was cruel in itfelf yet according to this
Doctrine it brought *Salvation* to all our *Race* And therefore there were a Sort of *Chriftians* in former Times,
who worfhipped the Serpent that tempted *Eve*, becaufe
according to their *Faith*, that Temptation was the firft
Step to *Mankind's* Happinefs after *Adam's* Fall, and
they placed *Judas* (who betrayed *Jefus* to the *Jews*)
among the *Saints*, for having been fo particular an Inftrument in the World's Redemption

If *Jefus* be the *Saviour* of Men, it is abfolutely neceffary to believe in him   But whether he be, or be
not, the Faith of the *Chriftians* in that Point cannot
hurt them, fince our *Holy Prophet* himfelf has taught
us, That *Chriftians* fhall be faved, as well as the *Mufulmans* Whereas the *Chriftians* fay it is impoffible for
any to be faved, who follow the Law of *Mahomet* So
that they have our own Grant for their Salvation, which
they deny to us   This is a great Advantage on their
Side in the Controverfy betwixt us.

For my part, I tell thee ingenuously, were I convinced that *Jesus* was the Son of GOD, and that he suffered Death for the Sake of Men, I could readily embrace most of the other *Tenets* of *Christianity* without Scruple, I should not be frighted at their *Invocation* of *Saints* since it is the same as we do our selves practise, nor would their *Images* and *Pictures* startle my *Faith*, I should look upon these and a thousand more, as Things indifferent in themselves, and only made lawful or unlawful by the Sanction of *Divine Authority*

I should be most puzzled to know what *Church* to fix in among so many, all pretending to the right Way, I have examined their different Opinions, and find Reason or something very like it, on both Sides I admire the *Abstinence* of the *Greeks*, *Armenians*, and generally of all the *Eastern Christians*, yet their Ignorance disgusts me I honour the *Learning* and *Politeness* of the *Roman Church*, and could almost vail to their Pretensions of *Antiquity*, *Catholicity*, and *incorrupt Doctrine*, but I am highly scandalized at their *Licentiousness*, *Pride*, and *Cruelty* There is much to be argued for the *Copts*, *Abyssins*, *Maronites*, the *Christians* of St *John*, and other *Churches*, but more to be said against them In fine, if I were to turn *Christian* I should be in a Wilderness, not knowing which Path to take, for fear of missing the right

In the State therefore wherein I am, I will think honourably of *Jesu*, as also of *Mary*, his Mother, who, at her daily Return from the *Temple*, found a thousand Sorts of Flowers in her Oratory I will not speak evil of any Person that has the Character of a *Saint*; but in general, will decline the Intercession of all that are near to GOD, t'is ten to one, if some of them do not vouchsafe to pray for me But whether they do or not, GOD hears me, and observes my Devotion, and if he please, my Petitions shall be granted As for the rest, I will endeavour in all things *to do as I would be done to*, keeping my Conscience free from Stain, so that I may die in Peace, and what becomes of me afterward, it is in vain to be solicitous, since the Decrees of *Fate* are irrevocable.   Tell

'Tell me now, my Friend, whether thefe Thoughts and Refolves be not more agreeable to Humanity, than to be a furious *Bigot* for I know not what   Is *that* a commendable Zeal for *Religion*, which under pretence of defending the Truth, flicks not to affert a thoufand Lies ? Or *that* a laudable Charity for Souls, which in order to their Salvation takes infinite Pains to fet the World together by the Ears, and embroil Mankind in perpetual Wars ? What elfe do thofe Difturbers of human Race, who not content with the Limits which the Fortune of their Birth has fet them, invade the peaceable Poffeffions of their Neighbours, commit all Sorts of Violences, Rapine, and Outrages, and all this under Pretext of reforming the Manners of Men, introducing Purity of *Religion*, and fulfilling the Will of *Heaven* ? As if it were a Mark of a Divine Commiffion, to be barbaroufly unjuft perfidious, and favage, and that the Height of Piety confifted in fhedding human Blood !

For my part I cannot approve of thefe Practices, and therefore think it fafer to ftand aloof from all *Religions* thus crue ly eftablifhed, than by entring into their inhuman Secrets, and fwearing to their fanguine Articles, incorporate my felf with profeffed Murderers, under the Notion of being a good Man

Happy are thofe innocent *Nations* of the *Eaft*, who from their firft Progenitors have kept inviolate the *Law* of *Nature*, who have never defiled themfelves with the *Blood* of Man or Beaft, but every one contenting himfelf with his native Home ftall, and the Fruits of his own Land, makes no Encroachments on thofe that dwell near him, nor butchers the harmlefs *Animals* to gratify his ill natured Appetite   Thefe fit under the Shade of their own Trees, and bath themfelves in the adjoining Stream, They go in Peace into the Houfes of their *Rural Gods*, and prefent them with Flowers, Rice, Fruits, and fuch as the Ground bringeth forth They never dream of foreign Conquefts, nor are troubled with domeftick Broils, but lead their Lives in a perpetual Tranquillity and Innocence   All that they defire of *Heaven*, is the Continuance of thofe harmlefs Delights

Delights the at prefent enjoy As for the tumultuary Pleafures of other Mortals, they have them in Contempt This is an Umbrage of the Felicity we are promifed in *Paradife*, where the Sound of the Drum and the Trumpet fhall not be hard, and the Inftruments of War fhall be of no Ufe

If thou chargeft me with Inconftancy in my Opinions, I neither deny it, nor am afhamed, it being better to change one's Thoughts every Day than to be fixed in Error all one's Life This to a Friend

Paris, 18*th of the* 3*d Moon,
of the Year* 1567.

LETTER IV

To Afis, Baffa.

THE Warriors and Mechanicks, Statefmen and Fidlers, Courtiers and Hufbandmen, Students and Chimney fweepers, are all taken up in difcourfing of the mighty Preparations the *Grand Signior* is making to befiege *Candia* They talk of fifteen thoufand *Pionec*, who are at work in order to this grand Undertaking, and that the City is blocked up by an Army of fixty thoufand Men That they have been raifing Batteries round about it ever fince the *Moon* of *December*, and that the *Sultan* is refolved to win this important Place, though he hazard half the *Ottoman Empire*.

This is refrefhing News to *Marmut*, who has heard nothing but improfperous Stories of the *Muffulmans* Arms thefe many Years Now I begin to lift up my Head and take Courage, when the *Empire* of *True Believers* makes fome Noife and Figure in the World whereas my Heart perpetually drooped before, I was like one among the Dead

It was but laft Year when the *Nazarenes* could boaft, That notwithftanding all the Menaces and Preparations

of

of the *Grand Signior*, yet the *Venetians* were the first in Field by *Land*, and appeared earliest with their Fleet at *Sea*, doing wonderful Things in *Dalmatia*, and blocking up *Carca* in the Isle of *Carly* Now it is to be hoped, they will change their Note, and begin to consider what a formidable Force they have provoked against them, even the Puissance of all *sia*, Men of *War* from their Nativities, an Army of select and chosen Soldiers, undaunted *Foot*, Sons of Thunder, magnanimous, invincible, and destined to vanquish the *uncircumcised* Nations

My Heart is revived within me at the Contemplation of sure and certain Victories, attending this glorious Expedition my Spirits are dilated with Joy, I celebrate a *Dunalma* in my Breast I am like an *Arabian* Horse, that foams, curvets, and paws the Ground in Fierceness, when he hears the Sound of the Trumpet, warning to Battle, his Eyes sparkle with martial Fire, a Smoak goes out of his Nostrils, he lifts up the Voice of his Courage, his Rider can hardly restrain him So I am all in Transport at these good Tidings I can hardly contain my self within the Compass of Moderation As old as I am, I feel a youthful Vigor stirring in my Veins, Methinks I long to be in the Heat of the *sacred* Combat, in the thickest Clouds of Gunpowder Smoak, to stand the Shock of Showers of Bullets, or with my Scymetar in hand to hew my Way to immortal Honour and Felicity For those who die in this Cause go strait to *Paradise* But I must be contented with this tame humble *Post*, and serve the *Grand Signior* in the Manner prescribed by my Superiors I tell thee, it is no small Mortification for an active Spirit to be thus confined But Refignation becomes every good *Mussulman*, and I willingly sacrifice my Passions to the Pleasure of the *Grandees* of the *Porte*, and the Interest of the *Ottoman Empire*

Here I sit, like a *Fox* in his Den, watching the Motions of the *Infidel* If any thing occurs worthy of Notice, out I bolt upon it, and make it my Prey, and send it as a *Present* to the august Ministers. I write to

all

all by turns, and therefore none has Reason to take Exceptions

If thou wouldeſt know what they are doing here in the *Court* of *France*, They are muſtering the *King's* Troops, they are revelling and feaſting at *Verſailles* the King's new Palace, where the Princes exerciſe themſelves with the noble Diſcipline, which they call *running in Squadrons*.   Whilſt Thouſands of People flock daily to *Verſailles* from *Paris* and all the adjacent Countries round about, partly to be Spectators of theſe Royal Paſtimes, and partly to behold that gorgeous Fabrick, which is eſteemed the faireſt and moſt magnificent in the World

Serene *Baſſa*, this Monarch has a vaſt *Genius*, whatſoever he undertakes he accompliſhes, and all his Performances are ſurprizingly great   He has a deep Forecaſt, and ſeldom fails in his Judgment of what will probably come to paſs   He is happy in do, born, and brought up   A Prince, one would think, deſigned by *Fate* for the *Empire* of the *Weſt*

Renowned *Aſir*, I kiſs the Hem of thy illuſtrious Robe, and with a profound Obeiſance bid thee Adieu

Paris, 20th of the 4th Moon,
of the Year, 1667

LETTER V

To Haſnadar-Baſſi, *chief Treaſurer to the* Sultan

IAM convinced it is now time for me to be reſolute, bold, and aſſured in my own Conduct   For it is in vain to aſk Counſel of the *ſublime Miniſters*   I have addreſſed my ſelf at certain Seaſons to them on that account, ever ſince I came firſt to *Paris*   But not one of them has vouchſafed me an Anſwer, or given me any particular Inſtructions how to deport my ſelf in an emergent Peril of Diſcovery   Whether I ſhould own my ſelf an *Agent* for the *Grand Signior*, or deny it, whether I ſhould boldly ſtand the Brunt of all Events,

or

or fly to Artifices and Evasions, whether I should per-
sist in acting the *Moldavian*, and continue to personate
a *Christian Student*, an *Ecclesiastical Candidate* under the
feign'd Name of *Titus*, or frankly tell them I am a
Mussulman, an *Arab*, and secret *Slave* of the *Sultan*

I ought to have been certified in these Cases, and
not left at Random to guess, at this vast Distance, the
Pleasures of my *Superiors* But since it is their Will
thus to make tryal of my Fidelity, Prudence and Skill
in warding off the Assaults of common Chance, Misfortune, and the Attempts of sly designing Men, I will
be as cunning as I can, without embarassing my Peace
with constant panick Fears and apprehensions of I know
not what No vain Endeavours to avoid the fixed Decree of *Fate* shall make me change my *Lodging*, or fly
from every menacing Contingency. I will rather trust
to *Providence* and present Courage, the Justice of my
Cause and Native Innocence leaving the Event to *Destiny*

By what I have said, thou wilt perceive I am in some
Trouble, and I can assure thee thou art not mistaken
I am hattered, hunted up and down, and persecuted
worse than the Foxes, Hares, and Hinds near *Adria-*
nople, I am an old Man, and yet they envy me the
Happness of a natural Death, they would not have
me go down to the Grave in Peace I have been imprisoned, threatened, dogged up and down the Streets,
assassinated in the dark, had my Chamber searched,
my Letters in danger of being seized, with those of
the *Supreme Ministers* I have run the risque of a Discovery, by meeting casually an *Infidel*, whose *Slave* I
once was at *Palermo* in *Sicily* I have been undermined by *Mussulmans*, as well as *Nazarenes*, by Strangers,
and by *Solyman* my *Cousin* Yet in all these Perils I
have acquitted my self faithfully, come off with Success,
and saved the Honour of my *Sovereign*, which is the
only Thing for which I am solicitous But for ough.
I know, my Care may prove in vain, and the Evils
which I have so long fortunately escaped, may now
surprize and ruin me As to my self, I care not what
becomes of me, and if the *Secrets* of my *Commission* be
revealed,

revealed, let the *Ministers* of the *Port* answer for that, who would never give me the least Direction

About two or three Years ago, I was forced to remove from my old *Lodgings*, where I had resided ever since my first coming to *Paris* The Dangers that then assaulted me, drove me to this House, where I still am, in a very obscure Place by the Wall of the City. Yet even hither am I pursued by watchful Enemies New Hazards threaten me on all Hands But I am resolved to fly no more, unless it be into the *City Ditch*, where I can find Admittance through my *Landlord*s Cellar. There is a private Passage, dug perhaps in elder Times, during some Siege, to serve the streight Necessities of those who then possessed this House It is so cunningly contrived, that human Wit can never discover it, unless by Chance, or by Direction of those that know it The Ditch is dry, the Door of the House always lock'd, and my trusty *Host* swears no body shall come in by Day or Night, till I have made a safe Retreat So that if all the *Officers* in *Paris* should come to search, I should have time to pack up my Papers, and slink away into my lurking Hole. And if they should by monstrous Accident find the concealed Avenue, I could soon slip into the Fields through the last *Postern* in the Wall and lock them in beyond the Possibility of Pursuit, whilst I took care to hide my self afresh, or leave the *Country*.

This is my final Resolution, if ever I am put to an Extremity again In the mean time, I desire thee to make it part of thy Care, that *Mahmut* shall not want for Money to carry on the *Sultan*'s private Affairs without a Baulk I do not demand unreasonable Things Let me but live, and have enough to defray the necessary Expences of my *Service*, and that is all I crave But let my Supplies be well timed and proportioned, that I may husband my *Pension* to the best Advantage Or else I must always press, and that is a Thing I hate I have writ to all the *Treasurers* that went before thee on the same Account, and with equal Boldness. Therefore take not in ill Part what comes from blunt Sincerity, and constant full Desire to serve effectually the

Grand

Grand Signior It will be very eafy for me to anticipate *Mahmut's* Expectations without exceeding the Orders which thou haft received   Money be obtained, if we could breathe and ferve our Friends, and carry on the Affairs of human Life without it   I am an *Afia* and could as frely pafs away my Time in harmlefs Rambles over the *Provinces* of *Afia*, as thus to be confined to narrow fretting Circumftances, the only Effects of too unfhaken unregarded, and incorruptible Loyal y

Wealthy *Difpenfer* of the *Ottoman Gold*, I afk no Alms, but my appointed Salary, in fending of which, I defire thee to remember the old *Roman* Proverb, which fays, *That he gives twice, who gives in Seafon.*

Paris, 9*th* of the 6th Moon,
of the Year 1667

LETTER VI.

To Nathan Ben Saddi, *a Jew at* Vienna.

I Know not whether I fhall live to hear from thee again, or to fend thee another Letter   Age, Sicknefs, Misfortunes, together with the Malice of Men, have laid a thoufand Snares for my Life, I am as it were, hunted by *Nature, Providence, Deftiny, a d Chance*, into the very *Toils* of *Death*, from whence it will be very difficult for me to efcape   Not to amufe thee, I am in danger of being difcovered, feized, imprifoned, and then thou knoweft, I can expect no lefs than to be put to the Torture, and racked with a thoufand Inventions of Cruelty, that fo they may force me to confefs what I am, and what my Bufinefs is in this *Kingdom* and *City*, where I have refided fo many Years

I was fufpected by *Cardinal Richlieu* for a *Muffulman*, as I have reafon to believe from feveral convincing Circumftances of that *Minifter's* Carriage to

me

me, ever fince his firft Acquaintance with me at *Paris*.
And the fame Jealoufy caufed his Succeffor, *Cardinal
Mazarini*, to put me into the *Baftile*, where I was
clofely confined for the Space of fix *Moons* And I
might have lain there till this Time, for ought I know,
had it dot been for the good Conduct and honeft *Fidelity* of *Eliachim* In fine, though I have hitherto efca-
ped Difcovery, yet I cannot flatter my felf that I fhall
always do fo. If they once lay hold on me again,
they will certainly fearch me for the *Scar* of *Circumci-
fion* , and then all the Arguments the Wit of Man can
find, will not be of force to blind them any longer, or
fave me from the Vengeance of the *State* They will
certainly put me to a cruel Death

However, I will baffle them if I can , and if I once
efcape, I will bid adieu to *Paris*, if not to the whole
Kingdom , being refolved not to truft any more to the
deceitful Security of new Lodgings in this City, and
a vain Removal from one Precinct and Houfe to another For the very Air of *Paris* is fatal to me   I am
never free from Terror, whilft within thefe melancholy
Walls The *Genius* of the *Place* is at Enmity with
mine Every Thing I caft my Eyes on, feems to low'r
and frown upon me I ftart at the Voices of Men going along the Streets, and difcourfing about their own
Affairs And if any one knocks at the Door, I am prefently upon my Guard, my anxious Soul ftill labouring
with fad Prefages of fome Calamity at hand, ready to
rufh upon me unawares

Perhaps I may go to *Lyons* where a Stranger may live
an Age concealed, and void of Peril, as in this City.
Or I may take a farther Journey to *Marfeilles*, *Toulon*,
or any other Sea-Port Town Where I will expect
new Orders from my *Superiors*

In the mean time, thou mayeft continue to addrefs
thy Letters as before For that Courfe can never fail,
let me be where it pleafes Heaven *Eliachim* will take
care of all Things, I writ to the *Hafnadar Baffi* on the
fame Account, defiring frefh Supplies of Money , which
I fuppofe will come by the Way of *Vienna* If fo, I truft
to

to thy Prudence in ordering my *Bill,* with fpeed, and the ufual Cautioufnefs

Nathan, adieu And whatever becomes of me live thou long and happily to ferve the *Grand Signior.*

Paris, *9th of the 6th Moon,*
  of the Year 1667

LETTER VII.

To the Venerable Mufti.

AS the poor injured Labourer, or *Slave* oppreffed by cruel and obdurate *Mofters,* as the defpairing *Client,* who can find no Juftice from the *Cheichs Cadis,* or *Cadilefquers,* fly immediately to the *Serait,* to make their laft Appeal, and feek Redrefs from the *Great Arbiter* of human Feuds So falls poor *Mahmut* proftrate at thy Feet, O *Sacred Oracle* of *Muffulmans,* begging from thy Authority, whom no *Believer* dares to difobey, what I could never yet obtain from any *Minifter* of *State,* or *Baffa* of the *Bench* That is, how I muft act in cafe I am difcovered, and barely fufpected, examined and put to my Oath, concerning my Bufinefs at *Paris* Lay thy fpeedy Commands on thofe whofe Care it ought to be, that no Intelligence, Advice, or Counfel be wanting to me the faithful *Agent* of the *Port,* refiding here *incognito,* a *Spy* upon the *Infidels* Or, at leaft, vouchfafe to fend me thy Inftructions, Rules infallible, Orders of perfect Wifdom, and divine Sagacity

I cannot for the future ftand the Brunt of long fuf pected Cafualties Events which glimmer from afar, like diftant *Ignes Fatui,* or other vagrant *Meteors* of the Night For fo Contingencies appear, which are to come uncertain, and remote, though fometimes near at hand, yet with deceitful Shew, they ftill miflead bewildered Mortals in the dark So the tired Traveller in *Libyan* Waftes, is tantalized by mocking Rays of Sands in drifted Heaps, or flying Bodies loosely wafted by the Winds, on which the *Moon* and *Stars* casting their Beams, create Refractions like Domestick Lamps or Tapers, and encouraging the disconsolate Man to hope for neighbouring Villages or Towns, where he may rest his weary Limbs, and find an hospitable Entertainment, secure from *Dragons*, *Lyons*, *Tygers*, or the more *Fierce* and *Cruel Race* of Men, who lurk in secret Places of the affrighting *Desart*, to rob unwary Strangers, as they pass.

It is sad, most *Holy Patriarch* of the *Faithful*, that Men are thus degenerate, and transcend the *horrid Nature* of the *wildest Beasts*! But sadder still, that *Cities*, first designed for *Sanctuaries* of the *Distressed*, should become worse than *Desarts*, and more *Inhospitable* than the Purlieu of *Dragons*, or the dreadful Haunts of *Lynxes*, *Crocodiles*, and other *Animals* of *Prey*. That *Men* pretending to be civilized, to live in Community and reciprocal Participation of all good Offices, incorporated by the same *Laws*, for no other end but to help, assist, and defend one another against all Foreign Enemies, should, instead of this, prove more barbarous than Savages, and more voracious than *Canibal*, whilst every *Citizen* preys on his Neighbour, and devours him whom he has sworn to protect. They all live by Robbery and Spoil. The Rich and Potent fleece those whose Wealth is not sufficient to defend them from Oppression. Thus are Towns and Cities, from celebrated *Refuges* of *Men*, become the *Den* of *Thieves*, and cruel *Murderers*. The whole Earth is stained with the Blood of the Poor. The Cries of Widows and Orphans pierce the *Heavens*. The Generations of Men are corrupted, with Fraud, Avarice, Perfidy, Ambition, Envy, and a thousand other Vices. Brother cannot trust the Son of his own Mother, Fathers are unnatural to their genuine Off-spring. Children think the Days tedious which prolong their Parents Lives. Self-Love teaches a Man to betray his Friend, for whom he rather ought to lose his Life. An universal Defection from Justice and sound Morality reigns every where.

But what is most surprizing, is, that even among those who bear the glorious Title and Character of the

True

True Faithful Mussulmans, there should be found a Crew
of Miscreants, Villains, and Traytors to GOD, his
Prophet, and their *Sovereign* I speak not of such,
whose *Genial* Inclinations tempt them to commit vulgar
Sins which injure no Man but themselves I tax no
Drunkards, Gamesters, and those amorous Persons, who
waste their Bodies, Time, Estates, and sacrifice their
Reputation to Volutpuousness These are but *Venial*
Sins, and soon washed off, by the appointed *Purifica
tions*, and *Penances* A little Water, Dust, or Sand with
Fasting, and devout Invocation, of the *Eternal Allah*, can-
cels these *Peccadilloes* , they are all put to the Account of
human Frailty , such is the Pleasure of eternal Good
ness But I accuse the blacker Crimes of those, whom
fretting Envy stimulateth to persecute their harmless
Neighbour , or base Ingratitude prompteth to betray
their Friends , or native Malice teacheth to seek out
all Occasions of doing mischief in the World A busy
restless Sort of Men buzzing about like Wasps or
Hornets, stinging every one they fasten on Or like the
Punes of *Paris*, a troublesome Kind of *Insects*, which
interrupt the sweet Repose of Men, creeping upon
them in their Beds and Slumbers, and silly biting
them, to suck their Blood

    Such are the *Men* of whom I now complain, who
flatter me from Statagem to Stratagem, from one Re
trenchment to another , whose Crime is double, in that
they are Persons of my own *Religion* , *Professors* of the
Genuine Faith brought down from *Heaven* , *Followers*
of the *Prophet*, who could neither *write* nor *read* , and
Subjects to the *Grand Signior*

    It is a long time since I had the first Occasion to ac
cuse some at the *Seraglio*, of private, sly Attempts to un
dermine and ruin me, that they might gain my *Post*
It will seem invidious, even in my own Defence, after
so many Addresses to the *Ministers* of the *Porte*, now
to repeat their Names, and discompose thy Sacred
Thoughts with black *Memoirs* of human Malice It
not Revenge I seek, but for the future how to escape
not prevent, the like Conspiracies. Nor is it for n

-felf alone, I cherifh this unufual Zeal and Care, but
'for my Mafter's Interefr and Honour

I have ferved near thirty Years in this precarious
'*Station*, and never made the leaft falfe Step, or, if I
have, it was not difcerned, which is the fame Thing
in effect   And I am very unwilling to mifcarry at
laft through the Treachery of my pretended Friends
at *Conftantinople*, or for want of full Inftructions from
the *Imperial Divan*

It is for this Reafon, I prefume to addrefs to the
Duft of thy Feet, *Supreme Judge* of the *Faithful*, begg-
ing the Interpofition of thy *Paternal* Authority on my
Behalf

There is one Thing more, which in all Humility I
recommend to thy Wifdom and Sanctity   I have often
writ to thy *Predeceffor* on the fame Account, befeeching
him to promote the *Tranflation* of *Hiftories*, and other
'Learned *Books*, out of Foreign *Languages* into *Turkifh*
or *Arabick*   That fo Knowledge might flourifh among
the *Mufulmans*, and the *Infidel* might have no more
Ground to call us *Barbarous*.   Let Men fkilful in *Lan-*
guages and *Sciences* be fought for   There are not
wanting fuch at *Conftantinople*, and in other Parts of
the *Empire*   Let them be employed in compiling an
univerfal *Hiftory* of the *World* in *Turkifh*, more ample,
true, and correct than any that has gone before it, in
Greek, *Latin*, or any other Language   This will bring
eternal Honour to the *Ottoman Empire*, and prove no
hard Tafk to them that fhall undertake it, fince it will
be only a choice Collection out of other *Authors*, a Gar-
land of Flowers culled from the various Fields of *Hif-*
tory, and compofed together with an Order full of Luftre and Beauty, the whole Work being interwoven
with a Chain of *Chronological* Years, which will not
only give it a fingular Grace, but alfo be of great
Advantage to the *Mufulman* Readers.

Succeffor of the *Apoftles*, remember, that though our
holy Lawgiver could neither write nor read, yet the
fucceeding *Caliphs* encouraged *Learning*   Benediction
on the Souls of them and their *Pofterity*   So will future

ture Ages blefs thy Memory, if thou vouchfafeft to en
courage this glorious Work   An *Ithuriel* the *Angel* of
Science, will make thee his *Affociate* in *Paradife*

With profound Submiffions I retire from thy *facred*
Prefence, begging thy *Abfolution* and *Bleffing*

Paris, *9th of the 6th Moon,*
of the Year 1667

LETTER VIII.

To Cara Hali, Phyfician, *to the* Grand Signior.

AMONG other *Difpatches* I could not forget
what I owe to the long continued Friendfhi
which has been between us   Having Leifure therefore
before the Poft goes, I will inform thee of a *Birth* which
has occafioned little Joy to the Parents, but much Ad
miration among all that hear of it, and raifed learned
Difputes between the Profeffors of *Phyfick* and *Sur*
ger,

In the Town of *Weesteed* near *Arderburgh* in the
Low Countries, a Woman was lately delivered of a mon
ftrous Child, with with two Heads, two Necks, four
Arms, and proportionably all Parts both outward an
inward double to the Navel, which feemed, to be the
Center of Union between the two Bodies   For from
thence downwards there appeared only the Proportion
and Shape of one Body, with two Thighs, Legs, and
Feet   The Faces were different, one fqualid and ir
regular, without a Nofe or Mouth, except a kind of
Orifice under the Chin, for the Eyes poffeffed the
Place of the Mouth, and a perfect *mafculine Genital* took
up the Room of the Nofe   The other was fair, and
made with Symmetry, having nothing extraordinary
faving two Teeth growing out of the Gums

Thi

This *irregular Production* has been curiously diffect-ed by a famous Anatomist, who found two Hearts, two Stomachs, and the other Vitals all fingle. What I have faid is attefted by five piofeffed *Phyficians*, who opened this wonderful Creature

There have been many Examples of extraordinary *Births*, efpecially in thefe Parts of the World   And I have read in a *French* Author, a Man of Credit, That in the Year 1592 of the *Chriftian Hegira*, a Woman of *Alfatia* brought forth at once an hundred and fifty Children, each but three Inches long

But what I fhall now tell thee, though it be not re-markable for the number of Children, yet has fome-thing fingular in the Circumftances that attend it

Irmetride, the *Countefs* of *Altorfe*, accufed one of her Neighbours of Adultery, becaufe fhe had three Chil-dren at a *Birth*, faying *She deferved to be tied up in a Sack, and thrown into the Sea*   Next Year the *Countefs* her felf was delivered of twelve Sons all at a Birth. And touched with Remorfe for the Sentence which fhe had pronounced againft the other Woman, conclud-ing it now a juft Punifhment for her felf, fent a Maid with eleven of thefe new born *Infants*, commanding her to drown them in the next River, referving only one to be the *Heir* of his Father's Eftate

Fate had fo determined, that her Hufband the *Earl* met the Maid as fhe was going to commit this execra-ble Villainy, and afking her what fhe had got in her Lap, fhe anfwered, *I am going to drown a few young Whelps*   The *Earl* being a great Hunter, and con-fequently a lover of Dogs, had a Mind to fee whe-ther any of thefe *Whelps* were of a promifing Afpect; when to his Aftonifhment he found eleven of human Shapes, all living and perfect, but very fmall. He preffed the Maid fo far, that fhe confeffed the whole Truth   Whereupon enjoining her Silence, and Affu-rance of a good Reward, he caufed her to carry them to one of his *Tenants*, where being all cherifhed and laid warm, he difpofed of them afterwards in conve-nient Places, to be nurfed and brought up till they

came of Age. Then he sent for them privately t
his House, having first apparelled them in the same
Fashion as their Brother was in who dwelt at Home

As soon as the *Countess* cast her Eye on them, and
observed their Number and Faces, so exactly resemb
ling him who had been always with her, she wept in
a Passion betwixt Shame and Joy, confessing her for
mer cruel Intention, and falling at the Feet of he
Lord, he pardoned her From these *Eleven* descend the
Family of *Whelps* or *Guelphs*, so renowned in *Germany*,
and bearing this Name from the Maid's Answer to the
Earl, when she had them in her Lap

Such strange Productions as these occasion various
Enquiries among the *Philosophers* here in the *West*
Whether *human Souls* be *generated* like the *Bodies* to
which they are united, or whether they are *created* by
the *immediate Power* of GOD Assuredly these *Infid*
are much in the Dark, and shut their Eyes against the
Light of the *Oriental* Sages If the *Prophets* should
rise from the Dead, they would not be able to con
vince these *Uncircumcised*, that all Things visible an
invisible are from *Eternity*, and that there is nothing new
in the System of the Universe, except the various out
ward Forms, which change indeed according to the
Laws of endless Transmigration, and sometimes ac
cording to the Frolicks of *Nature*, who loveth to mix
her Interludes and Antiques with the established Sense
of every Age

What I have writ is to divert thee But when sha
I have an Answer as from an old Friend ? Let not the
Honours of the *Serail* make thee forget those with
whom thou hast been once familiar My dear *Ha*
be not too much a *Courtier* Thy long Silence an
Reservedness forces this Language from me Sha
Constantinople blot out thy Remembrance of *Arabia*
Or the Blast of a Monarch's Favour be more valuab
than the durable Integrity of a Countryman, a Friend
If the *Sultan* trusts his Life in thy Hands, dost n
thou know that a fit of Gripes, the Stone, Gout, o
any violent Distemper, will turn all his Confidenc
into Jealousy ? I tell thee, he will suspect Poison i
thy very Looks. There

Therefore, continue to be the fame Man as thou wert formerly, and let not thy Improvements in *Phyfick* make thee go backward in *Morality*.

Paris, *23d of the 6th Moon,*
of the Year 1667

LETTER IX.

To Nathan Ben Saddi, *a* Jew *at* Vienna.

NOW I fee thou art a Man of Bufinefs! Thy Mind is cured of its religious Itch, and reftored to a found Complexion Perfevere and be happy.

Let no vain Scruples of Confcience moleft thy *Soul,* concerning the Peace that was lately made between the *Grand Signior* and the *German* Cares of this Nature belong to thofe who fit at the Helm, and direct the Steerage of the State As for thee and me, our Part is only to obey, without enquiring whether it be right or wrong that we are commanded Every thing is lawful to us that is enjoined by our Superiors And the *publick* Reafon ought to fuperfede our private narrow Sentiments. Whatever *Præmunires* we incur by our Obedience, the Confcience of the State will be our Bail, our Advocate, and our Ranfom Therefore, once more, go on and profper

Thou couldeft not have done the *Grand Signior* a greater Piece of Service, than by thus happily infinuating thy felf with the *Hungarian Faction* at *Vienna* For by that means thou becomeft *Mafter* of the Secrets of both Sides, the *Janus* that overlooks two oppofite Cabals at once And fo mayeft not only form thy Intrigues the better, but alfo give a clearer Light to the Minifters of the *fublime Porte*

I am difpleafed to hear of the frequent *Confpiracies* that have been made againft the *Emperor's* Perfon Not for any Love that I bear to him, or the Houfe of *Auftria*

ftria, for I wifh there was not a *Branch* of that *inceptuous Stem* left alive on Earth   But I never knew fuc Kind of Plots, if once difcovered and prevented, t take Effect again   Befides, they many times fpoil th main Defign   For what fignifies it, if this *Emper* were feized and put to Death, fo long as there is an one of that *tyrannical Race* furviving   They are a of the fame Blood and Intereft, educated alfo in the fame Principles and Maxims   In a word, they he all but one Game to play, which is, to aggrandize themfelves and their Pofterity for ever   And there fore thefe clandeftine Methods of Poifon or Affa fin, will but make them more watchful to prevent al Defigns of the like Nature for the Future

Remember, *Nathan*, that the Mark which thou ar to aim at, is to cherifh the Difcontents of *Hungary*, b all the Arts of a cunning Statefman   Count *Peter* a *Serini* is a fit Subject to work upon   The Death c his Brother and his own Difgrace at the *Imperi Court*, with the rifing Fortune of *Monticuli*, have fi led him with Sentiments of Revenge and Envy   H cannot behold Count *d'Avenfperg* in Poffeffion of *Cai ftadt* without much Refentment, having with fo gre Paffion begged that *Government* for himfelf

If this Prince can but be induced to revolt man thoufands of the *Croats*, *Dalmatians*, and *Sclavonia* will take up Arms under him, which will at on weaken both the *German Empire*, and the State c *Venice*   Befides the Marriage of his Daughter wi Prince *Ragotfki*, may engage the *Tranfylvanians* in h Party   Count *Nadafti* alfo, they fay, is not well ple fed with the *Court*, aiming to be *Palatine* of *Hunga* which has been refufed him.   This News comes t me but by Report   If it be true, thou art in the far Way to fucceed.   Such great Malecontents as the will puzzle the *Minifters* of State, and exercife the P licy of Prince *Lobkowitz*

Befides, if Things fhould not proceed to an op Rupture, yet, thou knoweft the *Hungarians* are offenc ed at the late Peace, which will not fail to put the upon committing perpetual Acts of Hoftility.   Th

Roma

stomach it extreamly, that the Town of *Newhaufel* is in the *Grand Signior's* Hands, and they will be always on their Guard in the neighbouring Parts patroling about, and skirmishing with our Foragers. Which will afford a good Occasion at any time for our Sovereign to break the Peace, whenever it is for his Interest. There are abundance of Consequences in such a Case, more than we can think of or foresee, yet all to our Advantage. As long as we go the right way to work, all things will succeed well. Make no false Steps, and there is no Danger of stumbling.

Remember still, that thy particular Charge is to foment a *Civil War* between the Court of *Vienna* and the *Hungarians*. It is no matter who gets the better of it. Let them quarrel to Eternity, and destroy one another in *God's* Name. Then shall the *Muffulman* Empire thrive.

Before *God*, you have a fine Opportunity, ye factious Comrades. But beware of fly Interlopers. Damn the Easiness and good Nature (falfly so called) of those who will admit any Man into their Cabal, provided he puts on a fair Guize of one of the Party. Ye cannot be too reserved and close. Do ye think the *Emperor* has not his Spies about in every Corner? A Pox of Stupidity, if you suffer this brave Design to miscarry for want of looking sharp. Damn you, for a Parcel of old thread-bare Fools, if after so many Experiences you do not furbish up your Wits, and look to your selves. There is *Gottendorf*, *Ralhauts*, *Sku*, the *Knight Baron Leipfem*, *Elnard* the *hereditary* Pretender to the Marquisate of *Thanu*, with many others whom I will not name in this Letter, By *Mofes* and *Mahomet* they are all Rogues, and if you trust them too far they will surely betray you.

Nathan, believe me, I would not write so paffionately were my Life at all precious. But I have no other End in protracting the Minute of my *Transmigration*, than to exalt as much as in me lies, the Majesty of the *Ottoman Lineage*, and to guard it from Dangers. I am placed here on purpose by Fate. And I will do my Duty, though the whole World should spatter their Venom against me.   C 3   O *Is-*

O *Israelite,* both thou and I muſt ſhortly leave this Earth ; or at leaſt we muſt change the Form of our Earth   We ſhall never ceaſe to be ſomething ; GOD knows what

In the mean time, be what thou ſeemeſt to be

Paris, 23d of the 6th Moon,
   of the Year 1667

LETTER X.

To the moſt Sublime and Magnificent of the Muſ-ſulman Baſſa's Achmet, *the* VIZIR AZEM.

MAY Chaplets of immortal Flowers crown thy noble Head, illuſtrious *Cuperli,* ſtrong Prop of the Houſe of *Etogriel,* main Buttreſs of the Tower of the *Zelzuccian Tribe* the Lineage of *Ottoman* Heir of the Heirs to *Iſmael,* the eldeſt Son of our Father *Abra-bam,* the Glory of Men, and the Beloved of GOD.

Not the unmatched Perfumes of *Arabia,* not the ſurprizing Odours of the *Perſian* Incenſe, which they offered to the Sun, not all the moſt ſkilful Compoſi-tions of *Eaſtern Aromaticks* put together are half ſo ſweet as is thy glorious Name among the *Muſſulmans*

I received thy Orders with a Reverence, ſecond only to that which is due to the *Grand Signior,* and will perform them with a loyal Alacrity   I perfectly com-prehend thy Deſign, and the Drift of the ſublime *Porte* For thou haſt ſtated the Caſe like an *Oracle*   It will not be difficult, I believe, to ſuggeſt under hand to the *French Court,* the Advantage they may make of the preſent Diſtractions in *Hungary* For they are already become the Subject of common Diſcourſe   *Lewis* the Fourteenth, by encouraging thoſe Malecontents, and ſupporting their Cauſe with private Diſburſements of Money, will doubtleſs facilitate his own deſigned Con-queſts on the Neighbourhoods of the *Rhine* For if the

Hun

Hungarian Lords proceed to an open Revolt and throw themſelves under the *Sultan*'s Protection, the *Emperor of Germany* will be obliged to turn all his Forces that Way which yet will not be able to withſtand the United Armies of the *Hungarians, Croatians, Heydukes, Tartars,* and the moſt invincible *Oſmans* So that by this means, the *Empire* will be weakened on both Sides, and in fatal Danger of it's final Diſſolution, whilſt the Strength and Power of the *Grand Signior,* and the King of *France,* his Noble *Ally,* will daily increaſe

Beſides, this will put all *Europe* into Diviſions and Parties, according as their Intereſts and Affections incline them, ſome ſiding with the Emperor, others with the *French King,* whilſt the Generality will ſtand Neuters, and contemplate the Iſſue of theſe Wars, without aſſiſting one Side or the other Than which, nothing can fall out more happy or more propitious for the Sacred *Monarchy* of the *Oſmans*

In obedience to thy Command, I have written to *Nathan Ben Saddi* on this Account, altogether as from my ſelf, not giving him the leaſt Ground to conjecture, that I had received an Order from the *Port.* I frequently take the Liberty to counſel that honeſt *Jew* in many Caſes; inviting him to Projects in general Terms, and to do ſome extraordinary Service for the *Grand Signior.* So that he will imagine my writing now is only of Courſe, without ſuſpecting any thing elſe.

I beſeech thee to ſend me all the Inſtructions that are needful for me, not only to carry on this Affair proſperouſly, but all others relating to the *Port* I will be careful to tranſmit thy Commands to *Nathan Ben Saddi,* in ſuch a Diſguiſe, as he ſhall not dream they are any other than his own Propoſals Since thou doſt not think it fit that the Majeſty of the *Port* ſhould appear to be concerned in a Buſineſs of this Nature, eſpecially ſo ſoon after the late *Peace* concluded with the *Emperor.*

It is an invaluable Honour thou haſt done me, in truſting to my Conduct an Intrigue, whoſe Effects for ought I know, may reach all the *Nations* of *Europe,* and laſt till the Day of *Doom.* Queſtion not my Fidelity, for it is of Proof Besides, it many times tempts a Man to be false, when he knows he is suspected to be so

I am *Slave* of the *Slaves* of those who stand near the *Sultan*'s Person, and confess *Mahammed* to be the *Apostle* of God More particularly I am devoted to those who have the Honour to serve thee, the Grand Pillar of the *Ojman Empire* God perpetuate thy Felicity

Paris, *23d of the 7th Moon,*
   of the Year 1667

LETTER XI.

To the Selictar Aga, *or* Sword-Bearer *to the* Sultan.

THESE *Parts* abound in Action at this Time, Couriers run up and down from *Court* to *Court* with secret *Dispatches*, and Matters of deep Import. The Death of the *Queen* of *Poland*, and of *Pope Alexander* VII occasion this new stirring and bustling in *Europe*. She died on the 10th of the 5th *Moon*, He on the 22d Every *Kingdom* and *State* in the *West*, have some Interest to make or preserve, some Design to form or to carry on, the Success of which many times depends on the well managing the Consequences of these great and fatal Breaches, which Death makes in the Families of mighty *Potentates*, *Houses* of *Royal Descent*

The *French Court* were all dissolved in Joy, for the Marriage of the *Duke* of *Guize* with *Madammoiselle d'Alencon* They were in the midst of the Nuptial Triumphs, and Festival Solemnities, when the Black Expresses came, which soon turned all their Mirth to Mourning, at least in outward Appearance For it was not decent for the *Sons* to continue longer revelling, when the *Greater Father* lay embalmed in order to his Sepulture Therefore, to prevent Idleness, the

King thought fit to change the Paſtimes of the *Court* for more neceſſary Buſineſs , and the ſoft Entertainments of *Hymen*, for the rugged Toils of *War* He cauſed his Armies to march into *Flanders*, to give his *Queen* Poſſeſſion of certain *Eſtates* fallen to her in thoſe *Parts*. This ſurprized the *Low Countries*, who began to demoliſh ſeveral *Places* of *Strength* that had not ſufficient Garriſons to defend them

The *King* was himſelf in Perſon at the Head of his Army, which gave immerſe Courage to his Soldiers So that *Tournay* quickly ſurrendered to him on the 24th of the 6th *Moon* , and *Doway* not many Days after In the mean while, the *Mareſchal d'Aumont*, with another Army takes the *Bergue Furnes* near *Dunkirk* Then he beſieges *Liſle*, which was taken alſo after ſeventeen Days , but not without the *King's* Preſence , who appeared indefatigable, always on Horſeback, or in his Coach, going the Rounds, and ſurveying all the Works He ſlept in his Coach that Night the Town was taken, on a Bridge not far from *Gaunt*. They have alſo taken *Courtray*, *Ordenarde* and *Aloſt*. They have defeated the Prince *de Lingen*, and *Count de Maran* In a word, they have done ſo many great Things this Campaign that all *Flanders* is ſtupified, as at a *Miracle*

Illuſtrious *Aga*, I have in a Sort of Miniature preſented thee with a true *Effigies* of *Weſtern* Affairs at this Juncture Let not my Abruptneſs diſpleaſe thee , ſince this *Epitome* deſcribes the Truth as lively, as if I had filled an Ell of Parchment up with Words.

Paris, *2d of the 8th Moon,
of the Year* 1667.

LETTER XII

To Dgnet Oglou.

I Know not whether I have reafon to rejoice or b fad in my prefent Circumftances, fo ambiguou are the Events of Human Life Even the moft bla difhing Gifts of Fortune, and fuch as we are extremely taken with, many times prove like the *Trojan* Horf, only fair and gay in outward Appearance, whilft, like that deceitful Engine of the *Grecian* Craft, they carry a Army of hidden Calamities within, which in the mid of our fecure Repofe, when we leaft dream of any Evi rufh upon us from their concealed and unfufpect Ambufcades, put us all in Terror and Confufion

However, fince I have had a fufficient Share o Trouble, Grief, and Melancholy, now let other fprigh ly, chearful Paffions take their Turn, be the Ever how it will, I cannot always bear the Burden of loaded Spleen, crammed and puffed up with melar choly Winds, the *Embryoes* or Vehicles at leaft of hor rid Thoughts, perplexing Cares, and black Defpai Befides, methinks, I have a fit Occafion to be merry being by a very pleafing Accident, at once rid of great many vain Doubts and Anxieties, (which ha difturbed my Peace for thefe three or four Years) ar reftored to the charming Converfation of *Daria*, who thou mayeft remember I fo paffionately loved in t Days of my Youth

Know then, that one Day as I was walking in t Streets, I met that lovely *Greek* in *Mourning* Su prized above Meafure at the Sight of a Perfon, fo whom I had formerly cherifhed fo great an Efteem, ftood ftill at firft, like one Thunder-ftruck I coul not forbear queftioning my own Senfes, and givir the Lye to my Eyes, which affured me it was fa Neither Age nor Abfence had effaced her loved I from my Memory, or fo much changed her Face, b that I eafily called to mind the Object of my Amo ous Defires   Yet my Aftonifhment was fuch at this unthought-of Interview, that I had not Refolution e- nough to believe my felf, and her Amazement feemed no lefs than mine , whilft neither of us had Power to fpeak, but ftood like Fools. 'Till I, afhamed longer to lofe my felf in fuch an effeminate Confufion of Spirit firft broke Silence, not without fome Rapture and Emotion, crying out, " Is it *Daria* or her *Ghoft*, I " fee ? Has *Fortune* bleffed or mocked me at the fa- " tal Hour ? Or do deluding *Nymphs* and *Fairies* haunt " the Streets of populous Cities, walking about in bor- " rowed Forms, and mixing with the Throng of Mor- " tals, to tantalize our fofteft Hopes with a falfe Shew " of fome dear Lover, Friend or Perfon highly wifh- " ed for, never to be enjoyed ? It may be true, that *Cy-* " *therea* left her *Heaven* (as *Virgil* does relate) and in " a *Tyrian* Drefs met the *heroick* Off fpring of *Achilles* " in the Fields, amufing him with a difguifed Sem- " blance of Mortality and human Race, until her *hea-* " *venly* Voice difcovered that fhe was a *Goddefs*   So " ufed *Diana* to defcend in dead of Night, and mix " the Slumbers of *Endymion* with Immortal Dreams ; " ftealing foft Kiffes from the lovely Youth, and whif- " pering *Cæleftial* Words into his Ears, more forcible " than the Songs of *Orpheus*, when he moved the " Trees and Rocks to Paffions of *Platonick* Love   At " other times they would come down, and take the " Air of cool Mount *Hæmus*, or the lofty *Ida*   Thus " *Melpomene, Clio*, and the reft of the *Sacred Nine*, " would often vifit the refrefhing Heights of their " beloved *Parnaffus*, from whence defcending to the " fhady Banks of *Helicon*, with more than mortal Voi- " ces, would awake and tempt the wanton *Ecchoes* to " ftrike up, like *Unifons*, and join in *Confort* with them, " whilft they chant the Praifes of fome *Demi God* or " *Hero*, whom they love   But that a *Goddefs, Nymph*, " or *Mufe*, did ever frequent the common Crowd of " *Mortals* in a City, is not to be credited   Therefore " unlefs I dream, it is *Daria* I behold

My *Dianet*, I was running on higher Ecftafies at mentioning of her Name but that fhe fmiled, and in-

terrupted

terrupted me with an obliging Reservedness, and said,
" *Malmut*, if you are the Man I take you for, and
" would have my Esteem, be less passionate, and leave
" off this wild Way of Raillery We both are past
" the Vanities of Youth Our Years should now re
" tain no remnant Froths of early boiling Blood, and
" young, green, foolish Passions '

I took this only for a female Banter and Essay of
Woman's Craft, to try the Sense and Humour of a
Man   For, thou knowest the greatest *Princess* loves a
truly passionate Address, though not a puling, whining
one , besides, it is the Fashion here in *France*, to use
Romantick Forms of Speech, when they make Love.
However, in regard it was inconvenient to lose more
time, in open Street, by this Sort of Discourse, I in
vited her to a House, where we might converse with
more Freedom   She accepted the Motion, and I con
ducted her to the House of *Fhachin* the *few* It is plea
santly seated on the Banks of the River *Seine*, and has a
fair Garden belonging to it   *Chachim* happened to be
abroad, which gave us a better Opportunity of im
proving of Time, without the necessary Interruption
of Salutes, Compliments, *&c* usual in such a Case
And I had the Command of his House, as though he
had been there himself

I being in the Heat of *Summer*, I led *Daria* into a
little, shady, green Retreat, in the midst of the Gar
den out of the Reach of curious Ears , where under the
cool refreshing Shelter of a wide spread Beech, we sat
down and called to mind our former Acquaintance and
Friendship *Daria* still retained her Native Modesty
and Prudence, neither had the external Beauty of her
Face suffered any great Detriment, than what befalls
the fairest Roses, Violets, or other Flowers, which
even in their most decayed Estate, merit the Character
of amiable Sweetness   However the Lustre of her
Wit, and the Goodness of her Humour, supplied all
other Defects

I protest, my *Dgnet*, it was impossible for me to see,
and not to love again, a Person whose *Idea* was once
so domestick and familiar to my *Soul*   And I was the

more animated to make my *Court*, when she told me, that
she was a *Widow*. It was easy to forget, or banish
from my Thoughts, her former faithful Treachery, in
acquainting her Husband with my Amour. Love soon
removes all puny Obstacles: it is ready, prompt, and
dexterous to find Excuses for the greatest Faults a
Friend can ever commit. Much more ingenious to
palliate the *Peccadilloes* of a Mistress. This Generous
Passion, by a peculiar Force, extirpates all Revenge,
and blots out the *Memoirs* of past Unkindnesses. It
ever springs and blooms with fresh desires, young vigorous Inclinations. Like to the Palm oppressed with
Weights, it higher grows. It would fain increase, dilate, and stretch itself to Immortality. There is no
Consideration, but that of Honour, can pretend to
match, or stand in Competition with the divine Regards of Love. And yet the most exalted Human
Glory often vails to this soft Passion. The Conquer-
ors of the World suffer themselves to be overcome by
Women.

Wonder not therefore, that I who am Flesh and
Blood as well as other Men, could not now defend
my self from fair *Dara*'s Charms.

Excuse me in that I cannot now give thee any farther Account of this Adventure, being interrupted by
a Messenger from *Elhachim* the *Jew*, who brings me
Word, my Mother is very sick, and wants my Company. Expect another *Dispatch* speedily.

Paris, 15*th of the* 10*th Moon,*
  of the Year 1667

LETTER XIII.

To the Pesteli Hali, *his Brother,* Master of
the Customs, *and* Superintendant *of the*
Arsenal *at* Constantinople

IT is written in the *Fates*, That Man should once at
least be vanquished by a *Woman* in his Life. But
it is my Chance to be twice subdued by one of the
fair Sex. I know not whether I acquainted thee with
the Love I formerly bore to *Daria*, a beautiful *Greek*
Lady sojourning in *Pera*. Neither have I at this In-
stant an Opportunity to look over the File of my Letters, they being in my Lodgings and I at *Ehachir*
House, where I writ this Letter, for the sake of a Con-
venience, which offers it self, of sending thee a small
Present of *Watches* and *Oriental Stores* by a *Jew,*
Merchant, who is just departing for *Constantinople*.

However, if thou art curious to know the Circumstances of this Amour I speak of, our Friend *Oglou* can
inform thee of it. In the mean time, suffer me to vent
some of my Thoughts concerning Women, and the
Love of them rooted so deeply in our Hearts by Na-
ture. None of our Sex could ever escape this gen-
Passion it being mixed and blended in our very Original *Embryoes*, and after cherished with our Mother
Milk. It was the peculiar Mystery of our Nurse
by a thousand Female Tricks and Arts of necess-
Tenderness, to blow and kindle up the little Sparks
this immortal Fire within our infant *Souls*, whilst fro-
their Breast were sucked and guzzled down inebri-
ing *Philters* and *Love-Potions*, more forcible and durable than those the *Grecian Maids* compound
Magic' Files when they wou'd captivate some Lov-
Youth within their Snares. Our Blood thus fed v
early sympathetick Draughts, becomes the Seminary
a thousand amorous Inclinations, general, unform-
volatile Affections to that Sex. Till Time and O-
portunity fix our loose Desires on some particul

Maid, whom *Fate* or *Chance* has brought into our View. At the firſt Glance, ſhe darts from her enchanting Eyes, the perfect Image of her *Soul,* which penetrates like Lightning our moſt Interior Faculties   The ſwift *Idea* transforms us into its own Similitude, like melted Wax we take the momentary Impreſſion of a Figure, which may laſt as long as we, or if we melt again, it is but to receive ſome other Stamp of Love   Thus our whole Life paſſes away in an enchanted Circle of Amours

However, it is the Part of a wiſe Man to regulate this Paſſion, and not ſuffer it to degenerate into Dotage.   There is much to be ſaid in Praiſe of Women, and not a little in their Diſparagement   As we are *Riddles* to our ſelves, ſo *that Sex* is in a higher Degree *Myſterious* and a *Paradox*

It would be a kind of ſacrilegious Envy to conceal their Excellencies, and the Advantages they have of us in many Regards, whilſt our partial Pen ſhall only publiſh their Defects and Infirmities   Some *Hebrew Doctors* from the different Names of *Adam* and *Eve,* draw Arguments to prove the Dignity and Perfection of the *Female Sex,* in that *Adam* ſignifies [*Earth*] but *Eve* expreſſes [*Life*] For they affirm, that every Name which GOD impoſed on any Thing, deſcribes its *Nature* and *Qualities,* as a *Picture* repreſents the *Original* Therefore by how much *Life* is more to be eſteemed than *Earth,* by ſo much more excellent, in the Opinion of thoſe *Rabbies,* is *Woman* than *Man*

They go farther alſo, from the Affinity between *Eve's* Name and the *Sacred* Name of GOD, the ineffable *Tetragrammaton,* the *Cabaliſts* borrow Proofs in Confirmation of their *Doctrine*

I know not whether ſuch Critical Obſervation be of any Moment or no, in this Caſe yet thou knoweſt that all the *Faſtern* Languages are full of hidden Myſteries, each Word and Letter being impregnated with ſome *Divine* or *Natural* Secret, beſide the common obvious Senſe Thus *All Zerbi,* the holy *Muſſulman Doctor* ſays, there is Magick in the Sacred Name of *Jeſus,* and that whenever it ſhall be once pronounced through the

great

great Tube or Trump of *Michael*, it shall cause all the
Powers in *Heaven*, in *Earth*, and *Hell*, to bow the Knee.
This *Globe* whereon we tread, shall tremble, and all the
Elements melt away, the *Firmament* shall be snatched
up like to the Motion of an *Eastern* Antiport Veil, or
Curtain The wide stretched *Orbs* above shall warp
and rowl together as a scorched Skin, or a Piece of
Parchment does before a Fire So forcible will be the
Energy of that tremendous *WORD* by which the Uni-
verse was made, when God designs to rend this visible
World of ours in Pieces, that he may reveal his nobler
Works, the Worlds invisible and eternal This mighty
Frame on every Side, will bow, and yield, and vanish
not able to support the crowding 'Train and Luftre of
immortal Glories, radiant, bright *Essences*, descending
in a Body from the high *Palace* of God, the infinite
Solitudes and Recesses of the *Omnipotent*

Thou hast no Reason to be scandalized at what I
write as if I were a *Christian* Thou seest I have
Doctors of the *Arabs* for my *Author* A *True Believer*
and reputed Saint Besides, if I am worthy to advise
thee, let not the common Practice of *Mussulman* Professors in the *Imperial* City tempt thee to despise the
Bleffed Son of *Mary*, of whom our *Holy Prophet* speaks
so honourably How many *Chapters* in the *Alcoran* do
celebrate his Praise ? I rather counsel thee to imitate
the honest *Turcomans*, who are esteemed the best of
True Believers Thefe honour both *Jesus* and his
matchlefs *Virgin-Mother* So do the *Chupmessiass*, and
all good *Mussulmans* As for the rest, they are either
superstitious and morose *Fanaticks*, profligate *Renega-
does*, or loose, wild *Libertines*, who fear neither God
nor Man

And now I have mentioned that incomparable *Mary*, *Mother* of the *Messias*, of whom the mighty *Alcoran*
speaks fuch venerable Things, it is a fit Occasion to
return from my Digression, and proceed in relating
what the *Jewish Rabbies* say farther in Commendation
of the *Female Sex*

They consider the Order which God, according to
the *Writing* of *Moses*, observed in the Creation viz that

among his Works, some are incorruptible aud immortal, others subject to Corruption and Change, and that as he began in the noblest Species of the former, to wit, pure separate *Spirits* , so he ended in the most illustrious of the latter, that is *Woman* , the last of all his Works, and the most perfect of compound Beings For in her are centered and consummated the Nature of the Heavens, the Earth, Air, Fire, and Water, with Minerals, Plants, and Animals, and whatsoever else was made before her This is the Opinion of some *Hebrew Writers*, who believe, that GOD having made *Eve*, and then surveyed the *System* of his Works found nothing more excellent or divinely framed than *Woman* Therefore in her he rested and commenced the *Sabbath* as if his Power and Wisdom now were tired and foiled, and that he could not start the *Idea* of another Creature more perfect than her Or, as if he did not esteem the *Universe* it self compleat without the last and most accomplished of his Works For they hold it absurd to believe, that GOD would finish such a prodigious and admirable Task, in any mean or abject Thing. They also illustrate this by a Similitude, asserting, that the World being as it were an entire Circle, it followeth by necessary Consequence, that it was finished in that Part, which by the most intimate Union couples the first Atom to the last

They endeavour to strengthen this by the common Principle of *Philosophy*, which teacheth, that the End is always first in the Intention, and last in Execution. *Woman* therefore being the last Work of the Creation, it is evident, say they, that she was the chief Design and Aim the *Almighty* had in building this immense Fabrick, which he first furnished and adorned with infinite Riches and Delights, and then introduced *her*, as into her own native, proper Palace, there to reign an absolute Queen over all his Works

Besides they take Advantage from the particular Place of her Creation to exalt *her*, in that she was formed in *Paradise* among the *Angels*, whereas *Man* was made in the Common Waste among the *Brutes* And therefore they say, *Woman* have this peculiar Privilege, that
when

when they look down from any eminent Height o
Precipice, they feel no Dizziness or giddy Sym,
toms in their Head, no Mist or Dimness in their Ey
being, as it were, nearer their proper Element, or lof
Birth-place, whereas it is common for Men to b
troubled with these Accidents in such a Case

But the most prevailing Argument they use, is take
from the stupendous Beauty of that *Sex*, which like t
finer Sort of Clouds in Summer, seems to engross th
Splendors of immortal Light, and so reflect them o
the World How matchless is a *Woman*'s Form? Wh
dazzling Majesty environs her from Head to Foot
Gaze on her lovely Countenance without Astoni
ment or fix your Eyes on hers without an Ectass
those Lights which do mislead the *Morning Stars*, an
cause the *Gods* to ramble from their *Heaven*, if wh
the *Antient Poets* say be true So did *Apollo* for h
Daphne, and *Jupiter* for others of that charming *Se*
Neither need we wonder at this, since the *Written* Law
it self records, that *Angels* fell in Love with admirabl
Maids of *human Race*, and took them for their Wiv
or Concubines, from whom the *Progeny* of *Giants* cam
Thus more modern *Writers* testify, that incorpore
Spirits and *Dæmons* of all Ranks and Qualities, bot
good and bad, have been inflamed with ardent Pa
fions for some *Mortal Virgin* Which is no false o
vain Opinion, as the incredulous Part of Men wou
fain insinuate, but a known Truth confirmed by mar
Experiences.

Indeed, so admirable is the Figure, Voice, and Mi
of a fair *Woman*, that he is wilfully blind, who do
not see, whatsoever Beauties the whole World is o
pable of, concentered in that *Sex* And for this Re
fon it is, that not only *Man*, with *Angel, D*
mons, Genii, Satyrs, and the whole Series of *Ratio*
Beings, admire a fair *Woman*, but also the ver
Brutes are struck with a profound Amazement at h
Sight With Sighs and silent Vows the *Animal Ge*
rations pay Homage to her, and adore the state
Idol Every Thing in *Nature* is enamoured, and h
prostrate at her Feet. She alone commands the U
verse.

Yet after all my Brother, they have their dark Side too, lke the reſt of mixed *Beings* They are the Frontier Paſſes of the World above, and that below , the Gates of Life and Death, the very Avenues to Heaven or Hell, according as they are uſed. Like Fire they will warm and refreſh a Man, if he keep at a due Diſtance , but if he approach too near they will ſcorch and bliſter him, if not conſume him quite Or, like that other Element of Water, they are very good and ſerviceable, whilſt kept within their Bounds , but let them once break down the Banks of Modeſty, they will threaten all with Ruin In a word, 'tis neither ſafe to vex them in the leaſt, or humour them too much. The Exceſs of Fondneſs, as well as the Defect of natural Love, may equally undo us Prudent Generoſity is the only Method of making ourſelves happy in the Enjoyment of this *Sex.*

Dear *Peſteh*, let us reverence ourſelves, and then we cannot fail of due Reſpect from our *Wives* and *Concubines* For they love a Man that is truly maſculine and brave.

Paris, 15*th of the* 10*th Moon,* *of the Year* 1667.

LETTER XIV.

To the ſame

JUST as I had finiſhed the other Letter I was alarmed afreſh with new Diſcoveries of *Solyman's* Treachery. That barbarous *Dog* is certainly an *Imp* of *Hell*, a *Devil* in human Fleſh , an adventitious Plant, plucked from the Drery Banks of *Phlegeton*, or *Cocytus*, and engrafted in our noble Stock, on pupoſe to ruin and deſtroy us The whole *Tribe* is bound to curſe him with immortal Execrations He induſtriouſly ſeeks and ſtudies all Occaſions to do miſchief His Veins ſure ſtream with fierceſt Venoms, rather

than

rather than with human Blood The Poison of D
gons, and *lives* under his Tongue, and the Gall
C o'hes within his Lip His Lungs breathe
thing but infernal Smokes; the Spirit *Negrides* tr
the *Systole* and Diastole of his Heart, and his wl
Body is a Den of Fiends, as foul and black, as th
which guard the Throne of the Great *Prince*
Da kn /s

I cou'd have easily forgiven his sly malicious
tempts upon my Life and Honour, his interlopi
Tricks and *Plots*, his *Calumnies*, with all the Train
his perfidious *Actions* But that he should abuse t
virtuous *Fatima*, Daughter to our Uncle *Useph*, is an
jury, I cannot put up, or pardon That innocent L
dy never deserved such cruel, unmanly Usage at l
Hands The Dregs of a thousand bitter Curses be
Portion to drink in *Hell*, unless he repent of this pr
digious Baseness, and make honourable Satisfaction

Thou wilt wonder, perhaps, what is *Solyman's* Crim
that fills me with such implacable Resentment Kno
then, that *Fatima* s Husband being called to the Gr
Signior s Service in the *Wars* of *Dalmatia*, and for th
Reason forced to tarry from her above these fourte
Moons, she entrusted *Solyman* with an Affair of gr
Importance, a Matter which concerned her Life, H
nour, and Welfare in the World It seems she had
Quarrel with an old *Grecian Hag*, who sought to pr
stitute her to the Great *Cadi* of *Smyrna*, where
lives This *Grandee* had by a strange Accident fe
Fatima in a Bath, frequented only by Women of Q
/ty However, through some Neglect of the Servan
he was not spied himself, but went away deeply
Love That Passion thou knowest, makes every Bo
restless, that is tormented with it He knew not ho
to ease himself, but by communicating his Thoug
to the forementioned *Grecian* Widow, whom he h
often made the Confident of his Amours T
through paced *Bawd* soon promised him Relief,
that she would accomplish his Desires However
failed, and found herself mistaken, when she came

tempt the inviolate Chastity of *Fatima* For all her glittering Promises, her softest *Rhetorick* could never corrupt a Heart established firm in Virtue

Mad at her Repulse, she studied how to be revenged, conceiving it not impossible to bring her Designs about by Violence, since fair Persuasions would not do. She frames a formal Accusation against *Fatima* before the *Cad*, taxing her with *Witchcraft* and other Crimes upon Oath The *Cadi* having learned his Lesson, would not hear the Cause in open *Divan*, but pretending Indisposition of Body, caused her to be brought before him in his private Bed chamber The *Greek* had ready by her several suborned *Witnesses*, to depose most horrid Things against the innocent Woman. When the *Cadi* professing an entire Respect to *Fatima's* Husband, seemed to take Pity on her Circumstances, and waved the farther Prosecution of the Cause till another Time, keeping *Fatima* Prisoner in the mean while in his own *Palace*

All this was managed so privately, that no body in the Town took notice of it, save an Acquaintance or two, of the *Grecian* Widows, and *Solyman* our worthy Cousin, who happened to be at *Smyrna* in this very Juncture among his other Rambles

Persons in trouble are willing to fly for Refuge to any Friend, desiring their Assistance *Fatima*, all in Tears at such an unexpected Change of her Condition, had Leisure and Opportunity to speak to *Solyman*, conjuring him to go to certain intimate Friends of our *Family*, living in *Aleppo*, and tell them her Circumstances Instead of this, the Faithless Villain goes to her Husband's Friends at *Tripoli*, telling them the utmost shameful and scandalous Things of *Fatima* his Malice could invent, and that by her lewd Courses she had well-nigh ruined her Husband, producing at the same time forged *Bills* and *Letters* as from him, whereon he raised a thousand *Zequins*, with which the perjured Villain is gone no body knows whether, to make his broken Fortunes once again, and lay a Foundation for new Cheats Whilst the poor injured *Fatima*, is forced to bear the Reproach and Infamy of Things whereof she never was guilty But Time

I

I hope, will clear her Innocence, and bring that cu
Vagabond to Shame

I counselled him indeed long ago to travel, and see
various *Regions* of the Earth, But I never advised hi
load his *Soul* in such long Voyages with the Guilt of
Ingratitude, barbarous Malice, Perfidy, and other
of the greatest Hue The smaller Frailties, Stains,
Blemishes of human Life, are too great a Burden f
generous Heart to bear without Complaints and Sigh
that has but a Spark of Virtue in him, blushes for e
Peccadillo he commits If tempted by good Comp
or in hopes to banish melancholy Thoughts, he inc
himself a larger Draught of Wine than what is ordin
and so insensibly boil up his Blood to irregular He
and Superfluities, he is all this while no body's Foe
his own, He plots no Mischief against his Friend, i
lation, harmless Neighbour or Acquaintance A
Enmity he shews is to himself, and in his Cups he is
aware of that For which Reason afterwards, to expia
criminal Advances he made to Self Murder, he will
scums off the grosser Ebullition of its heated Vein in f
tent Weeping A Flood of Tears runs from his Eyes,
generous *Libations* at the Foot of the *Altar*, to pacify
Wrath of God, whilst the lighter Part evaporates in
Sighs and Vows Thus this Pollution vanishes like Smo
and he is soon made clean again And so in other Vic
is the same with Men disposed to Virtue, they endea
to root out the evil Habits they are accustomed to T
try all Ways and Stratagems to reform themselves
wicked Men, by Inclination, sin on without Remo
They never study to retrench the Evils they comr
Ever propense to Vice, they chuse is Ways, and c
the Opportunities of doing impious Things. The
natively Unjust, and cannot live at ease without pre
ditated Crimes; It is their Element to be proje
Mischief And such a one is *Solyman* our Cousin

God inspire him with more grateful Sentiments tow
his Friends, more Natural and Affectionate to those c
Blood, and a more just Deportment to all Men Or
he may be like *Cain* who for murdering his Brother
condem

condemned to be a *Vagabond* on Earth ; and like *Zeuli Bazar* the *Perſian*, who falſly accuſed *Hoſain* the *Prophet*, and for that Reaſon was troubled with a *Palſy* in his Head as long as he lived.

Paris, 14*th of the* 10*th Moon,*
    of the Year, 1667

LETTER XV.

To the Mufti's Vicar

I Sent an Account to the *Port* of the Death of the late *Rumb g,* or *Pop,* who is the Great *Patriarch* of the *Nazarene* Now the *Cardinals* have choſen another to ſucceed him, whom they call *Clement* IX A Man of a great Character for Learning and Piety, and one from whom the *Fari* expect glorious Things to be done for the Publick Good of *Chriſtendom*

Theſe *Popes* ſeem to inherit the Authority and Honour of the Ancient *Pontifex Maximus,* or *High Prieſt* of the *Romans* in the Time of *Paganiſm* Nay, they aſſume a far more ample and uncontroulable Power. For thoſe *Gentile Prelates* always ſubmitted to the *Imperial* Authority, from which they received Protection and Maintenance But theſe *Chriſtian Fathers* acknowledge ro *Superior* on Earth *Kings* and *Emperors* do Homage to them, and perform the meaneſt Services ; as to hold the *Baſon* whilſt the *Pope* waſhes his Hands , to hold the *Stirrop* whilſt he mounts or alights from off his *Mule* Sometimes Great *Princes* lead his *Horſe* by the *Bridle,* whilſt at another Seaſon they carry him on their Shoulders It is recorded, that *Eumenes* King of *Pergamus,* came to *Rome,* and pulling off his *Turbant,* humbly laid it on the Ground before the *Senate,* confeſſing he received his Liberty from them And *Pruſius,* King of *Bithynia,* uſed to ſtile himſelf the *Roman Senate's Slave,* and bow down to the Earth before them. But this is nothing to the Reverence which

greateſt

greateſt *Monarchs* pay the *Pope*, when crawling on th
and Knees, they kiſs the Sandal on his Foot

He can make and depoſe *Kings* at Pleaſure, abſo
Subjects from their Allegiance, bind and remit Si
open and ſhut the Gates of *Paradiſe, Purgatory,* a
Hell, or at leaſt he endeavours to make the World b
lieve ſo

He has Seventy *Cardinals* for his Aſſiſtants a
Counſellors, all equal to *Princes*   A hundred and
ty *Archbiſhops* under his Obedience   A Thouſand
Seventeen *Biſhops*   A Hundred and Forty Four Th
ſand *Monaſteries* and *Religious* Houſes ; Three H
dred Thouſand *Pariſhes* obeying his Will, and ye
ing Homage to him   So that if he were reſolved
carry on ſome laſting *War,* he need only lay an I
poſt of Six Crowns a Year on every *Monaſtery,*
Fifty Two on every Pariſh, and it would amount
Sixteen Millions of Crowns yearly Income   And f
of every *Monaſtery* he choſe out Ten Men, he wo
have an Army of Fourteen Hundred and Forty Th
ſand Men   Which is more than any *Potentate* in
World can do beſide

Thou wilt ſay, it is a Wonder then he does no
this in Practice, and ſo wage *War* with the G
Signior, who has fleeced him of many flouriſhing Co
ties formerly under his Obedience

O Sacred Oracle of the *Muſſulmans, God* has tied
his Hand, he cannot do it   Theſe are but c
Speculations, impracticable Projects, fantaſtick i
deas.   The mighty Train of his *Archbiſhops, B*
Pariſh-Prieſts, with *Jeſuits, Monk,* and *Friars,* tho'
never ſo willing to obey his Orders in ſuch a Caſe,
cannot ſtir a Foot without the Leave of their reſpe
Sovereigns   For they are diſperſed through d
Kingdoms, States, and Principalities, where the
ſubject to the Laws and Government in Force
that unleſs he could unite the Hearts of all the C
t an *Princes* one with another, and with his c
to undertake ſo grand an Expedition, it is impoi
ever to effect his Will   Each *Nation* has an Int
of its own to purſue which makes them deaf to t

Proposals as may embarrass, if not ruin them. No *Peter* of the *Dysart*, rambling up and down from *Court* to *Court*, with his Religious Harangue, will ever again prevail to raise another *Crusade* That Zeal is out of Fashion now in *Christendom*, Kings, in these latter Ages have not half the Attach and Veneration for the *Pope* they had in former Times When *Pope Boniface* VIII claimed a Temporal Jurisdiction in *France*, *Philip* the *Fair* being then King, sent him this short Answer, *Let thy Great Sottishness know, that in Temporals we are subject to none but God alone.* And a *French Ambassador* at *Rome*, speaking something boldly to the *Pope*, the *Prelate* reproached him, *That his Father was burnt for a Heretick*, whereupon the *Ambassador* gave him such a Box on the Ear, that he fell down as dead But it was a tart Message indeed which the *Eastern Bishops* sent to *Pope John* III who claimed an Universal Authority over all the *Churches* in the World For, they say, *We firmly believe thy Absolute Authority over thy own Subjects, but we who are not subject to thee, cannot bear thy Pride, nor are we able to satiate thy Avarice. The Devil be with thee, and God with us*

In a Word, all *Denmark, Swedeland, Norway, Holland, England, Scotland, Geneva, Ireland*, half the *Empire*, and half *Switzerland*, are fallen off from their Obedience to the *Pope* within these Two Hundred Years And those *Kingdoms* and *States* which yet continue under the Yoke, are ready to shake it off at every Turn, when they are never so little galled and vexed *France, Spain*, and *Venice* often huff the *Pope* into Compliance with their Demands Nor dares he to refist, but winks and puts up all, like an old decripid *Father*, for whom his Sons are grown too strong

Holy Successor of the Prophet and Messenger of God; thou art the *Infallible Interpreter* of the *Law*, and *Judge of Equity*, yet dost not arrogate a *Power* above thy *Commission* The *Grand Signior* honours thy Wisdom and Sanctity, and thou obeyest with humble Submission to the *Imperial Edicts.* He is thy Lord, and

thou his *Guide* and *Tutor* in the Way to *Paradise* May
God increase thy illuminations with thy Years, and in
spire me and all the *True Faithful* with sincere Loy
alty to our *Sovereign*, and devout Obedience to thee,
without the least Allay of Treachery or Superstition

Paris, *2d of the 11th Moon,*
   of the Year 1667

LETTER XVI.

To Nathan Ben Saddi, *a Jew at* Vienna.

NOW thou seest I am a truer Prophet than the
New Messias, that *Impostor Sabbati Sevi.* And
yet, though I am so in effect, I do not aspire at the
Title. I claim no Character above that of a Mortal,
who has not quite forfeited his Sense and Reason
However if thou wilt yet retain some Veneration for
his Person, shew it by imitating his Example and em
brace the *Mussulman Faith* as he has done. At least he
outwardly professes it, and had the Honour to do so
first in Presence of the *Sultan.* I know not whether
thou hast heard of this or no. Thy Brethren perhaps
may be unwilling to disperse the News of a *Conver
sion* bringing so much Infamy to all your *Race.* It is
possible they are ashamed to own or publish to the
World, the Tidings of their own egregious Folly, in
giving up their *Faith* to such a Cheat as this, a Cheat
as one would think grown stale and fetid enough, to
make a Man that had the smallest Grain of Sense recoil,
considering how oft your *Fathers* have been bubbled be
fore by such upstart *Messiacs,* such spurious *Prophets* as
this

I commend the Wit of *Sabbati Sevi,* in that he
would not stand the Brunt of the *Grand Signior's Archers,*
or by a vain Presumption hope for Miracles from Hea
ven to skreen his naked Body from a Shower of fatal
Snafts. Had he been so rash, I should esteem him the
                                        greatest

greateſt Miracle of Stupidity that ever was extant on
the Earth If thou haſt not been yet informed of theſe
Paſſages, Fame will quickly bring them to thy Ears,
and then my Letter will not ſeem obſcure In the
mean time, aſſure thy ſelf, he denied his *Apoſtleſhip* to
ſave his Life, and this before the *Grand Signior*, with
the chief *Grandees* of the *Court* Where at the ſame
Time he confeſſed *One God*, and *Mahomet* his Meſſen-
ger If thou art his *Diſciple* therefore, thou oughteſt
to be ſtedfaſt, and tread in his Steps, giving Glory to
the *Eternal One*, who has ſent *Prophets* into all Nations,
to lead Men in the right Way, as he ſent *Moſes* to the
Houſe of *Iſrael*

Na *han*, ſuffer no narrow Principles, no partial Prejudices to ſhut up thy *Soul* from the bright Splendors of
Immortal Truth, which ſhine on every Man The
Light of *Heaven* is not confined to one particular Lineage It is copious, large, and infinite, ſpreading a-
broad its Univerſal Rays, enlightning all the Families and Nations on Earth

It is true, I grant, the *Omnipotent* firſt ſent *Moſes*
with the *Written Law* to the *Poſterity* of *Iſaac* Had
they obeyed the *Sacred Inſtitution*, it is poſſible your
Race had now been bleſſed above the reſt of Men
Perhaps your *Fathers* would have ſtretched their *Con-
queſt* far and wide to the utmoſt Limbs of the *Land*,
from *India* to the *Weſtern* Shores of *Africk*, and from
the remote Borders of the *South* to *Nova Zembla* in the
Arctic Circle Then devout Princes, would have travelled from the *Four Angles* of the World, and made
long *Pilgrimages* to *Jeruſalem*, there to perform their
Vows, and offer *Sacrifice* to the *King of Heaven*

But alas, your *Anceſtors* turned *Infidels* and *Idolaters*,
even at the very Foot of Mount *Sinai*, whilſt the tremendous * Echoes* of the *Thunders* yet were in their Ears.
They made themſelves a *Calf of Gold*, and adored the
Idol of their own *Workmanſhip* So did their *Children*
worſhip *Adonis*, *Venus*, *Diana*, and almoſt all the *Rabble* of the *Gentile Gods* and *Goddeſſes* For which Reaſon, the Wrath of *Heaven* was kindled againſt that *Generation* *God* rouzed the Mighty *Monarchs* of the

Eaft to take up Arms, and punifh fuch a *Wicked Race*
of Men How oft was fair *Jerufalem* facked, and all
the *Jews* deftroyed or carried away *Captives* by *Perfi
ans*, *Medes*, *Affyrians*, or the *Kings* of *Babylon* How
many *Prophets* were fent to tell them of their Errors,
and reclaim them ? But the obdurate Sons of *Jacob*
ftopped their Ears, being refolutely bent on Wicked
nefs, the Meafure of which being once compleat, *Fate*
figned the *Edict* of your utter Ruin For then came
Jefus the *Son of Mary*, the True *Meffias*, who foretold
the irrevocable *Cataftrophe* of *Jerufalem*, which came
to pafs accordingly in that very Age, when the Victo
rious *Roman* Army laid it all in Afhes, not fo much as
fparing the Glorious *Temple* of *Solomon* Ever fince
which, the *Jews* have been difperfed abroad through
all the Earth Each *Nation*, *City*, or *Province* where ye
live, account ye Execrable *Fugitives* and *Vagabonds*

In they mean while, the Fame of *Jefus* fpread a
broad, his heavenly *Doctrine*, perfect *Life*, and mighty
Miracles, fubdued the Hearts of Men *Chriftianity* took
Root in the World It grew and branched itfelf through
out the *Continent* The *Roman* and the *Grecian Empires*
tamely fat down under the *Church's* Shade within Three
Hundred Years, and quickly after, other Nations fled
unto the *Sacred* Shelter But in Procefs of Time, this
Religion alfo, like to yours, degenerated in o Error,
Superftition and Idolatry And then *God* raifed up
Mahomet, our *Holy Lawgiver* He fent him down the
Book of *Glory* by the Hand of *Gabriel*, and command
ed him to teach it to the Houfe of *Ifmael* firft, and
then to all Men that were willing to embrace the *Unde
filed Faith* but to chaftife with Fire and Sword, the *In
fidels* who fhould oppofe his *Miffion*, and refift the *Truth*

How foon the *Muffulmon Law*, took place, and
gained Ground in *Arabia*, *Perfia*, *Syria*, and the adja
cent *Regions* of the *Eaft* ? Nothing was able to ftand
before the Warlike Troops of *True Believers*. How
bold and matchlefs were the Actions of the Valiant
Hali ? How wife the Counfels of Sage *Omar*, and
Abu Bacre ? How eloquent and forcible the Words of
the Chafte and Generous *Ofman* ? The *Prophet was*

happy

happy in the Company of all the *Calphs* They fought
and conquered all before them

Where er the Heavenly Banner was difplayed,
Trembling and Horror feized the *Infidels* Showers of
incefate Arrows ftreight were fent, againft which the
Chriftians could not ftand, much lefs could they
fuftain the near Approach and dreadful Shock of our
Invincible Cavalry Their faint Battalions quickly
fled, and pofted from the Field, whilft ours, un-
mindful of the Spoil, purfued the Chafe, and ftrewed
the Ground with flaughtered Carcafes of flying Mif-
creants Conqueft attended the *Tiue Faithful*, whenever they drew their Swords Thus for above thefe
Thoufand Years has Religion made its fortunate Advances on the Earth And if another *Law* fhould be
revea\led, and fome new *Prophet* rife to check the farther Growth of *Muffulman Faith*, and undermine the
Empr. of the *Faithful*, we ought not to reflect on *Mahomet* for this, as though he were an *Impious Seducer*,
any more than we do on *Mofes* for your Calamities, or
on *Jefus* the *Son of Mary*, for the declining State of
Chriftendom

It is not impoffible, but that the *Omnipotent* may
have hidden Referves of *Precepts*, yet to be divulged.
He has had his various Methods and Difpenfations in
all Ages and Parts of the World Neither is it fit for
Mortal Man to limit the *Eternal One*, or fet him
Rules His Methods are to us incomprehenfible.
He fent *Mofes*, a Man bred in all the Sciences and
Wifdom of the *Egyptians* To *Jefus* he committed his
hidden Power and Knowledge, and the *Apoftles* fpake
all *Languages* But *Mahomet* could neither write nor
read, and yet thou feeft his *Law* has profelyted many
mighty *Kingdoms*, *States*, and *Empires* Who knows,
but that in future Times he will convert the *Apoftate
World* by fome *Dumb Perfon*, who can neither hear nor
fpeak? or by fome blind Man, who could never fee?
Or is it not impoffible, but that he may employ fome
Maid of admirable Beauty, Gifts and Learning in the
Myfterious Work So were the *Sybils* of old infpired
with *Sacred* Wifdom and Foreknowledge of Things to

come

come All filled with inward *Blaſts* of ſome *Immortal Wind,* the pregnant *Virgin* ſoon conceived deep *Myſteries* of *Fate* which they writ down on *Leaves* of *Trees* For they were *Eremits,* and *Twelve* in Number, as Ancient *Records* ſay One of them lived at *Cuma* in *Italy,* where her *Cave* is ſhown to *Travellers* at this *Day* They foretold what ſhould happen in After-times, particularly the *Birth* of *Jeſus* the *Son* of *Mary* But they never ſaid a Word of *Sabbeti Sevi,* or of any other *Meſſias,* to come after the Firſt Theſe *Holy Men* were had in great *Veneration* by the *Gentiles,* who gathered up the ſcattered *Leaves* whereon they writ their *Prophecies,* and tranſcribed them carefully on *Paper,* that ſo the *Sacred Memoirs* might be delivered ſafe down to *Poſterity*

By what I have ſaid, *Nathan,* thou mayeſt perceive that I aim at nothing elſe, but to wean thee from the ſuperſtitious, fond *Conceit* of your *Nation,* and to make thee ſenſible, That though *God* once favoured the *Jews* with *Oracles* of *Light* and *Reaſon,* yet they have for many *Ages* forfeited this *Privilege* Since which, he gave the *Goſpel* to *Jeſus* the *Son* of *Mary,* the *Alcoran* to *Mahomet,* and at all Times has ſent *Meſſengers* and *Prophets* to every Nation and People on Earth

There are no partial *Biaſſes* in the *Divinity* which made the *Worlds.* He is an inexhauſtible *Abyſs* of *Love,* of *Light* and *Life ,* where every *Creature* drinks its *Fill* of *Natural* Happineſs, according to the different Ranks, Capacities, and Deſires of Things He veſts the *Sun* with an *Immortal Robe* of *Light,* the *Train* of which is born up by the *Moon* and *Stars*

When *Phœbus* is upon the *Wing* by *Day,* his *Garment* covers all the *Sky ,* the Golden *Fringes* of it dangle to the *Globe,* and *trail* along in the *miry Soil,* yet never gather the leaſt *Speck* of *Dirt* They are *dipped* and *plunged* in *Rivers, Lakes* and *Seas,* without being *wet ,* and yet they drink up *all* the *Ocean* by *ſucceſſive Draughts* This lower *World* rejoices in the *glittering* Shew , the *Elements* with every *Being* compounded of them, *baſk* in the welcome *Rays* So do the *Planets* above,

above, who take a singular Pleasure to *fold* some *Part* of the *Illustrious Dress* about them   They *wrap* themselves *half* up in *borrowed Light*, and then, like *Western Frail*, the foot it too and fro in their beloved Walks above, giving the necessary Salutes and *Conge*'s to each other *Passent*, and to the Sedentary *Signs* and fixed *Stars*, to see if any of them mind their *Courtly* Garb and Mien   For they are the Sun's *Domestick Pages*, the *Favourites* of his *Seral*   At other Seasons they stand still, perhaps to gaze upon themselves, in Contemplation of the Majestick Figure they make

So have I seen a proud, conceited *Spanish* Trumpeter, after he had blown a *Levet* pretty well lay down the Silver Instrument with a disdainful Gravity   His Cheeks all blown with inclosed Air, and Soul puffed up with Arrogance, he struts and curls his black *Mustaches.* Then with big Looks, surveys himself from Head to Foot, casting an Eye of Scorn upon the silent *Tube,* conscious that he alone can make it sound so well

Thou wilt say, I wander in my Discourse as much as those *Heavenly Bodies* I am speaking of.   It is true, *Nathan*, our Thoughts are free, and not confined to Rules and Forms   We easily slip from one Imagination to another.   And since I have made this *Planetary* Digression, suffer me now, like them, to run retrograde, and come to the Point from which I roved.

Doubtless, each individual *Being* is filled with its *Essential* Bliss   The Fire has its Specifick Happiness, so has the Air, the Water and the Earth, with all the living Generations on it   And when the *Most High* distributed the *Sons* of *Human Race* through all the various Climates, Zones, and Provinces, he furnished every Region of the Globe with Gifts and Products, Riches and Delights, agreeable to the Inhabitants, with this *Proviso*, that they should live in Innocence, Justice and according to Reason   From which Eternal Law, if any People swerved, they should forfeit their Privileges, and be subdued, if not extirpated, by some more virtuous Nation

From

From hence fprung all the Revolutions of Mighty
Kingdoms and *Empires*, one fucceffively fupplanting an
other to this Day   And the Sins of your *Nation* being greater, it feems, than thofe of any other, *God* has
difperfed you over all the Earth, without fuffering you
to inherit or poffefs a Foot of Ground

If ever therefore *Fate* defigns to reftore the *Jews*
again to the *Holy Land*, wherein their *Fathers* lived,
never expect it, till your erroneous Minds and vicious
Manners are reformed   For *Palestine* was never feat-
ed fo delicioufly for bloody Zealots, Hypocrites, and
cruel Ufurers to enjoy.

Paris, 2d of the 11th Moon,
    of the Year 1667.

LETTER XVII.

To Dgnet Oglou.

*D*ARIA is a Quean, a Jilt, and I am once more
      cured of my Dotage   There is no Truft in
Woman's Beauty, Faith or Wit   They are deceitful
as the Fruit of *Afphaltites*   They are perfect *Riddles*
and *Paradoxes*, and have more unlucky Tricks than
crofs grained *Elves* or *Fairies*.   When a Man over
heated by his Amorous Paffion thinks to embrace a
Goddefs, he meets with *Ixion*'s Fate, and only hugs
gaudy *Cloud* or *Meteor*

I will not make thee fick with a particular Rehear-
fal of my Second Folly, in being fo fond of one who
had betrayed me formerly   I will not repeat the vain
Addreffes I made, the kind obliging Things I fpoke,
nor her deceitful Anfwers.   I will not tell thee how
fhe drilled me on into her Snares, and led me Captive
in an Amorous Circle   Content thy felf to know,
that I have been *Twice* her *Cully*, and if ever I am the
Third Time, it will be my own Fault, as the *Italic*
                                                      fay

fays No, my *Dgnet*, I have done with that *False* Sex
Henceforth for ever, I abjure all Amorous Regards of
Woman   I will fhun them, as I would a Peftilence I
will either fhut my Eyes, or turn them another Way
at leaft, whenever I meet a *Female*   I will not think
of them, but with Difdain and Hatred Finally, I am
off f om them to all Intents and Purpofes

However, as the *Arabian Proverb* fays, *That Wind
blows from an unlucky Point of the Compafs, which wafts
n Good to fom body* , fo from *Darra's* falfe and feigned
Smiles, I reap fome Benefit I have learned a Secret,
which has rid my Spirit of a Thoufand Cares, Difquiets
and Agonies

In the Year 1664, of the *Chriftian Hegira*, I fent a
Letter to the noble *Kerker Haffan Baffa*, our Countryman , wherein I informed him of an Affaffin
mroe upon me in the Dark, as I was going to my
Lodgings, and how I killed the Ruffian that attempted
on my Life I told that generous *Grandee* all my
I d ufes and Conjectures on that Subject , how I
fufpected fome of my Enemies at the *Porte* to have a
Hand in the Defign , or elfe, that my *Sicilian Mafter*
was concerned in it I knew not well what to conclude.
But now I am fatisfied it was *Darra's* Hufband, who
refenting deeply my former Amour with her, which fhe
difcovered to him at large, could never be at reft till
he faw *Paris*, where he defigned to be the Executioner
of his own Revenge, and lay in wait accordingly for
my late returning home For he was not ignorant of
my Lodging His Wife knew nothing of his Defign,
he having pretended other Bufnefs at the City And
it was from accidental Words in her Difcourfe, that
I collected this great Secret For when I afked her of
her Hufband's Health fhe told me, he was killed at
fuch a Time by Night, in an Alley of *Paris*, by
whom fhe never yet could learn   But I ftreight blufh-
ed with Confcioufnefs, and took the Hint I dropped
fome neceffary, carelefs *Quer s* by degrees And all
her Anfwers ftill confirmed me, as to Time and
Place with other Circumftances, that he muft be the
Man I murthered in my own Defence fo long ago

I kept this Secret locked up in my Breaſt, nor could my doting Fondneſs melt me into ſuch a ſoft and eaſy Temper, as to betray my ſelf to her   But I took inward Pleaſure at the Thoughts of my Deliverance from that ſudden violent Death, and from my After Cares and Fears by this Diſcovery   Henceforward I will ſuſpect no *Muſſulman*, though my Enemy   Nor ſhall I be ſo fearful of my *Sicilian Maſter*   No panick Terrors ſhall confine me to my Chamber, and make me ſpend my Days in fretting and conſuming Melancholy   I will not be ſurprized when Strangers knock at the Gate, or when I hear the bluſtring Voices of the Pariſh Officers below, or the Collectors of the King's Revenues—Yet theſe before were dreadful as the *Sultan*'s *Atteſcheriff*, or *Fatal Warrant*, when he demands a *Baſſa*'s Head, ſo forcible is Jealouſy and ſuſpended Thoughtfulneſs, ſo black the Influence of miſgrounded Apprehenſion, and miſtaken Guilt

My *Dgnet*, this mortal Life is a dark *Labyrinth* of croſs Everts   Bewildered Man gropes up and down he often trips and ſtumbles at Contingencies, he ſtrays about in thorny, rugged Paths, not knowing where he is, or which Way to turn himſelf   Sometimes an *Ignis Fatuus*, with its deceitful Light, miſguides him in miry Places, Fens, and Bogs, where he is in danger of being ſwallowed up, or leads him to the Brink of an high Precipice, where, if he advance but one Step more, he is gone beyond Recovery, he falls and daſhes himſelf to Pieces on under growing Rocks

Reaſon is the only Clue that can conduct us ſafe thro' all the Windings of the perilous Maze   Heav'n grant that thou and I may never let go our Hold of this ſo neceſſary Faculty, until he has conducted us ſafe to *Paradiſe*

Paris, 15*th of the* 12*th Moon,*
    of the Year 1667.

LETTE XVIII.

To the Kaimacham.

LAST Year I gave thee an Account of the Birth of a young *Princess* of *France* Now I shall inform thee, that she was baptized on the 21st of this *M..r* *Baptism* with the *Nazarenes* is equivalent to our *C..rc..m..sion*, nay, it is something more *D..vine*, if we may believe them They call it the *Sacrament* of *Initiation* the *First Mystery* of *Christian Faith* But when it is applied to the Children of *Royal* Extraction, the Sons or Daughters of *Kings*, it looks more like a *Ceremony* of *State* than a *Mystery* of *Religion* However, be it what it will it is performed with Abundance of Pomp and Magnificence And at this *Ceremony* it is that every *Christian* receives his *Name*, which is given by the *Godfathers* and *Godmothers*, that is, Persons who stand *Suret* for the Child's Education in the *Christian Religion* This *Princess* was named *Maria Theresa* by the *Dutchess Dowager* of *Orleans*, and by the Duke of *En-g..."*

On the same Day the *Cardinal Duke* of *Vendosme* had *..ence* of the *King* and *Queen*, in quality of *Legat de Lat..* from the *Pope* It seems, the *King of France* had desired the *Pope* to stand *Godfather* to the *Dauphin*, which the good *Prelate* accepting, sent this *Cardinal* as his *Deputy* and *Representative* to perform the *Charge*. He is to give the *Dauphin* his *Name* In the mean while, he stands much upon *Punctilios*, requires vast Respects and submissions from the *French Bishops*, and carries himself with as much State, as if he were a *God*, or an *Angel*, looking as big, as if he were the *Emperor* of the *U....e* and well he may, since during this *Legatio..* he has as much Power as the *Pope* himself, that *Soveraign Prelate* having invested him with all his own *Infernal full Authority*, which he would make the *World* believe, is greater than that of Earthly *Kings* and *Emperors*. And yet he stiles himself the *Servant* of the

the *Servants* of GOD A fire Piece of *Ecclesiastic Hypocrisy!* the Ways of these *Infidels* are double The Practice runs counter to their Profession They would fain appear as *Saints*, when in effect they are little better than *Devils*

There has been a great Alteration lately made in *Portugal*, the *Estates* of that *Nation* having compelled their *King* to renounce his *Government*, and confer it on *Don Pedro* his Brother. The *Spaniard* laughs at this privately, hoping from their intestine Animosities to draw Occasions of advancing his own Interest, and of recovering that *Crown* again

Accomplished *Minister*, there is nothing new under the *Moon*, but a perpetual Circle of the same Events What we admire in this Age as a Novelty, has been acted over and over in former Times Peace follows War, and War treads close upon the Heels of Peace, Faith, Perfidy, Sedition, Obedience, Virtue and Vice, are the reciprocal Off-spring of each other There is nothing fixed or stable, but the World turns round upon Eternal Vicissitudes

Paris, 30*th of the* 1*st Moon, of the Year* 1668.

LETTER XIX.

To Abdel Melec Muli Omar, President *of the* the College *of* Sciences *at* Fez.

I Received thy invaluable *Dispatch*, containing marvellous Things, Revelations of a sublime Rank, Mysteries heretofore undiscovered, Yet I was not much surprized, having all along presaged some vast Improvement of Learning from thy accomplished Spirit, O thou *Terrestrial Star* of the *first Magnitude*, *Chief* in the *Constellations* of the *South*.

Glory

Glory be to GOD, who from infinite Darkneſs ſtarted the Eternal bright *Ideas* of the Univerſe, and on the Womb of everlaſting Silence, begat the W O R D by which he formed all Things Doubtleſs, there is no Blemiſh in his Works, no Botches, Knobs, or diſproportionable Unevenneſſes The World is a perfect Beauty

Were *Ptolomy* alive, thy *Syſtem* of the *Heavens* would put him to the Bluſh And *Tycho Brahe* would ſneak ou of his *Planetary* Frame, by ſome wild and more than *Eccentrick* Motion, aſhamed that he had been ſuch a Botcher in *Aſtronomy* *Copernicus* himſelf would ſink under the Burthen of the *Moon*, which the overloaded *Earth* would in revenge let fall upon him, for his unnatural Cruelty to his aged Mother, in burthening her ſo long, and all the World would celebrate thy Praiſe, who has thus happily reſcued *Heaven* and *Earth* from their Embarraſſments

Thy Thoughts are high and elevated to the *Heaven* of *Heavens*, yet thy Humility ſtoops to the *Centre* of the *Earth* But all Man'ind would be obliged to thee afreſh, if thou wouldſt vouchſafe to take the middle Path, and ſurvey with thy accuſtomed Accuracy the Surface of this *Globe*, whereon we Mortals tread *Geography* being already ſenſible of her elder Siſter's Happineſs, in thy Correction and Amendments of the former *Aſtronomick* Schemes, languiſhes alſo for thy Superviſal of her own Defects and Blemiſhes

Thoſe that have meaſured the Earth, cannot agree in ſtating her Circumference And there were few in former Times who did believe the *Antipodes* The *Miſſulmons* of *India* do aſſert, that the *Earth* is ſupported by eight mighty *Elephants* And thoſe of *Turky* ſay, it reſts upon the *Horns* of a great *Bull* If either of theſe Opinions were to be taken in the Literal Senſe, it would put the dulleſt *Philoſopher* to Subſmation, or at leaſt a Fit of Laughter But doubtleſs they are *Allegories*, under which are vailed ſome true and natural Secrets

However, let the *Globe* reſt where it will, on *Bulls*, or *Bars*, or *Elephants*, or *Camels*, *Dromedaries*, *Horſe*, or the Back of *Atlas*, as the *Gentiles* did affirm, I

would

would fain know, methinks, how large a Space of
Land we have to tread upon, and what Proportion is
allotted to the Sea

It is true, we have a common Notion of *Four Quar-*
ters of dry Land, *Asia*, *Africk*, *Europe*, and *America*.
Yet this is quarrelled at by those of later Times, who
add a *Fifth*, which they call *Magellanica*, or the *South-*
ern unknown Earth. From immemorial Times, our Fathers were acquainted with the *Three* First Divisions or
Precincts of the *Globe* But the two last were but of
late discovered, since the Improvement of *Navigation*,
and the Invention of the *Compass*

There is a vulgar Tradition every where in vogue
that after *Noah's* Flood, *Asia* fell to the Share of *Sem*
and his Posterity, *Africk* to *Cham*, and *Europe* to *Ja-*
phet Whether this be true or no, cannot be proved,
but is wholly owing to Conjecture However, this is
certain, th if it were so, there have been mighty
Changes in the Inheritance of *Noah's* Off spring, and
Alterations in their several Limits Insomuch, as now
they seem to be in Part blended and mixed together,
or at least Hed from one to another

Those who lived in the *Middle Ages*, made but *Two*
Divisions of the *Globe*, viz *Asia* and *Europe* And in
this they also erred For some made *Africk* only a
Province or Part of the latter, persuading themselves
that they were antiently joined together, tho' afterward
separated by a violent Irruption of the *atlantic Sea* by
the *Streights* of *Gibraltar*, which before was a narrow
Isthmus, or Neck of Land, but from the Time that
Bank was washed away, the *Mediterranean Sea* derived
its Origin Others made *Africk* a Part of *Asia*, there
being not absolutely parted by any Sea, though some E-
gyptian Kings and Roman Emperors attempted to make a
Canal between the *Mediterranean* and *Red Sea*

A third Sort divided the known Part of the World
into *Asia*, *Europe*, *Africk*, and *Egypt* While a fourth
placed *Egypt* to the Account of *Asia* making the River
Nile the Boundary between it and *Africk* But this was
incommodious, in regard it left that Part of *Egypt* on the
West of *Nile* to *Africk* Such was the Confusion of the
antient *Greek* and *Roman Geographers.*   A-

As for *America*, it takes its Name from *Americus Vesputius* a *Florentine*, who made the second Voyage to discover it. For it was first descryed by *Christopher Columbus*, a *Genoese*, in the Year of the *Christian Hegyra*, 1442, by the Order and at the Charge of *Ferdinand*, King of *Arragon* and *Castile*. This *Part* of the *World* is divided into two mighty *Empires*, the *Northern*, or that of *Mexico*, and the *Southern* or that of *Peru*.

Magellanica, or the *Southern Unknown Land*, derives its Name from *Ferdinand Magellan*, the first that ever discovered it, in the Year 1520, when he sailed quite round the *Globe*. About five and forty Years afterwards, *Francis Drake*, an *Englishman*, touched upon the same Coasts, and twelve Years after him, *Thomas Cavendish*, one of his Countrymen. Likewise *Oliver van Noord* a *Hollander*, undertook the same Voyage. But none made such Advances in this new Discovery, as a certain *Spaniard*, call'd *Ferdinand de Quier*.

God knows, what strange and unexpected Novelties this *Country* might afford, if Men were once acquainted with it. This may be the Sanctuary of the Ten Tribes of *Israelites*, which were led away Captives by *Salmanasar*, King of *Assyria*. Or perhaps the Inhabitants of this *Country* are of another Race than that of *Noah* and *Adam*. We may from them, it is possible, derive new Lights, as to the Pre existence of *human Souls*. Who knows, but they have Records more exact and antient than the *Indians* and *Chinese*? Be it how it will, I am clear for new Discoveries. There is a certain specifick Boldness in my Spirit, which prompts me to invade the pretended Modesty of *Nature*. I long to furl the Veil, which hides so many Secrets, and with a Philosophick Confidence, were I in Power, I would rumple up the envious Coverings of such desirable Wonders.

Oh! that some *God like Monarch* in this Age would in *Royal* Bounty equip a *Navy*, and man them with the most expert and resolute Mariners on Earth, with Vessels to transport an Army of Land Soldiers, with Tenders to carry Meat, Drink, Apparel, and other Necessaries for so vast an Expedition. Surely, the Event would answer

anſwer Expectation, the Gains would far tranſcend t Coſt, the Honour infinitely ſurpaſs the Peril and our known familiar World would be obliged by ſuch fortunate Undertaking

Sage *Omar*, it depends on thee to bring this Th to paſs Start but the Propoſal to ſome mighty S reign, thy Recommendation will be of Force Th wilt be more than a *Columbus*, *Magellan*, or *Pizar* In fine, thou wilt wind up the Searches of this inq fitive Age, and put a Stop to future Scrutinies

I only hint the Thing , do thou purſue it, and Generations ſhall celebrate thy Fame. GOD inſp thee with freſh Ardors

Paris, 7th of the 3d Moon,
    of the Year 1668

LETTER XX.

To Oſman Achooneth, Aſtrologer to th Sultan at Adrianople

OLD *Ptolmy* was much out of his Braſs , his wid irregular Fancy drunk with the Le of dark Opinion and Conceit, ſtumbled and ſtill aſleep up on the Thought of the *Earth* s being Centre to th Univerſe, and then the reſt of the *World* ſeemed to r round his giddy Head He often ſtrove to lift his he vy Noddle up, to ſee whether it were ſo or not B the befotting Load of Prepoſſeſſion weigned him dow again He ſlumbered, dreamed, and ſnorted loud ſtretched at large upon the fair Chimera

The ſtudious Candidates of Truth and Science, by his Example fell to the ſame Riot in *Philoſophy*, and continued the Debauch for many Ages Till too much furfeited and cloyed with ſuch a fulſome Entertainm bold *Tycho Brahe* rubs his Eyes, and wakes the Comp with a new Syſtem of the mighty Frame. Then beg

began to ftart and rouze, as at fome Prodigy. His
heavenly Gimcracks pleafed the Palate of the Age
His *Epicycles, Eccentricks, Perigæ*s and *Apogæ*'s, with
all the reft of his gay Whim-wnams, were received
with general Applaufe, till the more excellent *Copernic*
us appeared with fomething *Newer* ftill. And then the
blundring *Dane*, abafhed, flipped off the Stage, without
fo much as taking his Leave.

The Aftronomers foon fell in Love, and payed im-
plicit Adoration to the Idol which *Copernicus* fet up;
and it was but reafon, fince they had never feen a fairer
or a jufter Scheme of the World before.

Yet every Age improves it felf in Knowledge on the
Ruins of the former. And thus what *Ptolemy* never
found out, nor *Tycho Brahe* or *Copernicus* could mend or
match, if now they were alive, is very lately difcovered by the incomparable *Addel Melec Muli Omar*, Prefident of the College of Sciences at *Fez*.

The happy *Mufa Ab'ul Yatuftan*, Profeffor of Philofophy there, firft ftarted the Propofal of a Mathematical Experiment. And laying Heads together, the Pri-
mate of *Morofco* Doctors, Fathers of the *African Al-
faqu*'s living, found a true Demonftration in it.

I have lately received a Difpatch from that renowned Prelate, with an inclofed Model of this Planetary
Machine. A Copy of which I fend thee, drawn by
my own Hand. It reprefents the Original to a Point.
Examine it well, and thou wild find it is much more
regular and exact, than any of thofe antiquated
Schemes, and anfwers all the Queftions of *Aftronomy*
without the leaft apparent Blunder. Befides, it has a
perfect Symmetry and Proportion in every Part. It
makes the World appear a compleat Beauty. Whereas the Frame which *Tycho Brahe* made, was all deform-
ed with wild Unevenneffes. Nor was the *Syftem* of
Copernicus without a manifeft Botch, in making the
fmall Orb of the Moon alone to interfere with that of
the *Earth*. Whilft all the other Planets circulate in
their own entire and folitary *Spheres*, without an Inter-
loper to difturb them.

Befides,

Befides, he makes the *Earth* an *Atlas* to the Moo
whilft this poor weary *Globe* is forced in his Opinio
to drudge yearly round the *Zodiack*, with the vaft B
then of *Diana* on its Shoulders

If it be fo, it is no wonder that the Earth fo on
faints and trembles under the mighty Load   Her
forth we need not lay the Blame of *Earthquakes* to
celadus, as if the drowzy, fnoring *Giant*, turning
monftrous bulky Corps from one fide to the oth
were the fole Caufe of thefe Convulfions   When Ma
tals reel and ftagger, as they walk upon the Surfac
when Trees and Mountains rock as in a Cradle, a
whole Cities are fometimes fwallowed up.

No, let poor *Enceladus* fleep on, and take what R
he can in his *Infernal* Prifon   There was no Dang
of his ever ftirring again, after he had been once to
roughly fowed in *Lethe*'s All benumming Streams   C
pernicus is only in the Fault   Whenever we feel th
fatal heavings of the *Globe*, it was too unmerciful
Tafk he impofed upon it, efpecially in its Old Age

It would have grumbled in its early Day and ftur
Youth, had it been thus feverely ufed by *Orpheus*, H
mer, *Hermes Trifmegiftus*, or any other of the Primit
Sages   But now to be thus roughly handled by an u
ftart Infidel in its declining Years, when three Parts
its Marrow is decayed, and its once potent Nerves a
Sinews are fhrunk, its Liver wafted, and every V
winding away, almoft broke its Heart

Therefore thefe *African* Sages, in Duty to th
aged Mother the Earth, have found a Way to free h
from the Burthen of the Moon in her decrepit Sta
and yet to make the *Sun* the Centre of the *World*,
jufting at the fame time, with accurate Laws, and
unblemifhed Order, the Motions, Stations, and va
ous Poftures of the *Planets*,

This happy Revelation in *Aftronomy* is not to be d
vulged in Publick Writings, left fome inquifitive, c
rious Traveller, ambitious *Nazarene*, or envious *J*
fhould chance to light upon the facred Scheme, a
boaft himfelf the Inventor of it.

L

Let it be only communicated to Learned, Faithful *Mufulmans* of the First Rank For such Celeftial Myfteries ought not to be proftituted to the Vulgar Tell not the little *Jafmir Sigire Rugial* of it For if thou doth, all the *Frank* Merchants at *Aleppo* foon fhall be made privy to the matchlefs Secret Be it a perpetual *Arcanum* in the Breafts of fublime Men, exalted Souls, Friends of God, and little lefs than *Prophets* And be it, till all the Sages of the *Eaft* and *South* are firft made fenfible of it, and able to defend it againft the vain Attempts of the Uncircumcifed Nation Then let it be promulged in *Allah* s Name throughout the *Globe*, to the Eternal Honour of God, and the Glory of his Prophet, who could neither write nor read, yet has Difciple, to whom alone the pureft Reformation of the Univerfe is owing

Do but furvey with an indifferent Look the laft and lovelieft Portraiture of the World that ever was made by Man Fix thine admiring Eyes on the Magnifick Seat and *Palace* of the *Sun* Confider at the fame time the true and equal Forms, Dimenfions, Diftances, and mutual Interfections of the ambient *Orbs*, without the fmalleft Blur or Blot in all the Eternal Frame Then tell me thy Opinion, whether thou canft not calculate *Nativities*, erect all manner of *Schemes*, make *Almanack*, tell credulous Men their future Fortunes, appoint the *Eclipfes* of the *Sun* and *Moon*, fet *Venus* and *Mercury* together by the Ears, to ftir up a furious *Mars* to make a Hurly burly in the *Heavens* and *Elements*, or, if thou can' not wheedle the fowre Curmudgin *Saturn*, into a foft obliging Humour, or fret the noble *Jupiter* to Madnefs, by a damned *Conjunction* with his mortal Enemy, and a thoufand more *Aftrological* Enterprizes. Tell me, I fay, whether thou canft not perform all this and more, as well by the inclofed Effigies of the World, as by the old Threadbare, Weather-beaten, Worm-eaten *Italian* Clock-work of *Ptolemy*, or the later Inventions of *Tycho Brahe* and *Copernicus*

It will now no longer be a Secret, how thofe Birds difpofe themfelves, which at a certain Time of the Year are

are feen to gather in mighty Troops, and fly dire
upward out of human S at , not one of the whole
cies being left behind o found on any Part of
Earth, until the *Moon* is rolled full fix Times
the *Zodiack* When they return again in equal C
panies into this Globe, each *Species* to his native P
on For the intelligent *Fowls* exactly know the P
in which the Earth does its yearly Circulation
fect the neighbouring Orb of the Moon, and then
fnatch he Opportunity to quit the attractive *Atmo*,
and take the Air of the adjacent Planet

I have a great deal more o fay on this Subject,
I will referve for another Letter In the mean
thou venerable *Star-gaz*, adieu, and remember
private.

Paris *7th of the 3d Moon,
of the Year* 1668,

LETTER XXI

To the Venerable Mufti, *Principal Suppon*
Learning *and true* Science.

THE Orders of thy *Sanctity* came like a Mef
from Heaven, furprifing me at once with e
Pleafure and Aftonifhment Every Line increafed
Rapture And now I thought I had no more to
for n the World, fince the Great *Patriarch* of
Faithful has condefcended to embrace the Advice
mean a Slave as *Mahmut* It has been my paffion
Defire to fee Knowledge flourifh in the Renowned O
man *Empire*, that the *Infidels* may no longer repr
us with Ignorance and Barbarifm This was the b
fon that I fo often importuned thy Predeceffor to en
rage the Tranflation of Hiftories into the *Turk* L
guage Now thou art pleafed to begin this glo
Work, and to honour me, by requiring my Inftru

in the management of it   Nay thou haft commanded
me to lay the Foundation of fo Illuftrious an Enterprize, in prefenting thee a Pattern or Model of this
great Work, containing an Hiftorical Epitome of the
four Great *Monarchies*, with a brief Series of the moft
remarkable and famous Tranflations, Changes, and o-
ther Events in the World, with reference to the Nation and Age wherein they happened

As to the Advice thou demandeft of me, I think it
would be for the Honour and Benefit of the *Muffulmans*,
that a compleat *Hiftory* of the *World* fhould be collected
out of the moft antient and fincere *Writers*, and digeft-
ed into *Annals*, from the very Beginning of Time, down
to the Reign of our prefent *Emperor*, the Auguft Sovereign of the whole Earth   That fo whatfoever has been
done on Earth worthy of Memory, may be ranked in
its proper Time and Place, and we may not grope any
longer in the dark, when we would know in what Year
or Age any famous Warrior or Monarch lived or died,
or when any renowned City was built, befieged, taken,
and deftroyed, and by whom all thefe Things were
done   With many other ufeful *Memoirs*, in which the
Ottomans are now wanting

In the Beginning of this *Work*, it would be abfolutely necefiary to have recourfe to the *Chronicles* of the *Indians*, *Perfians*, and *Egyptians*, and to the *Writings* of
Orpheus, *Homer*, *Thales*, *Zeno*, and others of *Greece*,
Phrygia and *Thrace*   For tho' the *Nazarenes* of the
Weft defpife the Authority of thefe *Authors*, and calum-
niate all for *Fables* and *Romances* which was delivered
before the firft *Olympiad*, yet the more impartial Inhabitants of the *Eaft*, whether *Chriftians* or *Muffulmans*
reject nothing which has the undoubted Stamp of Antiquity   but rather feek to unriddle the myfterious Ex-
preffions of the *Poets* and *Philofophers*, who ftrove induftrioufly to cover all their Knowledge and Traditions
under dark *Ænigma*'s, Figures, Parables, that fo the
Divine Secrets of *Antiquity* might not be prophaned by
the rude and unpolifhed Vulgar.

It

It was ever the *Maxim* of some antient *Sages* and Politicians, thus to keep the People in Ignorance of paſt
Times, the better to aſſure their Dominion and Authority over them. They only revealed what was obvious
to every Man's Senſe, the manifeſt and viſible Influences of the *heavenly* Bodies of the Sun, Moon and Stars,
the Natures of *Plants* and *Animals*, with whatſoever elſe
was liable to any Man's Eye and Apprehenſion: but
as to the more abſtruſe and leſs conſpicuous Works of
Nature, they were like the Secrets of State kept under
a Veil.

Yet there wanted not Men of Wiſdom in other Parts
of the *World*, who ſtrove to unfold all Things, and render Mankind familiar with whatſoever fell under human
Intellect. Among theſe, the *Indians* and *Chineſe* de-
ſerve the firſt Place, who were never covetous of the
Gifts of *Nature*, but ſought to improve all thoſe of the
Nations in the Knowledge of the *Arts* and *Sciences*,
eſpecially in the Syſtem of antient *Hiſtory*. Theſe People ſhut up themſelves from the reſt of the World for
many Ages, fearing leſt Commerce might corrupt the
Simplicity of their primitive Laws and Inſtitutions.
Only *Alexander the Great*, and before him, *Semiramis*
Queen of the *Aſſyrians*, had ever Acceſs to them
in old Time. And *China* was never open till of late,
when their too potent Neighbours the *Tartars* brake
through their Famous Wall, and ſubdued the whole
Empire. And their Buſneſs was not with *Books* but
with *Men*.

For theſe Reaſons we may not wonder, that the Indian *Brachmans*, and the *Bonzes* of *China*, deliver an
Account of the *Origin* of the *World*, and the next ſuc-
ceeding *Ages*, ſo far beyond the *Fables* of all our
Hiſtorians, eſpecially thoſe in the *Weſt*.

For Events of later Date, the *Compilers* of this Work
may make Uſe of ſuch *Hiſtorians* as have written the
Annals of ſeveral *Nations* ſince the firſt *Olympiad*.

If thou knowest not what an *Olympiad* means, it is the Form of Computation used in the antient *Grecian Ægyra*, every *Olympiad* containing Four Years. And the First of these *Olympiads* began in the Year of the *World* 3228 At which Time *Chorebus* of *Elis* signalized himself, by winning the first *Race* that ever was run at the *Olympick Games* These *Games* were celebrated every *Olympiad*, and all the *Youth* of *Greece* flocked to them, to try their Skill in Running, Wrestling, and other manly Exercises

About this Time *Historians* began to write partially, and the Truth could hardly be discerned from the Fabulous Errors with which it was adulterated Yet this rather proceeds from a *Natural* Emulation, than from a Design to corrupt the *Antient Belief* However, thou mayest give Credit to *Thucidides*, who in the 80th *Olympiad* began to write his History of the *War* in *Peloponnesus*, between the *Lacedemonians* and those of *Athens*, which *War* continued one and twenty Years, as that Author testifies, who wrote *final* of it from the Beginning to the End And among other remarkable Passages, which he is very exact in recounting he mentions a famous *Eclipse* of the *Sun*, that happened in the First Year of that *War*, and was so great, that the *Stars* appeared at Noon-Day in the Sky *Plutarch* also speaks of this *Eclipse*, telling us, that *Pericles*, *Prince* of the *Athenians*, being at Sea when the *Sun* was thus darkened, and perceiving the *Master* of the *Vessel* in a great Fright, as at some Prodigy, he threw his Cloak over the Man's Face, and ask'd him, If he was afraid of that or looked upon it as a bad Omen? And when the *Master* answered, *No* *Pericles* reply'd, *What Difference is there between this Eclipse of the Sun, and that, since both are caused by the Interposition of a Veil between the Sun and thine Eyes, only that Veil is greater than any Cloak, it being the Moon which covers this Glorious Lamp from our Sight?*

Much about the same time lived one *Herodotus* and *Helanicus*, two famous Historians, Men of Integrity and Credit, and *Hippocrates*, the Renowned *Physician* of *Athens*,

thens. Thefe aie worthy to be tranflated into the *Tu*
ifh Language , as are alfo *Zenophon* and *Polybiu*,
wrote after them   They all, except the laft, lived
the Time of the *Perfian Monarchy*, and therefore
moft likely to deliver down a true Account of the m
morable Events that happened during that fo1mid
Empire.

As for the *Macedonian Monarchy*, the moft Emin
Writers were *Curtius, Arrianus,* and *Diodorius* S.
but this laft is frequently miftaken in his *Chron*
and therefore ought to be corrected by the oh
Plutarch alfo muft be confulted, and *Jofephus* the
with *Strabo, Appian, Livy, Juftin* and *Paufanio*
they either ferve to illuftrate one another, where
treat of the fame Matters , or elfe the one carries
the Thread of *Hiftory*, where the other left off
therefore thou needeft not wonder that I name fo m
Authors, fince they are worthy of Credit, and abfo
ly neceffary to the compleating an entire *Hiftory* of
World , whereas there are a Rabble of other li
who are fcarce worth the naming , much lefs their
thority to be trufted to, in compiling an univerfal
ftory, which is to give a new Luftre to the *O* t
pire, and raife its Credit in the Learned World

As for the *Roman Empire,* it will be neceffar
make ufe of *Jofephus, Tacitus, Suetonius, Pl*
Inus, Zonaras, Ammianus Marcellinus, Veller. Pa
lus, Seneca, Florus, Livy, and *Suidas*

Thefe will be fufficient Materials with which
Tranflators, Scribes, and *Compilers* may accomplifht
Illuftrious Undertaking, the Encouragement wher
I again earneftly recommend to thy Liberality
Munifcence

What concerns the Injunction thou haft laid on
to draw a *Pattern* or *Model* of this great *Work,* in
fenting thee with a brief Abftract of the *Rife* and
of the *Four Monarchies,* with fuch memorable E
as will be proper to direct the Undertakers in the
thod of digefting this Univerfal *Hiftory,* I will

another *Letter*, not having thofe *Books* by me which are requifite to affift me in this Affair

In the mean time, I pray *Heaven* profper this noble Enterprize, and grant that thou mayeft live the Space of many *Olympiads*, to fee the Effect of thy Bounty, when this Univerfal *Hiftory* being finifhed, fhall inftruct the *Mufulman*, and defeat the Calumnies of the *Uncircumcifed*

Paris, *2d of the 5th Moon, of the Year* 1668

The *End of the* Firft Book

LETTERS

WRIT by a

SPY at *PARIS*.

VOL. VII

BOOK II

LETTER I.

To Mehemet, *an* Exiled Eunuch, *at* Alc...
in Egypt.

THY Sufferings pierce my Heart, I owe th
Pity on the Score of human Nature, and
more Compassion as thou art a *M. fulm...*
but where is the Tongue or Pen that can defcri
the Sympathy of Friends ? Canst thou in a defpon...
ing Manner caft thy felf upon thy Bed, there to e
hale, in melancholy Sighs, that pungent Souro
which can fnd no other Vent, unlefs thofe Vapou
of the Spleen condenfe to Showers of Tears ? C...
thou do this, and I remain infenfible all the while
No ! I am a perfect Eccho to thy faddeft Groans
when thou weepeft, my Heart is not a Stone, that r
ters back again the Drops that fall on it, but it i l
Clay, that foftens with the gentle, folemn Diftill...
Believe that I fweat Blood, when thou diffolve

To

Tear   I am not capable of Moderation toward my
Friend   My Love, my Joy, my Grief and Anger are
all excessive, when such a one as thou occasioned't them
It is equal Pleasure to live or die in this magnetick
Point   For *Souls* of Friends are perfect *Unisons*.   Then,
if thou hast a Spark of Love of *Mahmut*, do not kill
me with thy sad Complaints   For whilst I hear that
thou art thus abandoned to Misfortune and Despair,
how can I live, without perpetual Deaths, more terrible than what we all must undergo by the Course of
Nature ? Dost thou delight to make a constant *Martyr*
of me ?

Thou art bred a *Courtier*, and so was I   Our Infant-
Blood was seasoned with the *Grand Signior*'s Bread and
S', we equally imbibed the Manners, Habits, Customs, Maxims and the Pride of the *Serail*, with the
Pilaw, the Milk, Sorbets, and other Nourishment of
our early Years   Since which, we have seen the various Revolutions of mighty *Kingdoms, States*, and *Empires*   We have beheld the invincible *Emperor* of *China* fall a *Victim* to the Perfidy of his *Slaves*, and to the
more propitious Fortune of the *Tartars*   After another Manner was the Glory of the *British Monarchy*
eclipsed   But no Foreign Story can match the barbarous Massacres of our Monstick *Sultans, Mustapha, Osman*, and *Ibrahim*, all within our Memory

O! *Mahomet*, we have lived too long after these Spoils
of *Royal* Blood   How can we repine at our own private Losses and Affections, whilst we do but sip the flat
insipid Reliefs of those tragical, sprightly Potions, brew-
ed for all the Palates of the greatest *Princes*   Henceforth let us live, as if we were among the Dead   Let
us hear, and see, feel, taste and smell these outward
Objects *en passant*, without being sensible what we do
or suffer   Let us anticipate by a wise Prevention, the
last Stroke of Death, by dying every Moment

Go to the *Pyramids*, my *Mahomet*, or would to God I
could go thither for thee, there to contemplate the
Fate of human Glory, the Mock Grandeur of this
World   Consider all the Race of the *Egyptian* Kings,
who built these costly and magnificent Structures ; or

their

their *Fathers* for them Who filled the hollow Pi
with Silver, Gold, and precious Stones, whilst, v
their Magick Laws, they lifted Legions of *Spir*
dwelling in the Air, Fire, Earth, and Water, oblig
them to guard the wealthy Sepulchres And tell m
then, what thou canst find in those superarnua
Vaults? Nothing but Stench and Darkness Old T
has filched away the sligher Glories of the Place, a
his younger Brother *Avarice* has plundered all ther
which was the more substantial Part He could h
done no less in common good Manners, than take t
Leavings of the Heir, the Elder of the two T
great *Al-ma-mun* thought to have the Gleaning
their Harvest, but he found the Gain would never a
ceed the Cost

But what is become of all the Founders of th
astonishing Fabricks Look in the *Tomb of Cheops*, w
is supposed to build the greatest of the *Pyramids*, a
thou wilt not find the least Relict of his Ashes Or
thou shouldest, it will be impossible to distinguish tre
from the common Dust of other Mortals though
meanest *Slaves* So mutable is human Glory, so
constant all the Smiles of Fortune

Do but reflect on all the glorious Conquests of *A*
ander the Great, and on the Triumphant Entry he ma
in *Babylon*, when the *Chariot* which carried him, w
an *Epitome* of all the Riches which the *Indies* could a
ford, and yet that *Chariot* ought to be esteemed bi
one Degree before the *Hearse*, which in a very fe
Days, with an Obscurity beneath the Merits of so gre
a *Victor*, conveyed him to his Grave

Consider *Cæsar*, who after four and twenty Battle
wherein he always got the Day, was drawn in a Tri
umphant *Chariot* to the *Capitol* by forty Elephants, ye
now his Name is hardly thought of

So *Epaminondas* thought to outvye the World in h
magnificent Insults, yet all this glorious Pageant
ended in Dust and Ashes *Aurelian* led the *Grand*
Captive with *Zenobia*, yet he himself at last became
the Prisoner of Death The pompous Galley of *C*
Patra, when she celebrated the *Cilician Triumph*, sen t

but to ment the Poop of *Charon*'s Boat, when she was
to be ferried to *Elizium*   So the proud *Sesostris*, whose
Coach was drawn by four vanquished *Kings*, at last was
fain to owe his uncouth Funeral to four sordid Slaves,
who tore his naked *Corpse* away from the designed Revenge of factious *Eunuchs*, and buried it in a Heap of
Camel's Dung

. but where is the Pen, or Pencil, that will to the Life
describe the unmatched Cavalcade of *Pompey*, when by
a prosperous *Cymar* he had extracted all the richest
Spirit and Essences of *Eastern* Wealth, to grace his
Entry into *Rome* ?

. The Front of the *Procession* dazzled every Eye with
the strange Lustre of Diamonds and Carbuncles mixed
in Chequer-wise   An *Oriental Figure*, or rather the
Substance of all *Asia* in *Epitome*.   Then followed the
Image of the Crescent *Moon* in massy Gold, with a
Train of Mountains of the same Metal, whereon were
Woods of Jet, Vines whose Grapes were entire Saphires, and Animals of Porphyry, grazing on Fields of
verdant Amethysts

To sanctify this glorious Shew, the Golden Images
of *Jupiter*, *Mars*, and *Pallas*, came next in sight, with
thirty Crowns of Gold, born up by the chief Captains
of his Army, as if so many Kingdoms were designed
for their Reward   And because *Gods* and *Goddesses*
should not want a *Temple*, Five hundred *Slaves* bore up
a *Fane*, built all of massy Silver, washed with Gold.
And at the Back of this appeared the Statue of the
Conqueror, on which no Eye could fix, being crusted
over with Hyacinths and Pearls

Behold, my *Mehemet*, an Exuberance of human
Glory   Yet wonder not to see a Man come after all,
a Mortal Man, I say, made Radiant as the *Sun* with
borrowed Jewels   And to compleat this fading Triumph, read these Letters, all pure jaspers on his Cha-
rot Wheels *Armenia, Cappadocia, Paphlagonia, Media,
Colchis, Syria, Cilicia, Mesopotamia, Phænicia, Palestine,
India,* and the *Deserts* of *Arabia*   All these were the
Conquests of this Triumphant Warrior, and yet his

Destiny

Deſtiny inſulted o him Poor *Pompey*, thou g
gone, and all thy ghty Territories in the *Eaſt*
now poſſeſſed by o o *Mahonet*, our glorious S
reign

And what need thee and I repine, after we ha
ſeen all this Let *Aſdrubal* aſtoniſh *Carthage* with
Glory of Your Publick a t Yet that Theatre
his Honour quickly prove the Stage whereon he
deguded ſtripped ſtark naked, and in Triumph
away by Death So *Marius*, ſuer he had been e
alted to the Top of human Felicity on Earth, was to
a naked, laying in a ſtinking Ditch

What is become o *Nero*'s Silver Gallery in the C
pitol? Or the pendant Gardens of *Semiramis*, whi
coſt no leis than twenty Millions of Gold? Where
now the glittering Hall of *Atabalipa*, King of *Pe*
whoſe Pavement was of Saphirs? Or the Garden of
Gyges, fenced round with Pales of Gold? Or *Caju*
Fountains garniſhed with *Dryads* of the ſame Metal
Where is the Ivory Palace of *Menelaus*, or the Cryſt
Louvre of *Druſus?* All theſe Things are vaniſhed wit
their Founders

How wiſe and happy then was *Saladine*, the gre
and moſt invincible *Conqueror* of *Aſia*, who triumph
over himſelf, and in his victorious Return, cauſed
Shirt to be carried before him on the Point of a Spear
with this Proclamation, *That after all his Glories, h*
ſhould carry nothing to the Grave but that poor Shirt
So *Adrian*, a *Roman Emperor*, to qualify the exceſſiv
Joys of his high Fortune, celebrated his own Funeral
and cauſed his Coffin to be born before him, when h
was to make a publick Cavalcade through *Rome* Thi
was a Sacred Triumph, an Heroick Inſult over i
ſelf and *Death*

Let thou and I, my Friend, imitate theſe ſage Ex
amples, and ever have the *Image* of *Death* before o
Eyes Then we ſhall never mourn for the vain Jo
fles we have loſt, or covet what we never enjoyed Bu
being ever content with what our *Deſtiny* allots us, l
paſs away our Time in a *Divine* Tranquility

Aſce

M.´ *met*, thou wilt find this to be a profitable and true Experiment. Try it, and the Issue will convince thee more than a thousand Counsellors.

Paris, 12*th of the* 5*th Moon,*
of the Year 1668.

LETTER II.

To Mohammed, *the Illustrious* Ermit *of* Mount Uriel *in* Arabia *the* Happy.

I Lodge in a House near the Wall of *Paris*, which gives me a daily Opportunity of surveying out of my Window the adjacent Fields. These extend themselves in a Plain for the Space of a League, or thereabouts, and then the Eye is arrested by a long Ridge of rising Ground, a Row of Hills or Hillocks, not meriting the lofty Name of Mountains, yet high enough to put a Valley out of Shape, and make the Horizon crump-backed.

These Hills are covered thick with Woods and Groves, among whose verdant, shady Tops, some stately *Palaces* lift up their glittering Crests, and make a sociable pleasant Figure in those Solitudes.

This Prospect represents so much to the Life the Valley of Adam in *Arabia*, the Place of my Nativity, that I could as well grasp Coals of Fire with naked Hands, and not be burned, as cast my Eye out of my Window on this lovely Landskip, and not be enflamed with secret Passions for my Native Soil, the Place where I first drew the Vital Air. It is a perfect Magnet to my Spirit wheresoever I am, attracting all my Wishes, Inclinations, and Desires. Methinks the Eastern Winds at certain Hours waft to my ravished Ears the Whispers of my Country. Methinks, sometime, I see the Faces of my Kindred, and their Rural Train, I hear their Voices, and converse familiarly

E 4   hastily

liarly with them, as though they were prefent Such
the Magick of ftrong Defire and Sympathy , it fe
the *Soul* away from it felf, and with fweet Viol
unites it to the beloved Object, tho' at never fo gre
a Diftance Thus when my wandering Thoughts ha
taken up their Refidence for a while in that delico
Vale where I was born, a far more powerful *Magi*
draweth them to thy Cave , Myfterious *Solitary*, M
of Virtues, Exemplary Guide of fuch as confecra
themfelves to God

Glory to *Him* that was before *All-Time*, the *Fathe*
Eternal Ages He changes not, yet is the Source of
defatigable and unwearied Revolutions He is the o
ly independent, true, and felf exiftent Being , the u
created Effence from whom all other Beings der
their Origin and Converfation He is the *Prop* and *Ba*
of the *Univerfe* He is but *One*, the *Primitive Un*
and cannot be divided into Fractions Yet every *Sp*
cies and *Individual Being* in the World participates
Share of his *Divinity* Immortal Praifes exhale from
all Creatures, and afcend like Clouds of Incenfe be
fore the *Throne* of his *Adorable Majefty*, or like Vapou
which the grateful Farth returns in a hot Summers
Day, by way of Acknowledgment for the Benefit per
petually flowing on her from the *Sun* So all the E
lements refpire their Thanks to Him that made them
The *Firmament* expands itfelf, and bows down to the
Brims of this low Globe   *Sun*, *Moon*, and *Stars* do
ftoop and kifs the Floor of the Earth, in Token of pro
found Humility and Devotion to the *Immortal Sour*
of *Light* Only ungrateful Man repays the Bounty
of the *Omnipotent* with Neglects, Contempts, Affronts
and Blafphemies I mean the general Part of Hu
man Race , excepting always from this Charge the
Juft, the Innocent and Pious , were it not for fuch as
thefe, the *Divine Patience* would be tired with the con
tinual Profanation of vain Mortals

Oh ' Venerable *Sylvan*, thou art the only pacifick
Victim of this finful Age Thy conftant Self-Denials,
Mortifications, Abftinences, and the whole Syftem of
thy accomplifhed Sanctity, ftop the Wrath of *Heaven*
from

from falling in large Cataracts on Mankind When
the *Eternal Eye* beholds thy Virtues, it drops down
Tears of Love and Mercy on the Earth, glad that a
Son of *Adam* yet survives, not stained with Vice Thou
art the effectual Propitiation for the sinful World
When Storms and Tempests of impetuous Winds,
when Lightning, Thunder, Hail, or Rain disturb the
Air, or Earthquakes menace more effectual Tragedies
to the Earth, I think of thee, the Favourite of *Heaven*,
and then repose in full Security Thy very *Idea* is
my Shelter from all Evils I shroud my self under the
Shade of thy inviolated *Beard*, over which the *Razor*
never passed I take Sanctuary in the *Umbrella* of thy
Arms, when stretched in fervent *Orations* Thy Remembrance is my certain Refuge in Calamity

I am impregnated with Sacred Emulations of thy
Virtue, I burn with fervent, passionate Desires to become thy *Disciple* I languish to withdraw my self
from this vain World, and from the contagious Society
of Mortals How happy is the Life that is led in quiet
Solitude? Where the *Soul* can feel herself, and being
awakened to a Sense of her Immortal Strength rouzes
and vigorously shakes off the heavy Clogs of Sleep and
Death Whilst the Divine *Afflatus* gently breathing on
the Intellect, and fanning the oppressed Sparks of Reason, which lay smothering under a Heap of Errors,
Lusts, Affections, and unlimitted Desires, kindles the
Mind into a perfect Flame of Light, which soon consumes the Rubbish of bodily Pleasures, dissipates the
Smoke and Mists of pampered Flesh and Blood, and
then a Man becomes all radiant within, shining with
unclouded Splendors

We Mortals seem to be ranked in a *Middle State*,
between the *Separate Spirits* and *Beasts* Our *Virtues*
make us like the *former*, our *Vices* like the latter For
when a Man has quite subdued his Appetites, and Reason sits Triumphant in her Throne, he is like an *Angel*
living above the Race of his Mortality. He does not,
with the *Stagyrite*, place *Virtue* in a *Medium*, or rank
the *Excess* of *Goodness* in the *Predicament* of *Vice*, but
makes direct and swift Advances to the *Zenith* of He-

roick Generofity, fcorning to halt or make lame mun-
grel Capitulations with himfelf, as if he were afraid of
being too Good.

I would afk a *Peripatetick*, whether it be a *Virtue* or
a *Vice*, in him that ftomaching the enormous Villanies
of wicked Men, boils up with an exceffive vehement
Anger? Or whether a Man can err in loving *God* too
much, or in conceiving too violent a Sorrow for his
paft Offences? Or, who can be too thankful for the
Favours of *Heaven*? No! the farther Diftance Virtue
keeps from this cold, earthly *Mediocrity*, the brighter
its Splendor. And fo on the other Side, the greater
the Barbarifm, Brutality, and infernal Stamp of Vice,
by how much more remote it is from this *Indifferency*.
In a Word, *Virtue* and *Vice* are two contrary *Extremes*.
So *Piety* is diametrically oppofite to *Prophanenefs*, *Intemperance* to *Sobriety*, *Fortitude* to *Cowardice*, *Incontinency*
to *Chaftity*, *Avarice* to *Bounty*, *Modefty* to *Impudence*,
Pride to *Humility*, *Enmity* to *Friendfhip*, &c.

Now the *Mediums* between thefe *Extremes*, are *Hy-
poorify* between *Virtue* and *Vice*, *Superftition* between
Piety and *Prophanenefs*, *Bafhfulnefs* between *Modefty*
and *Impudence*, and fo of the reft.

Yet after all, it is neceffary to obferve a *Medium* in
thofe Things which pertain to mortal Life, and to the
Perpetuation of Mankind. Such are Meats, Drinks,
Natural Paffions of the Body and Mind, proceeding
from the alternate Senfe of Pleafure and Pain. As
when we are preffed with Hunger and Thirft, we
ought not prefently to covet the plentiful Tables or
fuperfluous Banquets of the *Great*, but rather fuch a
Diet, as being eafily prepared, may fatisfy the Crav-
ings of our *Nature*, without naufeating and giving us
a Surfeit. To this End the *Divine Providence* has fcattered up and down the Surface of this Globe, an infinite Variety of Roots, Herbs, Fruits, Seeds, with all
Sorts of Corn and Pulfe. The Cattle afford us Plenty
of Milk, the Bees are no Niggards of their Hony,
the Fountains, Rivers, and Lakes abound with ever
fpringing frefh Supplies of fweet refrefhing Water.

also have the Use of Salt, Oyl, Wine, and other exhilarating Beverages, that being content with so many Benefits and Enjoyments, we might prolong our Lives in this World by Sobriety, as in a most pleasant Garden or *Paradise* of Health.

But alas, instead of gratefully acknowledging the Bounty of *Heaven* and pregnant Fertility of the *Earth*, instead of sitting mannerly down at the *Table*, which *God* has spread and covered for us with such a Train of Festival Dainties, we break the Rules of Hospitality, and rushing violently on the Creatures under his Protection, we kill and slay at Pleasure, turning the Banquet to a cruel Massacre, being transformed into a Temper wholly Brutal and Voracious, we glut our selves with Flesh and Blood of slaughtered *Animals*. Oh! happy he that can content himself with Herbs and other genuine Products of the Earth, that sleeps well in a solitary Cave, upon a Bed of Moss or Leaves, as in a Palace on a Couch of Down. He never wants, because he never desires what is not in his Power. He is not burdened with a Crowd of Servants and Retainers, nor his Repose disturbed with the idle Addresses of pretended Friends, officious Sycophants, importunate Petitioners, and other teazing Business of the World.

Why should I longer then demur or hesitate? What hinders me from presently embracing a Course of Life, that promises so much Happiness? A Discipline that will at once free me from a Thousand Tyrannies of Imperious Lusts, and Hostile Passions. I shall then have no need of Money, or the Help of cross-grained Servants. I shall not want a Multitude of Goods, the needless Pageantry of superfluous Ornaments to make a dazzling Figure, and draw the Eyes of People to a Reverend Admiration. I shall be free from sottish Drowsiness, and turbulent Dreams. My Lungs will in my Sleep respire the Air with Ease. Whilst gentle Slumbers, mixed with happy Visions, shall transport my Soul to unknown Worlds. No Fevers, Gouts or Diseases shall invade my Health, nor magisterial Processes of Empiricks bespeak my certain Death, unless

lefs

lefs I will patiently fubmit to all the needlefs Tor-
tures they are contriving for me, and tamely fwallo
down their new-invented Poifons, and be racked to
Death in Hopes of Eafe and Life From all whic
horrid Circumftances, a flender, innocent Diet, ro
ftained with Blood of any Animal, will fet me free

Holy *Eremite*, the Idea I have of this Manner o
Life, makes a profound and durable Impreffion on m
Soul I am ravifhed with the Sentiments of *Plat*,
and *Pythagoras*, and refolutely bent to undergo the
Difcipline of their Philofophy I will firft endeavor
to rid my felf of vain Affections, Habits, and pro
phane Negociations of the Earth I will graduall;
die to all Concupifcence and bodily Pleafure, that fol
may by equal Steps revive to the Contemplation of *Ce-*
leftial Things Then being free from every Spot and
Stain contracted in the Days of Security and Carelef-
nefs, my Thoughts and Works will be acceptabl
to *God;* who in return, will certainly infufe into my
defæcate Mind a fecret Virtue, the Magick of this Vi-
fible World, which purifying my Soul yet further, wil
prepare it for the laft and higheft Gift of the Eternal
Bounty to our Race whilft in this Life, to wit, a
Power of doing Supernatural Things, and of foretel-
ling Events to come

Do thou but pray it may be fo, and all the Powers
of Hell can never prevail againft me For thou haft
the Ear of the Omnipotent

Paris, *3d of the 6th Moon,*
   of the Year 1668.

LETTER III

To Hamet Reis Effendi, Principal Secretary *of the* Ottoman Empire.

IN this Time of Wars with *Nazarines*, when the Ottoman Fury is rouzed and provoked by *Infidels*, it will not be amiss to expose the Nakedness of *Europe* to the *Supreme Divan*, which is on Earth the close Committee of the Court above

I chuse to address my Letter to thee, in Compliance with my former Orders, wherein thou seemedst passionately desirous to know the present State of *Christendom*. God give thee a perpetual Serenity, *Scribe of the Scribes*. Mayest thou never be troubled with a running Eye, a shaking Hand, or the Tooth-ach As for me, I am a perfect Magazine of Diseases, a walking Hospital, the School of *Æsculapius* where the necessary God has Scope to vent his Skill on all the various Kinds of Maladies, which afflict our mortal Race Gouts, Fevers, Cramps, and horrid Dysenteries, are as common with me as my daily Diet

However, amidst all these Afflictions, I serve the *Grand Signior* and my Friends with a cordial Alacrity, never grudging to sacrifice my Ease and Health to the Interest of *True Believers*

The Face of *Europe* is much changed since the Decline of the *Roman Empire*, and the Usurpation of the *Popes*. The once mighty Monarch is now shrunk into a very narrow Compass, being shut up within the Confines of *Germany*, which formerly was but a *Province* of the Ancient *Empire* All *Italy* is revolted So are the *Swisses*, and the *United States* of the *Low Countries*. The *Hans-Towns*, which in Time past paid Homage to the *Emperor*, have now shaken off the Yoke, and are become Independent *Commonwealths Transilvania* plays fast and loose with him, according as their Interest requires. *Livonia* laughs at his Menaces, as appears by
the

the Anſwer they ſent to *Charles* V, when he dema
their Submiſſions, and that they would return to
Native Allegiance, otherwiſe threatning them with
and Sword   For all the Reply they made, was, Th
they knew the *Emperor* s Horſe would be foundered
fore he could reach the Frontiers of their Country

   'Tis a general Obſervation, That ſince the *R*
Rodolph I above Two Hundred *Principalities* and
have fallen off from the *Empire*   And thoſe that
continue in their Obedience, I mean the *E'*
Princes, claim ſo many Privileges, ſtand ſo much
Punctilio s and Prerogatives, that there remains now
tle more of the *Imperial* Majeſty and Power, ſave
bare Title and outward Pomp   It is remarkable,
within theſe Three Hundred Years, no leſs than N
German Emperors have been murder'd, and many
have been depoſed and baniſhed   To ſum up all
few Word   If we ſurvey the preſent State of the *G*
man Empire accurately, if we pry narrowly into
true Circumſtances we ſhall find, that after all the
ter of his noiſy Titles, the Emperor can call noth
properly his own, but his *Hereditary* Eſtate in *A*
which is hardly equivalent to the Territories of ſor
Lord whom he calls his *Vaſſals*,

   The *Germans* in general are a Rude, Unpoliſh d Peo
ple, greedy of Novelties, Inconſtant, Raſh, Perfide
and very Phlegmatick, much addicted to unnatur
Luſts, and inceſtuous Copulations   It is recorded
Barbara the Empreſs, Wife to *Sigiſmund* another
Jalira, that after her Huſband's Death, her Confeſ
adviſing her to reform her Manners, and live mo
chaſtly, like the *Turtle*, ſhe anſwered, *If I imitate*
the Life of Birds, why not of a Sparrow as well
Turtle? Her Brother *Frederick* was much ſuch anoth
For at Ninety Years of Age he murdered his Wife
the Sake of a Strumpet   And being adviſed to repen
and think of his Grave, he ſaid, *I am now ſtudying*
Epitaph, which I deſign ſhall be compriz'd in
Word

This is my Way to Hell; I know not what
I shall find there What I have left be-
hind me, I know I abounded in all De-
lights, whereof I carry nothing with me;
Neither my dainty Meats, or pleasant
Wines, or whatsoever my insatiable Lux-
ury exhausted

Drunkenness is said to be the Original Sin of *Germa-*
ny, from whence it spread it self into other Countries
They give this Character of a *German*, " That he is
" an Animal which drinks more than he can carry A
" Tun that contains more than he can express They
tell a Story of four old *Saxon*, who at one Sitting
drank as many Healths as they could make up Years
amongst them, which amounted to Three Hundred,
And 'tis recorded of a certain *German C t*, that he
used to make his Children whilst yet Infants, drink
hard, to prove whether they were of his own begett-
ing or no For if they grew sick after it, he presently
concluded them to be Bastards, but if the could bear
the Debauch well, he cherished them as his own true
Offspring In a word, thou mayest have the same *Idea*
of the *Germans* at this Day, as *Sigismund* the *Magnificent*
had in his Time who used to say, " I slight the *Ger-*
" *mans* above all other People of *Europe*, because they
" are always at Discord among themselves, nor can
" they ever be united any more than my Fingers and
" Toes They cannot endure Labour, and are the ex-
" cessivest Gluttons and Drunkards in the World They
' always maintain a Regiment of Whores in their
" Camp. Their *Generals* take more Pride in their
" *Feathers*, than in their *Military Arms*

In a word, the *German* is so over-run with all Kinds
of Vice, that he wants nothing to make him a compleat Devil, but only a little Tincture of the *Italian*
Qualities, according to the Proverb, *Tedesco Italianato,*

e 2n

è un Diabolo Incarnato, A German *Italianiz'd*, *is a De-*
vil Incarnate

It is certain, the *French* have so weakened them on
one Hand, and the *Swedes* on the other, that considering the frequent Troubles they meet with from the
Hungarians, *Bohemians*, and other Tributary Nations,
besides the Intestine Feuds of the *Electo al Princes*, we
need not fear the blunted *Telons* of the *Eagle,* which
are scarce strong enough to support her tottering State,
or prop her from falling into Ruin   So far is she from
being able to offend her Neighbours, that she never
makes War her Choice, or takes the Field but by
Compulsion in her own Defence

Illustrious *Hamet*, I pray God inspire the Victorious
Osman with prophetick Courage and Resolution, and
the final Conquest of *Germany* will soon be the Prize of
True Believers

Paris, 5th of the 10th Moon,
of the Year 1668

LETTER IV.

To Nathan Ben Saddi, *a Jew at* Vienna.

THE Friendship that has been contracted between
thee and me, ever since it was thy Fortune to
serve the *Grand Signor* in that Station, obliges us both
to mutual Sincerity   Besides, the Duty and Allegiance
we owe our Sovereign, requires Plain-dealing between
us   We ought to shun Flattery as the Bane of all friend-
ly Engagements, the Pest of the Courts of Princes, and
the General Contagion which infects chiefly the most
Effeminate Part of Mankind   Such as are these *Wes-*
tern Nazarenes, who abound in a Thousand little Com-
plaisances and false Civilities   Thus suffering their own
Integrity to be corrupted, their Virtue and Faithness
Spirit to be surprized and debauched, whilst their
Friends, by these Means, not seldom run or leap to

and fail into inevitable Ruin. In a word, they betray one another and themselves, out of a pretended good Nature

By what I have said, thou wilt comprehend, that I do not reprove thee out of Spight, Envy, Malice, or an affected Gravity, when I tell thee, that you took wrong Measures, in endeavouring to set the *Emperor's* Palace on Fire, or to poison him at his Dinner. I told thee once before, that these preposterous Methods will never take Effect. Besides, they will do the *Grand Signior* no Service.

Though thou art seemingly engaged in the Cause of the *Male-ontents*, remember, that thy Business is different from theirs. What signifies it to thee, whether the *Hungarians* have their Liberties, Rights and Privileges granted them, or no? Or what Reason hast thou to espouse the Interest of the *Evangelicks*, rather than that of the *Catholicks*, any farther than as an Umbrage to cover the greater Designs thou hast in Hand, as an *Agent Incognito* for the *Grand Signior*. Let the *Jesuits* pursue their own Game, and the *Protestants* theirs. Stand thou Neuter in the Main, and rather endeavour to keep both Parties in a Counterpoize, than to turn the Scales for either. For the *Sultan* will gain by the Divisions of the *Nazarenes*, let the Case go how it will between themselves. Besides, there are *Catholicks* engaged in the *Faction*, as well as *Protestants*. 'Tis rather a *Civil* Quarrel, than a *Religious* one. The *Nobles* and *Gentry* of *Hungaria* and *Transylvania* are concerned for their *Estates*, more than for their Churches. They see the *Imperial Court* wants Money, and it is a Crime for an *Hungarian* to be Rich. Those that have the *Supreme* Power in these Cases, will find Reason enough to condemn a wealthy *Lord*, whether he be guilty or not.

It is this puts them up caballing and entring into *Confederacies*, that so they might consult the Means of their own Safety, and be in a Posture to defend themselves.

I perceive the *Count de Serini* has made another Address for the Government of *Carolstadt*, and been repulsed, *Joseph* Earl of *Haberstein*, and Knight of

Maltha,

Maltho, being appointed to succeed the *Count d' t.* *sperg* in that Honour   Which is an evident Sign, the *Emperor* has no good Opinion of *Sei.at*, notw. standing all his former good Services   And th enough to alienate a Man of his great Courage a. Merit

Count Frangipani also has his particular Disconte. So has *Tattenbach*, with many other potent *Lord* *Hungary* and *Croatia*   Indeed, the whole Body those Nations are disobliged, and almost wearied with the continual Oppression of the *Germans*

Nathai, thou wilt find it no hard Matter to br. them to a Necessity of putting themselves under Grand *Signiors* Protection   It is thy Part to cher. their Discontents   As for the *Imperial* Court, t mayest perceive they are resolved to mortify th People, and to take from them all Opportunities the very Capacity of rebelling, by not suffering Natives of *Hungary* and *Croatia* to possess any Office Command

Every Party pursues its own Interest, and so mult ours. Self Preservation is the Root of all mutual S ciety and Justice   Take care of thy self, thy Friend and the Cause thou art engaged in, and then thou nea est not fear any Qualms of *Conscience*   In fine, I co. sel thee to put in Practice the Advice of one of t own *Rabbies, Jesus Ben Syrach*   *Be not over just.*

Paris, 17*th of the* 11*th Moon,*
of the Year, 1668

LETTER V.

To Pesteli Hali, *his Brother*, Master *of the* Gr Signior's *Customs*, *at* Constantinople

PRepare thy self for surprizing News, and rec with a Moderation becoming a Man   Ou our Mother is dead   One and the same Night lo

her in the Apartments of *Hymer*, and the Chambers of
Death　Before the Days of the Nuptial Solemnities
were over, the mournful Rites of her Funeral commenced　She made but one Remove from her Marriage Bed to the Grave

If thou wonderest, that a Woman of her Age, being
Seventy Five Years Old, and having already had Two
Husbands, should marry a Third, Know, that it was
no Dotage, but Discretion which prompted her to
take this Course　The Integrity, Wisdom, and prudent Conduct of *Eliachim* the *Jew*, had charmed her
Affection long ago, and improved her Acquaintance
with him into a strict and virtuous Friendship　As a
Mother, she owed him Respect and Love for his constant Fidelity to me　And on her own Account, she
could not but entertain Sentiments of Esteem and Gratitude for a Man, who had been so nicely careful to
preserve her Person and Honour from Injury and Violence, ever since she came to *Paris*　For he alone
among the many Myriads of People inhabiting this
City, was the only Confident both of her Secrets and
mine　In a word, these Regards, with some others of
Piety, Zeal, and good Nature, made her willing to become his Wife, who in all Things had performed the
Part of a Friend, and a Person of Honour

Besides all this, it was really her Interest thus to dispose of her latter Days in a *Foreign Country*, where she
knew no body but *Eliachim* and me　As for me, she
considered that my Life was not only subject to the
same Casualties with other Mortals, and that I might
be snatched away by a Thousand Deaths, but that my
Stay here was very precarious, and I might be suddenly recalled by my *Superiors* to *Constantinople*, or at
least be removed to some other *Post*, whither she could
not accompany me, being incapable of bearing at these
Years, the Hardships and Fatigues of Travel　That
after my Departure, she should be neglected contemn-
ed and abandoned by all, but those who would desire
her Death for the Sake of her Money, and Jewels

In thefe Circumftances, to remain a Widow, profeſ-
fing the *Faith* of *Mahomet,* and believing the *thin*
in a *Region* and *City* fwarming with *infidel* , would h
been but an uncomfortable, as well as a dangen
Condition   Wherefore having had Experience of *s*
acl m's Virtue, and incorrupt Manners, he alſo m...
Addreſſes of Love to her, and giving her Encou...
ment to hope that he would become a *Muſelme* , ...
yielded at laſt to the Thoughts of taking him fo...
Huſband, and they were married on the 7th of ...
Moon, in a private *Synagogue* of the *Jews*   For they ...
not allowed a *publick* one in this *City,* as they are ...
many other *Cities* of *Europe*

My Mother appeared neither too dejectedly fad, ...
profufely merry, during the *Nuptial Feaſt*   But co...
porting herſelf with a chearful Reſervednefs, feem...
to have her Thoughts rather fixed on fomething e...
than the vain Ceremonies, Noiſe and Mirth of th...
Company   It looks as if her Prophetick Soul was fe...
fible of its approaching Releafe   For, to be brief, fh...
was found dead in her Bed next Morning.

Brother, ſhe is now in her *Sepulchre,* at reft from...
the Toils of Human Life   Let not this News affe...
thee with fruitleſs Melancholy, ſince Death is the common Fate of all Mortals.   Rather advance the Bliſs ...
our deceafed Parent, with devout *Oraiſons* for her Sou...
remembring that before long we ſhall be in the fam...
Condition   For tho' Man, like a Moth, be paſſionat...
ly enamoured with the Light of this World , tho ...
flutter and dance about it for a while, baſking in th...
Splendor and Warmth of his good Fortune , yet ...
length he is confumed by the very Flame which g...
him Nouriſhment, and falls a *Victim* to his own Pl...
fure

Paris 9th of the 1ſt Moon,
   of the Year 1609

LETTER VI.

To Hamet, Reis Effendi, *Principal Secretary*
of the Ottoman Empire.

I Sent thee a Letter some Days ago, wherein I exposed the General Nakedness, Imbecility and lan-
guishing State of the *German Empire* in this Age   My
Dispatch abounded with Characters of their Vices   It
has described exactly the present Eclipse of ancient
Imperial Majesty, Power and Strength, the Revolt of
many *Principalities* and *States*, the Feuds and Discord
of those that yet remain in Obedience, and pay a seeming Homage to *Cæsar*, with many other Things,
which being well considered, may for the future prevent or at least diminish that Consternation and panick
Terror, which uses to seize the Hearts of *Musulmans*,
when we are in War with the Empire or
Now, as a farther Incentive and Encouragement to
take up Arms against the *Infidels*, as a Spur to certain
Victory and Conquest, I will unlock the Treasures of
the Country, without taking Notice of the Inhabitants.
And since nothing more excites the Resolution and
Valour of military Men, than the Hopes of Plunder,
and passing away a Campaign in Plenty of all necessary Comforts, I will give them a true Account of the
natural Dowry of these Regions, the Riches of the
Soil, and the Wealth, which Commerce with other Nations, together with the Spoils of former Wars, the In-
dustry of the People, and the Benevolence of Fortune
have added to their Store
Germany abounds in Generous Wines, and those
more lasting than any other in *Europe*   The *Rhenish*
Wines will keep above Fifty Years   The Wines of
the *Necker* are wholesome, and clear as Water from
the Rock   Those of *Franconia* are strong and opera-
tive, the *Austrian* Grape is sweet and luicious   Several *Roman Emperors* have preferred the Fruits of the
German Vintage to those of *Italy* and *Greece*   And
                                                    such

such is the superabundant Plenty of Vineyards, th
a Place called *Stut,ard*, there is a Proverb cur
that *They have more Wine than Water* If our 7
zaries knew this, they would be for an Expedition
Germany Nay, they temper their Mortar with W
in some Places, and slack their Lime with it

They have strong Beverages also made of Ba
Wheat, and other Grain, which they transport i
Braunswick, Breslaw, Delph, Dartzick, Lubeck,
other Places to most Countries in the *North* and *
Europe* They likewise make a Sort of Wine of
ney, as strong, and sweet as the Wine of *Cond,*

There is Abundance of Frankincense and M
in *Moravia*, of Saffron in *Austria*, of *Liquorice* in
coria, of *Madder* for Dyers in *Silesia*, of Amber in
ringia

There are innumerable Orchards full of all dea
ble Fruits, the Fields stand thick with Corn, the
tures are thronged with Cattle, and they have a B
of the stoutest Horses in the World They have 1
ber enough to serve all the Nations in the World
Shipping But that which s most inviting, is the
riety of Mines of Gold, Silver, Copper, Lead, Tin
Iron Before *America* was discovered, *Germany* was
Peru and *Potosi* of all *Europe* They have also le
of Marble as bright as Crystal

Besides their native and domestick Riches, the
mightily improved their Stock by Foreign Commerce
exchanging their Superfluities for Things more pec
and of greater Value Which in a constant Cour
Bartering brings into the *German* Coffers many h
dred Millions of Crowns in a Year In a Word
Cities are so rich that when they have been pilla
by an Enemy, the Booty of one City has been vale
at two Millions of Crowns in ready Money, beside
Plate and Jewels The common Soldiers have ma
Hilts for their Swords and Daggers of Gold and S
ver, nay, some would make their very Helme
the same Metals Publick Gaming Tables have be
set up in the Streets, and it has been common for

vate Trooper to win or lose Five or Ten Thousand Crowns at a Time, this would be rare Sport for our Jamzaries and *Spahies*

I tell thee, Serene *Minister*, considering the immense Wealth of *Germany* and the Degeneracy of its Inhabitants. *Providence* seems to invite our Arms to make a Conquest of those fertile Regions, and take from the Unarmed the Goods which surfeit them. They abuse the Gifts of Nature and Fortune, by employing them to the Ends of Vice, whereas the *True Believers*, were they once possessed of them, would turn them to virtuous Purposes, the publick Advantage, the Increase of the *Empire*, Glory of GOD, and Propagation of the *Faith Undefiled*.

Paris, 13th of the 4th Moon, of the Year 1669

LETTER VII

To Hebatolla, Mir Argun, *Superior of the Convent of* Derviches *at* Cogni *in* Natolia

IT was with a specifick Kind of Joy not easy to be learned, that I received thy venerable Dispatch. I perused the welcome Orders therein contained with a Delight not in the least inferior to his, who being abandoned to Distress and miserable Poverty has by good Luck discovered a hidden wealthy Treasure. For so my Spirit is ravished, to find in this degenerate Age, a rich Reserve of Piety and Devotion to the ancient Prophets of GOD

I am glad to hear the Character of *John* the *Baptist* which I sent thee formerly, was so well accepted by thee, and all the *Religious* under thy Charge, that thou make safest only to accuse the Shortness of the Relator, desiring a more particular Account of that Prophet's Manner of living, especially of his Abstinence, and what may be the most proper Interpretation of the

Grecian

Grecian Word αχριδας, mentioned in the History of
Life?

Praise be to GOD, who has inspired thee with
critical Regard to one of his most *Holy Messengers* I
vere thy learned *Soul*, and that accomplished Intelli
which is ever busy, prying into weighty and impo..
Matters   I honour thy impa.tial Mind, which scru
not to pay the Attach that is due to a *Saint*, tho' o
Christian Calendar   If we should reject all that the
lowers of *Jesus* do, we should neither Fast, Pray, gi
Alms, or perform any other good Work.   Theref
in this, thou art an exemplary Pattern to the rigid .
perstitious Sort of *Mussulman Fanaticks*, who bear
endless Grudge against all those that are not of t..
narrow Faith and dark Opinion

Glory be to GOD, with whom the WORD was pr
sent from the *Dawning* of *Eternal Light*, before .
Morning of his *Works* had peeped over the Moun .
of the ancient *Chaos*, or penetrated the dark Abys .
and misty Vale of *Nothing*, and painted the Tops .
the Creation, the highest Ranks of *Beings*, with Spk .
dors of the early Day   Before the *Sun* had drank .
immortal *Halo* in, and sponged up all the visible Beau
to squeeze them out again upon the *Moon* and *Star*
and on the lower World   That WORD remains f
ever, and at a determined Hour became incarnate, .
the Person of *Jesus* the *Son* of *Mary*, as the *Holy Alc..*
informs us

In those Days *John* the *Baptist* went into the Wilde
ness, and preached Repentance to the *Jews*, foretellr
the near Approach of the *Messias*   The sacred *Hero* ma..
a Cave his Residence, and at first, to wean his Bo..
from all Softness, he wore a Vest or Shirt of Came
Hair which was girt about him with a Belt made .
that painful and religious Creature's Skin to put h..
in mind, that he was born for *holy* Labours, Toils, a..
Mortifications   He had no Table spread with f.
fetched costly Dainties,   no Dishes crammed w..
bloody and large Inventories of Birds, four foo..
Beasts, and Fish   His Diet was simple, cheap, and .
nocent, easy to be got in every Wood or Field, w c

out the Detriment of his Fellow-Animals. For he either contented himself upon a Repast on Honey, which he found in hollow Trees or on a kind of *Manna*, a sweet *Dew* falling on their Leaves, and there condensed by heavenly Influence, Or else it was a kind of luscious Moisture, which he sucked from certain Plants, perhaps not much unlike our *Sugar-canes* For thus Interpreters do differ about the Words τὸ μέλι ἄγριον What ever it was we may conclude it to be some slender, light and easy Nourishment And when this Diet failed him, or his Stomach required a little more Variety, he banqued on what the *Grecians* call ἀκρίδες Some will have these to be a kind of *Locusts* or *Grashoppers*, a Meat indulged the *Jews* by *Moses* in the *Law*. The *Syrians* also counted them a Dainty, so did the ancient *Parthians*, as *Aristotle* and *Pliny* tell us And my Countrymen the *Arabians* eat of them to this Day Others are of opinion, that these ἀκρίδες were a Sort of little Shell-fish, such as *Crabs*, *Crawfish*, or *Shrimps*, which Nature has generally lodged in Holes along the Banks of Rivers A pleasant, temperate Sort of Diet, commended for their Virtues in expelling Poison, and being Remedies for the Strangury, and Antidotes to cure the Biting of mad Dogs

The divine *Prophet* therefore often frequenting the Waters of the River *Jordan*, wherein he used to wash his Converts and Disciples, these Men suppose, he took Occasion to allay his Hunger with these little Shell-fish, which he might easily take in mighty Numbers from their watry Nets And they endeavour to strengthen this Opinion, by asserting, That the Food which the Seas afford us, is much more pure and holy than what the Earth brings forth, in regard the Earth lies under the Malediction of God ever since *Noah*'s Flood, whereas the Waters never were cursed Hence, say they, it was probably, that the consecrated *Hero* would not defile his spotless Life with cursed Banquets from the Earth, but rather chose to appease his Hunger with the harmless, blessed, and wholsome Product of the Waters

If thou wilt have my Opinion after all, I am a
think these ἀκρίδες were nothing else but the ter
Tops of Plants, such as we call *Asparagus*, or perh
they were the wild Apples of the Wood, and then
may suppose there is some Mistake in the *Greek* Co
ἀκρίδες for ἀκράδες Or it may be, the *holy Pro*
in the proper Season of the Year, did use to crop
eat the Ears of the Barley, and then the Word shoul
καρποὺς For what could be more sweet and plea
to an abstemious Man, than to sustain his Life
Fruits, Grains, Herbs or Roots? Nor did the M
diction reach the *Vegetables*, but only the *Animal* G
rations, from which a perfect Man abstains

Certainly those, who out of an Aversion for P
Prayer, and Fasting, turn themselves from human
dies to Swine, and from religious Abstinence to sal
gormondizing on Flesh, seem to derive their Pedig
from a Race of *Devils* Especially, such as after
Manner of *Spiders*, gathering Poison from he Flo
of Piety, blaspheme this sacred Virtue of Abstinen
and call it by the infamous Name of Superstition

For if the Veneration we pay to God consist in
Knowledge, Love and Fear of his *Divine* Majesty,
Adoration and Praise of his Eternal Attributes, it
lows, that we ought to worship him with the most fer
vent Application of our Spirits But this religious A
cannot subsist in any Soul, whose body is not mortif
nor can the Body be mortified without Austerity, wh
always is accompanied with rigorous Fasting and Ab
nence from Flesh Wherefore if we ascend to God
the very same Degrees as we fall from him, it follo
that Abstinence is the first Step to Immortality and
preme Happiness

I do not mean by Abstinence, that natural Avers
which some Men have for Flesh, who never durst tast
of any in their Lives, compelled to this by some occu
Antipathy in their Stomachs For such a Necessity c
not make a Virtue, it being common to Men and Bru
there being many *animals* who fast from all Proven
certain Seasons of the Year, and others that take

ome Kinds of Food during their Lives So there are
ome Men to whom Wine, Flesh, Cheese, Apples,
Herbs, and other Things, are an Abomination from
their Cradles   There have been others, who, by a
Præternatural Necessity, have lived some Days, Weeks,
Months and Years, without either Meat or Drink   So
Plato records, That *Herus Pamphilius* lay ten whole
Days among the Dead Carcasses of Soldiers slain in
Batel, and when he was taken up to be laid on the
Funeral Pile, they perceived him to be alive. *Laertes*
tells us, That *Pythagoras* fasted forty Days and forty
Nights from Meat and Drink From whom *Apollonius*
Thyanæus learned the Art of keeping almost a perpetual
Fast   And these modern Times afford us the Example
of a *Spaniard* whom they call *Alcantare*, who every
Moon used to fast for seven or eight Days together So
a famous *German Maid* was diligently observed and
watched, whilst she passed away full seven Years Time
without Meat, Drink, Sleep or Excrements   *France*
also boasts another *Virgin*, who fasted above three
Years together

Such Abstinence as these are not to be put to the Account of Virtue, in regard they were not the Effects of
human Choice, but the *Decrees* of *Fate*   So would our
Abstinence be depraved, if we should only practice it, as
the old *Gentiles* did, who forbore to kill or eat some
certain Beasts, because they held them consecrated to
their *Gods* As the *Dog* to *Diana,* the *Tyger* to *Bacchus,*
the *Horse* to *Neptune,* the *Wolf* to *Mars,* the *Eagle* to
Jupiter, the *Peacock* to *Juno,* the *Swan* to *Apollo,* the
Dove to *Venus,* the *Owl* to *Minerva,*   Nor need we to
abstain on the Account of the *Soul*'s Transmigration ;
for so we ought to forbear the *Vegetable* Products of the
Earth, as well as *Animals,* since the *Soul* is indifferent
to all Bodies in its separate State

But our Reason in this Point ought to take its Rise
from the *Fundamental Law* of *Nature,* the *Original*
Justice of the *World,* which teaches us, *Not to do that*
to another, which we would not have another do to us
Now since it is evident, That no Man would willingly

become the Food of Beasts, therefore, by the same
Rule, he ought not to prey on them Next to this
Foundation of our Abstenence, we ought to build our
Aims at the Perfection of our Nature, which cannot be
acquired but by Degrees We must endeavour to abate
the Aliment of our Concupiscences, by exhaling the
superfluous and grosser Vapours of our Blood in sacred
Fasts and Oraisons Then we should refresh our fainting Bodies with Food affording little Nourishment and
Pleasure That so our vain Affections, Appetites and
Lusts, may gradually die, whilst the pure Mind revives, and being free from the gross Vapours arising
from too much, and too fattening Meats and Drinks,
the Films which darkened her Sight fall off and she
can better now discern the naked Forms of Things by
her own simple Institution, than before she could
through all borrowed Spectacles and other *Optick or
Book-Philosophy* Also she will more easily raise herself
to the Contemplation and Science of Divine Eternal
Things He therefore that in earnest will apply himself
to the Study of accomplished Sanctity, must first by Fasting exhaust the Marrow from his Bones, the Fatness
from his Flesh, the wild and rampant Spirits from his
Nerves, and then he must purge the Words and Actions of his Life from Vice When this is done, the
Soul becometh a pure *Tabula Rasa*, and is fit for the Im-
pressions of Celestial Virtue

    Those who labour under acute Diseases, run great
Hazard of their Lives, according to *Hippocrates*, unless
their Diet be accommodated with proportion to Regard
to the Quality and Time of the critical Fits or Parox-
isms But those who are entangled with Vice, do labour
under far more dangerous Distempers, than such as afflict the Body Wherefore the Prophet, our Holy Lawgiver, like a wise Physician, appointed certain Seasons
of the Year for sacred Abstinences, Fastings, Pilgrimages, Vigils, and other holy Exercises, especially the
mighty Fast and Vigil of *Ramezan*, wherein tho' we be
not forbid to eat of Flesh after the Stars appear at
                       Night,

Nor yet none but loose and indevout *Belevers* take this Liberty, whereas the better Sort content themfelves with an afcetick Diet. The *Hebrews* fasted with unleavened Bread, and a little Salad the *Christians* also tafte no Flesh on their prohibited Days. And shall the *Muffulmans* be greater *Libertines* than thefe *Infidels?*

Oh! how real now radiant is the Luftre of a Lamp when flaming through a clean, and fine, defecate Cryftal. So does the Soul difplay the Rays of her immortal Virtue round about, when fhe inhabits in a well purged chafte, and almoft pervious Body. Wherefore it is abfolutely neceffary for him to attenuate his Body with perpetual Temperance and Abftinence, who confecrates himfelf to Virtue and Devotion. He will not be enfnared or catched by any Baits of Luxury or Voluptuoulnefs, nor yet affrighted from his conftant, fober Courfe of Life, by any Pain or thwarting Accident. No Frowns or Menaces fhall divert him from his noble Purpofe. But he will fo nourifh his Body all his Life, that it fhall never be furfeited, or over-filled with Meats. And fuch is the Magick of this facred Virtue, that it can never be hurt, much lefs fubverted by all the Machinations of evil *Dæmons,* or the malicious Attempts of Men. But it proceeds from Strength to Strength, and fights the Combat valiantly, till having overcome at laft, it triumphs for ever, and receives the Palm, the Crown and Chaplet of Divine Reward in *Paradife.*

Holy Prefident, pray that I may practife what I fo admire, and not be felf-condemned for living contrary to my Knowledge. For God neither loves a double Tongue or Heart, neither delights he in Feet or Hands that are fwift and nimble to do Mifchief.

Paris, 13*th of the* 4*th Moon,*
   of the Year 1669.

LETTER VIII.

To Hamet, Reis Effendi, Principal Secretary
of the Ottoman Empire

NOW the *Christians* are in a general Consternation
for *Cand,* The Pope has sent Letters to all the
Princes that are in his *Communion,* inviting and pressing
them to succour that distressed Island. Levies are making
every where, and the King of *France,* who seeks all
Occasions of Glory, appears the most forward of all
to assist the *Republick* in this Fatal Juncture. The Duke
of *Beaufort,* and *Chevalier de Vendosme,* are appointed
to lead the Forces designed for that Service. They are
gone to *Toulon,* in order to embark. The *Pope* has sent
the Duke of *Beaufort* a *Brevet,* declaring him General
of the Troops *Ecclesiastick* that are to serve in *Cand,*
and for his greater Encouragement, he has sent him the
Pontifical Standard. In the mean while, there is a
Triple League concluded between the *Emperor* the King
of *Spain,* the King of *England,* the King of *Swedeland,*
and the States of *Holland.*

There is great Joy in *Portugal* for the Birth of the
Infanta, who is called *Elizabetha Maria Louisa.* She was
born the 6th of the 1st Moon, and on the 18th, the
Empress of *Germany* was also delivered of a Daughter.
These *Western* Queens are very pregnant, Not a Year
passes without the Birth or Baptism of some Royal In
fant.

This is all the News at present, but to oblige thee,
I will say something of *Italy,* which is esteemed the
Garden of *Europe.* Nay, *Constantin' Paleologus, Emperor*
of *Greece,* was wont to say, *Unless I had been assured by
very Learned and Holy Men, that Paradise was seated in
Asia, I should have sworn that* Italy *had been the Place.*

It is most certain, *Italy* is a delectable Country a
bounding in Riches and Pleasures. The Eye is not sa
tisfied with seeing the infinite Variety of Beauties, which
grace this happy Region. Such is the lovely Inter
mixture

mixture of Hills and Vallies, Groves and Plains, Palace and Gardens, that a Traveller is ravished as he passes on the Road But this is not all She is as rich as fair No Country in the World can match *Ital*, for the Plenty and Variety of excellent Wines , only they are of no long Continuance Above all the rest, Travellers commend that Sort which they call *Lachrymæ Christi* or *the Tears of Christ*, for its delicious Taste Which when a *Dutchman* once tasted he burst forth into this Exclamation, *O Christ, why didst not thou weep in my Country* At *Puzzia* there are a Kind of *Aromatick Grapes*, which leave a fragrant Odour in the Mouth of him that eats them It is recorded of a certain *Roman Lord*, That when he was in Prison half dead with Melancholy, he drank a Glass or two of this generous Wine, which so revived his Spirits, that instead of despairing, as he was ready to do before, he wrote a *Treatise, entituled, De Consolatione*

  Besides *Ital*, abounds in Cattle, Sheep, Fowls, Mines, Rocks of Alabaster Marble, Porphyry, Coral, Ophits, Agts, Chalcedonis, Azures, and innumerable other precious Stones Hence it comes, that in this Country are seen the most Glorious and Magnificent *Temples* of the World

  But this so fair and wealthy a Spot of Ground is inhabited by a very wicked Sort of People They are quite degenerated from the Virtues of their *Ancestors* They are a Base, Effeminate, Sly, *Sodomitical* Race of Men, Covetous, Revengeful, and Inexorable I have heard a Story of two *Italian* Brothers that were walking one Night in the Fields, it being a very serene Sky ; when one of them looking stedfastly on the *Heavens*, wished, *he had as many Oxen as there were Stars* The other wished, *he had a Field as large as the Firmament. What would you do with it ?* said the first *Let your Oxen graze there*, replied he But as they proceeded in this kind of foolish, loose Discourse, they kindled each other's Anger, and at length, falling from Words to Blows killed each other on the Spot Behold the Consequence of their covetous Desires ! They are extremely

addicted

addicted to Revenge, and are as dextrous at poisoning
as the *Indian* Prince. A certain *French* Author gives
us a very compendious Account of the Benefits a Stranger
gets by travelling into *Italy*, in these Words, *If
in Italy, says he, with incredible Charges, only to purchase
the mere Shadow of Civility, and we bring back from
thence the whole System of Vices* The *Milanese* teach
us how to cheat From the *Venetians* we learn Hypocrisy
Rome transforms us into perfect *Atheists* and *Libertines*
Naples turns us to *Satyrs* *Florence* instructs
us in the Artificial Methods of poisoning, There is no
one City, which does not tincture us with some Specifick
ill Qualities

Sage *Hamet*, in all my Letters to thee, I studiously
insert some Remarks on these *Western* Nations, that so I
may gratify thy Wishes Pardon the Want of Order,
for I write Things as they present themselves to my Memory
Accept all in good Part from *Mahmut*, who obeys
thy Commands chearfully, and honours thee without
Flattery

Paris, 12*th of the* 5*th Moon,*
    of the Year 1669

LETTER IX.

To Hamet Reis Effendi, Principal Secretary *of the* Ottoman Empire.

THOU mayest register in the Archives of the Sacred
Empire, That *Don John* of *Austria* is made
perpetual *Governor* of the *Low Countries* under the *Spanish*
King's Obedience He is also *Viceroy,* and *Vicar
General* of *Arragon,* *Catalonia,* and *Valentia.* But it is
fit for thee to know also, That this is so far from being
esteemed by that Prince a Happiness, that he counts it
his greatest Misfortune, in regard it is no better than an
honourable and irrevocable Banishment from the Court
    of

of *Spain*, where his Royal Blood and Merits are out-
matched by the *Genus* of a certain *Priest*, whom they
call *Father Nitard* This Man is very ambitious, always
aiming at high Matters, yet admired by no body for
his Learning, Beauty, or any other good Qualities Only
the *Queen* of *Spain* is pleased to make him her Favourite.

He could never buckle to the Humour of *Don John*,
and hence arose a secret Envy between them, which afterwards burst forth into open Animosities, Feuds, and
Quarrels So that at the last the Favourite got the Day,
and *John* was forced to quit the Field

It is possible to trace the *Sovereigns* of the Earth in
the Footsteps of their *Royal* Conduct, or else one would
certainly conclude, That so great a Prince as this, of
the same Lineage as the Queen herself, should have easily eclipsed the borrowed Lustre of an Upstart Minion.
But Princes have specifick Reasons to themselves,
which others cannot penetrate

This cunning *Priest* used a Trick like that of
a Soldier in the Army of *Alexander* the *Great* Who
being of a ambitious Spirit, and coveting to make some
greater Figure than that of a private Centinel, considered the Prince's Humour, and how to hit it. He knew,
that this Heroick Master took delight in any thing that
was bold and brave But how to come into his Presence,
he was ignorant At length, he pitched upon this Method One Day, as *Alexander* was debauching with his
beloved *Parmenio*, *Hæphestion*, *Lysimachus*, and other
Officers; this Fellow (whose Name was *Clitus*) put
himself into a mimick Dress of War, counterfeiting
himself Mad, and dancing the *Pyrrhick* Measures, with
his brandished Sword, killed five new-listed Soldiers
lately come from *Colchis* The Guards soon seized upon
him, and it being a *Tragical* Novelty, the News was
carried to the *King*, who caused the Fellow to be
brought before him And examining him on the Point,
(he answered, " Great *King*, those five Men, whom
" I have killed, had conspired to take away thy Life
" this Day, being hired thereto by the King of *Colchis*,
" and therefore sent into the Army Their Tent being
" next to mine, I had an Accidental Opportunity last

F 5   " Night

" Night of over-hearing their Difcourfe, when they
" were plotting together the Time, the Place, and Man
" ner of thy Death   I kept a Watch upon them, and
" obferved their Motions from that Moment   For, tho'
" I knew the Hour appointed by them for this execra
" ble Regicide, yet I was folicitous left fome ill Fate
" fhould prompt the *Ruffians* to antedate their own Re
" folves, and haften a Murder, whofe Delay might elfe
" difcover their Defigns, or at leaft prevent them
• Therefore I took this mad Difguife, to execute the
" fobereft and moft important Purpofe that ever I fram
" ed in all my Days, which was at once to fave the
" Life of the World's *Conqueror*, and get myfelf Im
" mortal Honour by the happy Deed "

After profound Deliberation of the Drunken Cabinet
Council, *Alexander* approved the Fact, and ordered
Publick Honours to be done to his Deliverer   Accord
ing to the *Macedonian* Cuftom, he vefted him with pur
ple Robes, and gave him a Chain of Gold, admitting
him to the latter End of the Banquet, and afterwards e
fteeming him above his moft Familiar Friends. 'Till fuch
another Debauch as this, but more unfortunate to *Clytus*,
at once deprived him of the *King*'s Favour and his own
Life   So inconftant is the State of Human Greatnefs

Sage *Hamet*, the Favour of *Princes* is like a Reed of
Egypt, which either tranfpierces him that leans upon it,
or flinches from the Burden, and fo gives him a Fall,
which moft times plunges him over Head and Ears in
the choaking Mire of popular Hatred

God grant thou mayeft never be crufhed to Death
from Above, by the Weight of the *Sultan*'s Difpleafure,
or undermined from beneath, and fwallowed up in an
Earthquake raifed by the Multitude

Paris, 18th of the 7th Moon,
  of the Year 1669.

L E T.

LETTER X

To Hebatolla, Mir Argun, *Superior of the Convent of* Derviches *at* Cogni *in* Natolia.

THOU wilt not be difpleafed to hear of a Mighty King, that having laid his *Diadem* and *Sceptre*, and abandoning the Height of Human Glory, has confined himfelf to a private *Religious* Life, vowing perpetual *Poverty*, *Chaftity*, and *Obedience*

Yet this is true of *John Cafimir*, late *King of Poland*, who from a Sovereign *Monarch* is become an Humble *Subject*, and having forfaken the Pleafures and Magnificences of his *Royal Palace*, voluntarily confines himfelf to the narrow Circumftances and Aufterities of a *Monk* Life

He chofe *France* for the Place of his Retreat from his own *Kingdom*, and the *Abby* of St *Germains* near *Paris* his *Sanctuary* from all worldly Affairs He was magnificently received and entertained in every City through which he paffed And on the 4th of the 11th *Moon* he made his firft Entry into the *Mofque* or Church of the *Convent*, where he made his Vows in Quality of *Abbot* or *Superior* of that *Houfe* For which they folemnly fung their *Te Deum*, or a *Song of Praife* to God. And the *Court* of *France* feems to be proud of the Honour this *Prince* has done it, in retiring hither, and making the *Theatre* of fuch pious Refolves, the laft Stage of his *Pilgrimage* on Earth, where he will bid *Adieu* to the vain Pageantries of *Honour*, Wealth, and Empire, and having fhaken off the Glittering Burden of a *Crown*, with all the other Clogs of elevated Mortality, he will the eather climb to *Paradife*

Abftracting from the particular *Superftitions* of the *Nazarenes*, I cannot but commend the fage Undertaking of *King Cafimir*, who in this feems to outgo the noify oftentous Action of *Adrian*, one of the *Roman Emperors*: for he only once celebrated in outward Pomp his own *Funeral*, by way of *Type* or *Figure*, making a fplendid

Caval

Cavalcade, before which his *Coffin* was carried in a kind
of *Mock Triumph* As if, after all his Victories, at last
he had led *Death* himself *Captive* Whereas this hindered not, but that he returned again to the Vanitie,
which in this publick Emblem he seemed to despise,
and from a *Dramatick Conquerer*, he became a real
Slave His personal Mortification in the Streets ended
in his ordinary Paffions at home And he had a strong
Inclination to the Bed of Voluptuousnefs at Night,
than he seemed to have by Day to his Grave

But this Heroick *King* of the *Poles* is really gone into
his *Sepulchre* [For no better is a *Monastery*, in my Opinion] He has tranflated the *Seat* and *Throne* of his
Kingdom to a *Tomb* , not for Three or Four Hours, to
make a Shew, but there really to lead a dying Life, or
living Death , and reign in *Funeral* Majesty all the rest
of his Days For to be thus *Recluse* from the World,
is to be buried alive

O Venerable and Benign *Dervich*, pardon the favourable Opinion I have of this *Chriftian Monarch* I do
not patronize his Friors in applauding his Virtue Besides, it is the General *Faith* of *Muffulmans*, That If
a Man be a *Chriftian*, a *Jew*, or *Pagan*, provided he
lives up to the beft Light he has, he fhall all be faved And
the *Holy Prophet* himself gave us Encouragement to believe fo

Thou wilt at leaft conclude this King to be more pious and worthy of Praife, than one of his *Predecessors*,
who ufurped the *Polifh Crown* This was *Uladiflaus* V
who having entered into a folemn League with one of
our former *Sultans* living in his Time, and taken an
Oath thereupon, giving also the *Eucharift* (or that
which they efteem the *Body* of *Chrift*) in *Hoftage*, yet
foon after broke the *Articles* that he had Signed and
fworn to, and for the Performance of which he had
pawned his *God*

This fo provoked the *Grand Signior*, that he had recourfe to his Arms for Juftice, and invaded *Poland* with that
mighty Force To repel which, *Uladiflaus* also levied an
Army, and met him in the Field. But juft as they were
going

going to give Battle, the *Sultan* took out of his Bosom the pawned *Eucharist*, with the *Capitulations* agreed upon, and sworn to between them Then holding the *Wafer* in one Hand, and the seals in the other he cried out, in the Hearing of both Armies, "O thou *Crucified* "God of the *Christians*, behold thy perfidious Adorers, "who have given thee to me as a Pledge of their "Faith and Truth in what they have sworn, yet in a "most impious manner they have violated their Oath "If thou art a God, chastise them now by my Means, "for their abominable Perjury and Prophanation of "thy Name" His Prayer was heard of *Heaven* For the victorious *Ottoman* gave a total Overthrow to the *Poles* and that blasphemous *Prince* was himself killed in the Battle

Whatever various *Forms* of *Religion* there be in the World, we know there is but *One True God, Creator* of *Heaven and Earth, Conservator* and *Governor* of *Men* He connives at the invincible Ignorances Frailties and Infirmities of our Mortal Race He accepts the Good Works and sincere Vows of *Pagans* and the *Uncircumcised* as well as those of the *True Believers*, and *Followers* of the *Prophets* But he abhors, and punishes all Injustice, Perjury, Treason both in One and the Other For he has no partial Regards for this Nation or Person, more than that They are all equally the Works of his Hands, and his Care is alike over all

The *Sun* runs from the *East* to the *West* In his daily Circuit he illuminates and warms this *Hemisphere*; and by Night our *Antipodes* enjoy his Favours, and welcome Influences At one time of the Year he comforts the *North*, at another he revives the *South* There is no Part of the *Globe*, which in due Season does not rejoice in his all chearing Beams

The *Moon* never slacks or deviates from her wonted Course, but from the *Crescent* to the *Wane*, observes the Laws of him that made her She is exact in timing the *Flux* and *Reflux* of the *Sea* And she guides the wandring Mariners by Night The Inhabitants of the *Arctick* and *Antarctick Circles* wait for her Light, when the

Sun

Sun absents himself for half the Year　As soon as the
see the *Chariot* of *Diana* appear on the Road of the
Heaven, every Man claps his Hands for Joy　The
rouze from their domestick Dulness and Melancho...
they come out of their Dens and Caves　With D...
and Songs they welcome the Approach of the Beau...
ful Goddess, knowing that she is but a Second Remove from the *Eternal Light*, the Mirror of the S...
in which that glorious Planet may see his Face
whose, by Reflection, we see the Face of God

So do the *Stars* keep on their various Tracts
through the *Heavens*　Each *Constel* ... faithful
maintaining its Post, each *Plan* ... pursuing its Ro...
Whilst all together, at so vast a Distance, appear ...
ing Camp, never setting up their bright Pavil...
but by Night and in the Morning, taking them ...
again　This may be called the Army of *Heaven*, ...
Host of *God*, enlisted in the H... to gu... his
Friends on Earth and to chastise his Enemies

To descend lower ye ... to our *Selves*, If eme...
we find the Rain, Hail, Snow, Winds, Thunder, Li...
ning, and other Meteors are impartially scattered up
and down the Climates of the Earth, I do not ...
by Chance but by the Universal Providence which go-
verns all Things　As the *Psalter* expresses it　" I ...
" he directs the Seasonal and Prolifick Showers ...
" Barren and Desart Places　Doubtless this is a Sig...
" of his *Divine* ... "

In fine, all Provinces and Corners of the Ea...
bring forth their proper Fruits in Season　And the
Negroes of *Africk* and *America*, though gross *Idolatr*...
and some of them worshipp... *Infernal Dæmons*, yet
enjoy God's Blessings, and live as plentifully, with ...
much Content and Joy, as we that adore his *Eternal
Unity*

Every *Nation* takes up their *Religion* on the Credit of
their Priests, and so long as they observe the *Natural*
and *Moral Law* imprinted in their Hearts, the ind...
gent *Judge* and *Father* of Men will dispense with those
that err, in Obedience to the Positive Laws of their A...

For Sedition is like Magick, odious to God and Man, and equally liable to Universal Punishment

Once more, O pious Father of the *Dervises*, I beg of thee to pardon the Freedom I take, in discoursing of *Religious* Matters in thy Presence, who art a Light to the Blind, a Guide to those that err, a Resolver of Doubts an Arbitrator of difficult Questions, the only Oracle of thy Province

I endeavour to inform thee, but to difentangle my felf from Error, and testify, that tho' I honour God and his Prophet, yet I think there is no need of a Falshood to defend the Truth

*Paris of the 2d Moon,
of the Year* 1670

L E T T E R XI.

To Useph, Bassa.

DEATH has of late celebrated a *Triple Triumph* in the Court of *France*, having led away Captive to the *invisible World*, the Cardinal Duke of *Vendosme*, a Dutchess of the same Title, and *Henrietta Maria* late Queen of *Great Britain*, being the Relict of King *Charles* I and youngest Daughter to *Henry* IV of *France*.

Thou mayest also report to the *Divan*, that *Casimir* late King of *Poland*, is now at this Court, having left *Poland*, as soon as he saw Prince *Wishourski* elected his Successor. The Dukes of *Lorrain* and *Neuburgh* had severally laid Claim to that Crown, and levied Armies apart, in order to make good their Pretensions. But the *Polanders* being aware of it, were resolved not to bring themselves under the Jurisdiction of any Foreigner, so long as there was a Prince of their own Nation capable of the Dignity, and one who being the Son of King *Casimir*, seems to have the best Title to his Father's Throne, whose Virtues he inherits

Here

Here is also arrived the Prince of *Tuscany*, who has travelled through all *Europe*, and takes *France* as the last Kingdom in his Return Homewards. Protestho does this in good Manners, as preferring *France* to the Nations in *Christendom*. Indeed, he could do more in good Manners, than make this Apology, which sounds very flat to a Court so refined as this, who might have expected his first Visit, as a Token of Regard, since, tho' in Domestick Processions There and Coronations, those of highest Dignity take the Place, yet in Foreign Embassies and Visits, it is usual for Princes to address those first, for whom they have the greatest Esteem.

The Politicians here keep very secret the News comes from a *Courier* which makes all Men conclude is none of the most prosperous. It is generally reported for a Truth, that Admiral *Beaufort* is either killed, or taken Prisoner by the Ottomans, and that the French have lost near Two Thousand Men in the late Duel king.

I wonder why the Paint is always describe Death the form of a bare Skeleton, a starved Syster of a Body. Whereas one would think, he ought to be pourtrayed as a Monster, a Miracle of Fatness, since he is the greatest Glutton in the World, hourly gorging on all manner of Flesh, and is the very Original, the several Cannibals of Nature, who from the beginning of the World has feasted himself with human Bodies. Besides perhaps neither a bad Digestion, and not of all his meat and bloody Diet will afford Nourishment enough to find so much as a poor skin to cover his Nakedness, and therefore it is he is always drawn in this lean Figure.

Courteous Reader, suffer me in this vein Jest to into a serious Reflection on our Mortality, and the State of Human Race.

Man is but a thin Vapour, first exhaled from the Earth, and afterwards advancing, is condensed to a Cloud that to his Frailness may be concealed under the Covert of a Skin, there in Secret to engender Thoughts, Meteors of Fiery Passions, Lusts, Concupiscence extravagant Thoughts. Which in time burn forth,

but

troune a'l the World   Yet end at laſt in empty Smoak,
Rain, Hail or Wind, and are extinct almoſt as ſoon as
they are formed

The Elements of which we are compounded, may
ſerve as Mirrors to repreſent the conſtant Mutability of
our Nature   So the devouring Fire, when all its Fuel
is ſpent, decays and dies   Earth, Air, and Water, all
are ſubject to Corruption, and from thence our Generation takes its Riſe   Likewiſe thither we return
again   This is the Eternal Circle of Natural Products.
The Trees the Flowers, with all the Vegetable Race,
the Birds, Beaſts, and Fiſhes, with every Species of Animal, are ſo many Remembrancers of our Mortality
Which way ſoever we turn our Eyes, they are preſented with ſuch Image of Human Weakneſs   And the
very Breath which doth prolong our Life, helpeth
equally to ſhorten it, ſince every Reſpiration carrieth
away ſome Portion of our Subſtance   Our finer Particle gradually vaniſh into Smoak and Air, whilſt the
more groſs Remainder ſcums off in noiſome Excre-
ment   And if there appear a Shew of any thing ſolid
in us at our Death, it is ſoon reduced to Aſhes, Dirt,
or Worms   Our Bodies, of which we make ſo great
account whilſt Living, are loſt in an Abyſs of Univerſal Matter ſoon after Death

What were the greateſt Prince the happier, though
he poſſeſſed the whole Circumference of this Globe ?
'Tis but a mighty Heap of Dirt or Dung, perpetually
falling or crumbling away   It is one of the Diſhes
which compoſe the Banquet of all devouring Time
and whilſt the inſulting Monarchs of the Earth trample on it in Diſdain, ſpreading their Armies far and
wide and boaſting that their Empires have no Bounds,
each does but haſten to be ſhut up himſelf within a little obſcure and putrid Hole, not much ſurpaſſing the
ſame of a Mole hill

Good Loya, let not the Honours and Dignities thou
enjoyeſt, make thee forget the Miſeries to which thou
art liable each Hour   But remember thou art a Man

Paris the 11th Moon,
of Lent, 1699.

L E T-

LETTER XII.

To the Kaimacham.

HERE is arrived a *Mutafaraca*, called S[...]
Ismael, with Ex[...]esses from the Gra[...]
It was no small Refreshment to see his publick [...]
which appeared like a little *Epitome* of the [...]
Grandeur and Magnificence. The young R[...]
as curious to be Spectators of the [...] Ca[...]
as the *Romans* were fond of beholding the S[...]
which were exhibited but once in an Age. Nay P[...]
ple of all Ranks, Ages, and Qualities, filled the s[...]
the Windows, and Battlements of their Houses [...]
because they never saw such a Sight before, o[...]
despairing that they should live long enough [...]
Witness of such another

Yet with all their Curiosity, none but the M[...]
State are able to dive into the least Secret of h[...]
structions. These willingly communicate the [...]
which that *Great Arbiter of the Earth* gives the Fr[...]
King. That so not only his Subjects, but n[...]
ing Nations may conceive the profounder Vene[...]
for him, without penetrating the Measures he t[...]
This is an Artifice common to all States to turn [...]
best Side outermost, only the H[...]ders excepted, [...]
in the Days of their *Revolt* from the King of [...]
could not so much as put a good Face upon [...]
Matter. But were forced to expose their P[...]
and *Nakedness,* as well as [...] under it, adur[...]
themselves to *Elizabeth,* then Queen of *England* [...]
Character of *the poor Distressed States of* Holland, [...]
so begging her Assistance

However, *Solyman* has faithfully imparted to m[...]
Affairs, as I have Reason to believe. He is too [...]
born and bred, possesses more Reason and Wit, t[...]
to amuse *the Old Man in the Cassock* (so they cal[...]
here in the Streets, who know me not by a[...]
Chara[...]

haracter , so private is *Mahmut* in *Paris*, at this Hour,
ot thstanding all his publick Sufferings)

I esteem *Ismael* is one fit to represent the *Grand Sig-*
r Person among better People than *Infidels.* Yet I
ll nee the *French* are the most refined of all the *Wes-*
n Goths

In a understands the Force of the Civil Laws which
l uned from *Justinian* s Code, and other Books For
perfect in *Greek* and *Latin*, and has bestow'd some
s in reading their Books both Prints and Manu-
ps

He makes a very Personable Figure, being tall, full-
died, well shaped, and not of an ugly Face, which
erugh to be sid of a Man designed for Business
d not only for Love He is never in danger of fal-
g under *Cato's* Censure, who seeing two Ambassa-
s ir from *Rome* to a foreign State one of which
d his Head so little, that it could hardly be distin-
ished from that of an Owl , and the other such a
pple, that he could not walk without Stilts , cried
, *Here is an Embassy which has neither* Head *nor*
il

And then our *Muta-faraca* is rich He supports the
arges of his Commission with extraordinary Muni-
ce His House is already become the Sanctuary
all the distressed *Levantines*, whether *Greeks, Arme-*
, or *Followers of the Prophets* And he speaks
r as readily as a Native Yet he dissembles his
perness in that Language, to keep up the State and
evedness of the *Ottoman* Empire, which disdains
condescend to any other Speech than *Turkish* or
k Besides, he has the Advantage, by thus al-
cilly shutting his Ears that he can at one Time
th *Hear* and be *Deaf*, *Understand* and be *Ignorant* of
soever is said by the Spies of the *French* King
d this is no small Gift in a Man of his Character
Irut For he had need of an *Angel*, or a *Devil*
s Elbow, that thinks to over-reach this Court.

About

Above all, I believe our *Solyman* would never
guilty of the Error committed by the Ambassado
from *Tenedos* to one of the *Roman* Emperors, I am
he is not yet. For those Gentlemen had seen the De
of the Emperor's Son, Eleven Moons and For
Days, as the Story says, before they knew it was
Duty to make an Address of Condolence. Or,
least, before they called it to mind, for the;
drowned in the *Roman* Luxury. So that, when the
came to perform that *Devoir*, the Emperor could
forbear to scoff at them in these Terms. *I nut*
ment, said he, *the Love of the Renowned* Hector, *.*
Country-man, and Champion, whom Achilles *the Gro*
killed above a thousand Years ago

I speak this in a particular Regard to *Solyman*
portment here. For, when he first came to this Co
he found them all in Mourning for the Death of
King's Aunt the late Queen of *England*, and of
High Personages, (particularly those that were slain
the late Action at *Candia*) whereof I have already
ven an Account to the *Sublime Porte* in another Let
Without Instructions he very demurely accosted
King, and told him, " There could be no *Disastr*
" the *Ottoman* Empire, for the late Success at *Car*
" so long as the *French* Court were Mourners

This was a sensible Touch to those that underst
it, and from that Moment, the Grandees and M
sters of State have made a Difference in their Ent
tainment of this ingenious *Muta faraca*, and t
which they used to give to the *Chiauses* formerly
from the *Porte*

I can assure thee, he is, at the same time, very
and very elegant in his Discourse. There is Fire in ev
ry Word he utters, to warm and refresh, if they
it at a due Distance, but if they approach too near,
scorches their Spirits, and puts them into a Choler
dare not shew. They consume inwardly in their o
Despight. Yet cannot help themselves

Doubtless, the King of *France* is the greatest
narch, the most powerful and victorious Prince in

..., the only *Invincible* Emperor of the *Western*
... Yet he veils to our *Majestick Sovereign* Lord
...he whole Earth. And our *Eunuch* will not part
...h a Tittle of his Master's Honour, or give any Ad-
...ge by an Easiness worthy of Blame, in a Case
...may be turned to a Precedent He is very happy
...n Repartees, as thou wilt perceive by the Answer
...gave to a *French* Lord yesterday, when he asked
..., Whether he thought it not a Violation of the
...al Law, for Ambassadors to be imprisoned, as they
...re in the *Ottoman Porte* ? *No,* (says *Solyman*) it
...... the *Ambassador* is guilty of Treason or Cri-
...l. to Majestatis But, if it were, you Frenchmen
...e least Reason to accuse us of it, since we first learn'd
...his in from the Back of your Salick Law, where
...t an fed And then he produced twenty several
...tances of this Kind in the Court of *France*
...In a word *Solyman* has hitherto acquitted himself
...th marvellous Success in every Thing, tho the
... Grandees often set upon him, to try what Metal
...s made of, having generally a mean Opinion of
...........s, because Learning is so little countenanced
...ong us
...I have no Matter of News to acquaint thee with,
...... a violent Plague broke forth not long ago at
......, and a terrible Earthquake in *Sicily,* frighted
...Inhabitants of *Catanea,* and the adjacent Towns
...their Habitations , after one whole Village had
... swallowed up
...And who were curious to pry into the Cause of
...e particular Convulsions, and that affrighting Over-
...w perceived, after diligent Search, that it proceed-
...from a new Eruption, or Breach in *Mount Gibel,*
...but two Miles from *Catania* Where the *Horrid*
......n vomited forth Floods of Fire, with Flaming
......, which being carried violently through the Air,
...he Space of near a League round about, at last fell
...wn in Flaming Showers or *Cataracts,* producing sad
... calamitous Effects in the neighbouring Country

Serene

Serene Minifter, it is evident, that the Judgmer
God are upon thefe *Infidels* Yet, they will r
converted from their Errors and Vices They h.
the fame Tempeft of Fire which overwhelmed th-
Cities of the Lake *Afphaltites* Yet, they remain
fible and obdurate Surely, they will be extermir
from the Earth.

Paris, 4*th of the* 12*th Moon,*
    of the Year 1669

The End of the Second Book

LETTERS

WRIT by a

SPY at *PARIS.*

VOL VII

BOOK III.

LETTER I.

To Mehemet, *an* Exiled Eunuch, *at* Alcair *in* Egypt.

BE no longer melancholy, my Friend, nor fink under the Burthen of thy Misfortunes. Give not thy Enemies an Occasion of double Triumph in that they have driven thee from thy felf, as well as from the *Grand Sign or's* happy Presence. Thou haft Money and Jewels enough left to purchafe thee a competent Felicity any where. Or, at leaft thou haft Virtue which renders every Place a *Paradife.* Afociate thy felf with the other *Exiles* in that City, Victims to a *Royal Caprice,* fuffered with all their immenfe Riches, to make a pompous and magnificent Entry into that Metropolis of *Egypt,* but foon after ftripped of all their Wealth, and facrificed to the *Court Avarice.* So were the confecrated Bulls of old, dreffed up in ftately E-
quipage,

quipage, their Horns and Hoofs all gilded over
Gold, adorned with Ribbons of coftly Silk, their
dies covered over with Mantles of Brocade and Tu
embroidered with Pearls and precious Stones,
trailing on the Pavement of *Apollo*'s Temple, w
the Priefts ftood ready at the Altar to difpatch w
Hecatombs of thefe gay Sacrifices

Your Cafe is not fo bad at *Cairo*, in that your L
are fpared, and you at Liberty to carve new For
to your felves, where-ever you pleafe You ought
aid and counfel one another in your Misfortunes I
a Comfort to the Miferable, to have Companion
their fad Eftate Infinuate thy felf into the *Ba*
vour He may do fomething to alleviate th G
He will meafure thy Circumftances by his own,
fidering that he has but three Years to enjoy his
fent Wealth and Grandeur

Go to the banifhed *Mufti*, if he be living at C
defire his fpiritual Advice Perhaps thou may'ft
into the Bargain fome Temporal Advantages fro
He has a greater Influence on fome of the *E*
Beys, than the *Grand Signior* has himfelf You
alike embarked in one Affliction, whofe Effence
confift in being degraded from your former Hon
(though in different Degrees) and being feparate
your Friends, that bafk in the immediate Luftre of
perial Dignity It is your Bufinefs therefore no
find out fome new Source of Happinefs To m
new Friends, fince you have loft the old, or, at l
to prop up one another by a mutual Friendfhip m
be broke or diffipated, but by a *Deftiny* equal to
former And then you have no more to do, but
fecute your feveral Interefts, and be refigned to *Fa*

As for thee, I am particularly folicitous, being
gaged together from our Youth, by a Reciproc
ticipation of good Offices, which was the Effect
deep rooted and ftrong *Sympathy*. The Agreeabl
of Humour united firft our Souls, and taught us
myfterious Leffons of *Platonick* Love We live e
other, and were ftreight infpired with facred Inch

ions   My Eye no fooner fixed on thine, but through
that Perfpective, I could fee the inward Virtue of thy
Soul, which immediately produced a Ventilation in
my Breaft   And I foon found our Hearts bore Time
to one another   This generous Paffion afterward increafed as we grew up , and what it loft of its firft Violence, is gained by acquiring a more lafting Strength,
more durable Integrity, and conftant Faithfulnefs   Our
Joys and Griefs were ftill the fame.   No profperous or
adverfe Fortune could ever change our Minds, to warp
us either to Flattery or Contempt   But with an even
Mind we ftill fuftained the different Accidents of human Life, and propped up one another with a right
Affection, till it was the Will of Fate to feparate us,
I being made a Slave in *Sicily,* whilft thou enjoyedft
the Smiles and Favours of thy Infant-Fortune, which
introduced thee firft to the *Serail*   Afterwards I gained my Freedom, and returned to the *Imperial* City,
and to the Palace of the *Sultan*   But was not fuffered
long to enjoy that Happinefs, being appointed for this
hazardous Poft in *Paris*

I tell thee, *Mehemet,* I reckon my Cafe far worfe
than thine, in that I am forced to take my conftant Refidence up among thefe *Infidels*   Could my propitious
Stars encourage me but with the fmalleft Hopes to
charge my prefent Courfe of Life, I would never repine at what was paft, but pleafe my felf with flatter-
ing Profpects of fome future and unknown Felicity.
But to be irrevocably chained down to the Oar, without a Glimpfe of any Sign that I fhall ever be relieved,
is worfe than Death it felf.

Whereas, on the other Side, thou art difpofed of in
the happieft Region of the Earth, *Egypt,* the Mother
of *Sciences,* the Midwife of *Celeftial Secrets,* the Nurfe
of *Sages, Saints,* and *Prophets,* the Granary of the
Mufulman Empire , and the Refuge of Diftreffed Mortals   Oh ! *Mehemet,* prize the vaft Advantage thou
haft of me, and others of thy Fellow-Slaves. Improve
thy Privilege and Opportunity of ranging where thou
lift   Go, vifit all the Antiquities of *Egypt,* and trace her
Borders to the *Weft* and *South*   If this will not divert

thy Melancholy, go farther yet, and fearch the migh
ty *Cataracts* of the *Nile*, which deafen Mortals wit
their Fall. Go view the Mountains of the *Moon* i
Æthiopia Or, fee the Defolation of the *Smoaky Vah*
and of the Cities, whofe Inhabitants were in a Minu\
metamorphofed in to Stones, as a Memorial of Etern\
Vengeance againft crying Sins.

But, after all, my *Mehemet*, depart not from th\
Reafon, Loyalty and Faith For thefe are Armo\
Proof againft the Affaults of Chance and Deftiny,
Men and Devils, of Earth and Hell And when th\
Travels are finifhed here on Earth, thofe Virtues \
not fail to carry thee to Heaven.

Paris, 5th of the 4th Moon,
of the Year 1670

LETTER II.

To the Same.

I Cannot forbear giving thee the Trouble of anoth\
Letter by this Poft, that I may yet more encou\
thee to a virtuous Refignation to the Will of F\
which thou knoweft is inexorable.

There is an Eternal Law fixed in the Univer\
which admits of no Repeal No Prayers or Tear\
Paffionate Mortals , no Vows, Alms, Pilgrimage\
any other Supererogating Works, can move the D\
ftinies They are more inflexible than the Judges\
the old *Athenian Areopagus*. And the unchanged
Edicts of the *Median* Empire might fooner be reverf\
than the Decrees of *Fate*.

If thou couldft make *Corban* with an hundred tho\
fand Sheep, and feed the Poor of all the *Eaft*, accu\
ing to the *Muffulman* Practice or facrifice as ma\
Bulls, afer the Fafhion of the antient *Gentiles* , coul\
thou monopolize all the *Aromaticks* of the *Orient*,

compo-

compound the moft exalted Incenfe, and make a *Pyramid* of odoriferous Smoke afcend high as the Shadow of the Earth at Midnight, whereby the Heaven of Heavens fhould be all perfumed, and every fleeping Deity fhould be awakened by the fragrant Smell, couldeft thou bribe the Choirs above, to tune the Spheres anew, and raife the fweeteft Harmony that ever reached the *Eternal Senfe*, yet all would not prevail to alter tne Refolves of Heaven, or re-inftate thee in thy former Honour. No! my *Mehemet*, thou art loft for ever at the *Serail* The Face of Things is changed, fince thou haft been in *Egypt* Thy Friends are all difperfed abroad in the World, or dead, which is but another kind of Separation There are no Hopes now left thee, of ever returning again to that proud City, which inherits the Character of antient *Rome*. *The Lady of the Earth*, I wifh the *Roman* Luxury be not alike entailed.

Rouze up, my Friend, and look not on thy State, through the deceitful *Opticks* of thy Paffion, but let Reafon light tne *Profpect* Thou wert before a Slave; now thou art free, and Mafter of thy felf. However, to rid thee of tre very *Idea*, or fancied Mifery, I counfel thee once again, to travel.

Go, make the fpeedieft Retreat thou canft out of the Limits of the *Ottoman* Empire that thou mayeft forget thy Cares and Fears Take not the Way by *Barbary*, nor covet to fee the Place where antient *Carthage* was fituated, be not curious to enquire after Queen *Dido*, *Ænai*, or *Hannibal*, or to heai fome Stories of the famous *Scipio* Nor would I counfel thee to pafs the kingdoms of *Morocco* and *Fez*. For, though thofe realms pay no Obedience to the *Sultan* yet they are his allies, and that Reflection will always keep thee in pain Befides, the Sight of *Muffulmans* will terrify thy mind, and fill thee with a thoufand Apprehenfions

Go rather the directeft Way thou canft, unto the kingdoms of the *Negroes*, or Black People inhabiting the *Torrid Zone* But, take this Rule Be fure to coaft along the River *Nile*, as near as the Roads of *Africk* will permit That fo thou mayeft avoid the horrible and

G 2   affright-

affrighting Defarts of *Lybia*, *Nubia*, and *Zanfar*, w
other inhofpitable mountainous Parts between the *T*
pick of *Cancer* and the *Equinox*   For, thou wilt
find it very pleafant to encounter and converfe w
none but Dragons, Bafilifks, and other Monfter
thofe Regions   And yet, for ought I know, it is be
ter than to fall into the Hands of human Savages

I know not how to give a general Character of
Southern Blacks, fince every Province varies in its p
ticular Principles, Cuftoms, Laws, and Inftitutio
The *Abyffines* are *Chriftians*, fo are the Inhabitant
Congo, *Songo*, *Angola*, and other Countries bordering
the Upper *Æthiopia*   Thofe that dwell along the
Sea, are generally *Mahometans*   They difcourfe alfo
a very populous Country thereabouts, poffeffed by *J*
alone   And there are Authors who affert a Fer
Kingdom, a Nation of *Amazons*   It is certain, on
Weftern Side they are all *Pagans*

It will be worth thy Labour to obferve the diff
Humours of thefe People, and make comparifon b
tween the Antient and this Modern *Gentilifm*, to
ftract their Morals from their Superftitions   And t
me then, whether they do not better deferve the T
of *True Believers*, than we *Muffulmans*, fince they
according to their Faith, whereas we go by a qu
contrary Method   They believe no other *Gods*
their Domeftick Priefts, and thefe they never will
offend, Whereas, whilft we profefs the *Eternal Lr*
we fcruple not to fin againft him every Hour   Th
circumcife, wafh, pray, abftain from Meats, give Al
as well as we.   Their Juftice is as ftrict, their Mei
foft as ours   In fine, they are Men differing from
only in Colour, Education, and the peculiar Maxims
their Country, which they rigoroufly obferve, and h
for Happinefs thereby, as we do by obeying the L
brought down from Heaven

Mehcmet, Our Holy Prophet has faid, " That w
" foever lives innocently, and does Juftice, whethe
" be a *Chriftian*, *Jew*, or *Pagan*, fhall be faved as w
" as his Difciples "   Therefore in all thy Travels,

pife not any Man for his Religion, be it never fo ridiculous in Appearance, provided he be good and honeft
in his Converfation, much lefs contemn thofe *Africans*
for their Colour, fince *Black* and *White* are all alike
to him, who firft gave Man the Power to know the
Difference

Mahomet, If thou accepteft my Advice, take alfo my
Wifhes for thy good Voyage and Profperity

Paris, 5th of the 4th Moon,
of the Year 1670

LETTER VII.

To the Mufti, *Venerable* Patron *of* Learning *and* Knowledge.

FROM thy Clemency I will not fear a Charge of
Negligence, in that I have delayed to perform
the Tafk thou enjoinedft me   Thou knoweft my Circumftances, and will confider, That though I have
read *Books*, yet I have not a *Library* of my own, It is
true, I often frequent thofe of this City, but my Seafons are limited, either to thofe Hours when the *Libra-*
ries are opened, or to thofe I can fpare from the Affairs of my Commiffion   I cannot ferve the *Grand*
Signior, and follow my Studies both at once   Yet I
have outpaffed Frugality, and turned a Niggard of my
Time, that I might obey the great *Oracle* of *True Be-*
lievers, and promote a *Work*, for which I have fo
affionate a Regard

The enclofed Paper contains the Size of the Volume, which I conceive will be moft proper for fo
great a Work, with the Contrivance of the Pages,
which I have divided into Columns, that fo the Years
of the World, the Date of the Olympiads, with other
remarkable *Æras*, may be ranked in Order, each
parallel with the reft, and all with the Matter treated
of at fuch a Time

This

This I have done in the enclofed Paper, not thinking it proper to interrupt the Series of my Letter with
a blank Scheme, which is for the Ufe of the Comp-
lers, but to prefent thee with a tranfient View of the
Four Monarchies, which have made fuch a Noife, in the
World, wherein thou needeft not fear the Fatigue of
a tedious continued Hiftory, for I defign only to cull
out fuch Paffages as are moft diverting, and worthy thy
Perufal

To begin then with the *Affyrian Monarchy*, which
was the Firft of the Four This Nation was, for
a great while, contented with its own Bounds
without feeking to encroach on the Territories of o-
thers And *Ninus* was the Firft of the *Affyrian Kings*,
who enlarged his *Dominions* by *Conqueft*. He fubdued
the greateft Part of *Afia*, and raifed *Affyria* to the Title
of an *Empire*

After his Death, *Semiramis* his Wife took upon her
the Government, counterfeiting the Perfon of *Ninus*
his Son, who was yet but a Child She wore the Habit
of a Man, and being like her Son, paffed for him, and
the lawful Succeffor, unfufpected This *Virago* enlarged the *Conquefts* of her Hufband, and fpread her
Empire from *India* to *Æthiopia*, and to lay the Foundation of an immortal Fame, fhe built *Babylon*.

To her, fucceeded *Ninyas* her Son, of whom nothing is remarkable but his Effeminacy For neglect-
ing the Affairs of War, he fpent all his Time among
his *Concubines*. And the fame Stain is faftened on his
Succeffors, even to *Sardanapalus*, in whofe Death the
Affyrian Monarchy fuffered an Interruption, being Cantonized into Petty Royalties by the *Governors of Provinces* Among whom, thofe who affumed the Crown
of *Babylon* were of moft Note, in regard they firft reco-
vered the broken Empire to its old Grandeur and Unity

By a Succeffion therefore of many Kings, in reference to whofe Actions Hiftory is filent, the *Monarchy*
defcenced to *Merodac Baladan* In whofe Days happened that wonderful Retrogradation of the Sun, mentioned by *Hebrew Writers* and others, which occafioned
the

those Famous Controverses among the Philosophers and Astronomers of that Age, mentioned in the *Persian Chronicles.* For they observing, that not only the Sun, but the whole Planetary System, and all the fixed Stars went back at the same Time, or at least seemed to do so, began to revive that curious Question, about the Motion of the Earth, which the *Chaldeans,* and Gymnosophists of *India* had started before, when the Sun and Moon stood still at the burning of *Ida* And it was concluded by some of them, That the Motion of the Earth being granted, its standing still or going back at these extraordinary Times, would solve all the Astronomical Appearances better and in a more Natural Way, than by supposing such a prodigious Stop to be put to the whole Celestial Frame at one Time, or that the Everlasting Spheres should be rowled backwards at the other

This Dispute was the Occasion of that famous Conflux of the *Eastern Sages* to *Babylon,* mentioned in the *Persian Poets* and *Historians.* For *Baladan* being very inquisitive after Knowledge, and particularly desirous to be informed in the Grounds of this Preternatural Appearance, sent Messengers into *India, Ægypt, Persia,* and all *Kingdoms,* where Learning flourished, inviting the *Astrologers, Priests, Magicians, Prophets,* and all that had the *Character* of *Wise Men,* to come to his *Court* of *Babylon,* where they were magnificently entertained; and when they had fully satisfied all the King's Demands, he sent them away laden with Gifts and Presents, every Man to his own Country

Asbanus succeeded *Baladan* in the *Kingdom* of *Babylon,* in whose Time *Ecbatan* was built To him succeeded *Belithus, Aphronadius, Rigibelus, Messissimordacus,* after whom the *Kingdom* was again translated to the *Assyrians,* in the Reign of *Escharhaddon,* in the 3323d Year of the World, and 24th Olympiad During the Empire of this *Escharhaddon,* the *Assyrian Monarch, Chalcedon* that lies over-against the *Imperial* City, was built by the *Thracians,* in the 25th Olympiad, and the 3329th Year of the World.

To *Efcharraddon* fucceeded *Soafdachinus*, *Chyladan*, *Nabopolaffar*, in the Reign of which laft, *Accho*, K. of *Egypt*, attempted to cut a Canal from the *Nile* to th. *Red Sea*, wherein he employed an Hundred a. Twenty Thoufand *Egyptians*, but difcouraged by t. flow Progrefs they made, and the vaft Expences was at, he gave it over

This *Nabopolaffar*, once more raifed the Kingdom *Babylon* to an univerfal Monarchy, for before his Tir it had been for fome Years in the Hands of the *A. rian*, but he fubdued all *Syria*, *Phœnicia*, *Juda*. and *Egypt*, and expelled the *Scythians* out of *Afia*

To him fucceeded his Son *Nebuchadnezzar*, w dreamed of the *Four Univerfal Monarches*, that were fucceed one another   In his Reign was born t. *Grand Cyrus*, who raifed the *Perfian Monarchy*   C him it is recorded, that one Night he dreamed, *That* Sun *ftood at his Feet, whom when* Cyrus *Thrice attempt to lay hold on, the* Sun *as often difappeared*   Which th *Magi interpreted* as a fure Sign tnat he fhould Rei; Thirty Years, which came to pafs accordingly

During this Reign, there waca not able Duel fough between *Pittaccus*, one of the Seven Wife Men *Greece*, and *Phrynon* the moft renowned Combatan . thofe Days, for he always won the Prize at the Olyn pick Games   He was General of the *Athenians*, a. being puffed up with his conftant Succefles, he der. any Man to a fingle Combat   *Pittacus* the *Sage* a. cepted the Challenge, and when they were hotly e gaged in the Field, he fuddenly threw a filken N. over *Phrynon*'s Head and having thus entangled hir thruft him through with his *Lance*.

This was that great *Nebuchadnezzar*, who have befieged and taken *Jerufalem*, burnt it down to th Ground, razed the Walls, and carried away all th *Jews* with their Riches into Captivity to *Babylon*

Afterwards, having conquered all the Neighbouring Nations, he new built *Babylon*, and enclofed it with Three Walls   He alfo built thofe *Pendulous Garde* renowned

enowned throughout the Earth, and made those Brazen Gates which were reckoned among the *Wonders* of the *World* But at length being puffed up with the Thought of his Magnificent *Works*, he was Metamorphosed into a *Satyr*, or *Silvan*, and dwelt Seven Years in the *Desarts* of *Arabia*, being a Companion of the *Brutes* My *Countrymen* shew the Places of his wild Haunt to this Day, having received it by *Tradition* from their *Fathers* They say also, that *Paremel*, the *Angel* of the *Woods*, when the Term of Seven Years was expired, interceded with God for *Nebuchadnezzar*, who thereupon turned him into a Man again, and reftored him to his *Empire* He died peaceably in the 34*2*d Year of the Word, and the 43d of his Reign

To him succeeded *Evil Merodach, Neriglissor, Laborosoarchod*, and *Labynitus*, in whose Time there was War between the *Babylonians* and *Persians*, when *Cyrus* after many victorious Campaigns, at laft laid Siege to *Babylon*, took the City, and tranflated the *Empire* to the *Persians* and having fubdued all the *Weft* of *Afia*, even to the *Red Sea*, he died at Seventy Years of Age, Commanding his Servants not to embalm his Body, nor ufe any coftly Pomp at his *Funeral*, but burying him decently like a Man, fhould cause this *Epitaph* to be writ on his *Tomb*

O Mortals, I am Cyrus who laid the Foundation of the Perfian *Monarchy, and was Emperor of all* Afia, *Therefore envy me not a Grave.*

To him succeeded *Cambyses* his Eldeft Son, who marching with his Army into *Egypt*, and laying Siege to *Pelufium*, caufed a great Number of Cows, Apes, Birds, and other Animals, to be placed in the Front of his Army, knowing that the *Egyptians* worfhipped fuch for *Gods*, and consequently would forbear to fhoot their Arrows that way By which Stratagem he took the City, and afterwards conquered all *Egypt*, carrying

away

away many Thoufands of the *Egyptians*, with Foreign
ers refiding there, into *Captivity*, among whom wa
Pythagoras the *Philofopher*

After this *Cambyfes* fent *Spies* under the Notion of
Ambaffadors to the *King* of *Æthiopia*, with rich *Prefents*.
But the *King* fufpecting what was then Bufinefs, took
a *Bow* in his Hand and bent it, as though he would
fhoot, and giving it to the *Spies*, he bid them carry
to their *Mafter*, and tell him, *That when he and his Per*
fians *had learned to bend* Bows *of that Strength, he might*
think of invading Æthiopia, *and not before, for that the*
Æthiopians *were Giants in Vigour* And when the *Spies*
returned to *Cambyfes*, there was no Man found among
his Soldiers which was able to bend that *Bow* Yet
he marched directly towards *Æthiopia* with a great
Army, part of which was overwhelmed in the Sands
of the *Defarts*, to the Number of Fifty Thoufand, and
the reft being reduced for Want of Provifions, to a Neceffity of eating one another, he returned in a great
Rage to *Memphis*, where he flew *Apis* the *God* of the
Egyptians, and caufed his *Priefts* to be maffacred He
alfo flew his own Brother, and killed his Wife, becaufe fhe mourned for him He fhot *Prexaipes* through
with an Arrow, and commanded Twelve *Perfian Nobles*
to be buried alive He fet Fire to the *Temple*, blaf-
phemed the *Gods*, and at laft killed himfelf by an Accident with his own Sword

After his Death, the *Magi* crowned one of their own
Order, and fet him on the *Throne* of *Perfia*, giving
out that he was *Smerdis* the younger Son of *Cyrus*,
who had been murdered by the Command of his Brother *Cambyfes* And it was eafy to carry on the Fraud,
in regard the *Perfian Kings* rarely fuffer themfelves to
be feen which is a Cuftom, thou knoweft obferved
by all the *Monarchs* of the *Eaft*

One *Oftar*, a *Perfian* Prince, firft difcovered the
Cheat, by means of his Daughter a *Concubine* of the
King's For fhe, by his Inftruction, found out, that
the *King* had no Ears, which was a convincing Argument

ment that he was one of the *Magi*, whose Ears *Cam-ly-s* had commanded to be cut off

This *Ostan* drawing six other Princes into *a Conspiracy*, they rushed into the Palace, and killed all the *Magi*, and singled out of their own Number, one *Darius* the Son of *Hystaspes*, to succeed in the Throne. This was not done by Election, but by Lot For they agreed to meet all together, one Morning before the Palace Gates on Horse-back, and that he whose Horse first neighed after the Sun was up, should be King This fell to *Darius*'s Share, by the Stratagem of his 'Squire, or Master of the Horse Then the other Princes crowned him, and made him swear by the Sun and Fire, that he would never put them to Death, or deny them his Presence

But *Darius* finding himself curbed by these Princes wa resolved to rid himself of such dangerous Companions Wherefore he caused a Stove to be built on purpose for a *Banquetting-House*, and so artificially contrived, that the Fire place being under the *Banquetting-Chamber*, should, in so many Hours, burn asunder the Pillars that supported the said Chamber, and cause the Floor to fall down into the Fire. Then he invited these Princes to a Feast, which he held in his *Banquetting-House*, and was merry with them till the Signal was given him to depart At which Time he left them in the Midst of their Mirth; and within a while after he was gone, the Floor of the Chamber fell down, with all that were in it, into the Fire underneath, where the Princes were soon consumed to Ashes.

After this *Darius* managed all the Affairs of his Empire without Controul He ruled over all the Provinces of *Asia*, from *India* to *Æthiopia*, containing above an Hundred Kingdoms He extended his Conquests to the Provinces of *Greece*, and setting forth a prodigious Fleet, he sailed into the *Mediterranean* and *Archipelago* He conquered the Islands of the *Ægean Sea*, reduced *Chalcedon*, and all the Cities along the *Hellespont* and *Propontis*, even *Byzantium* itself, the present Seat of our *August Emperors*. At length, having reigned

prosperously

prosperously Thirty Six Years, he died, and left *Xerx*
his Son to succeed him in the Throne

Thou seest, great Guide of the Faithful, that I have
not yet reached to the End of the *Persian Monarchy*,
whereas I thought to have comprehended all the For.
in one Letter, for I have only touched upon the mo
remarkable Passages, omitting the main Body of the
History, which it would be too tedious for thee to pe
ruse

If thou approvest what I have written, I will conti
nue thus to abbreviate the History of the *Persian*, M
cedonian and *Roman Empires* in other Letters But
thou thinkest what I have already writ to be a suffi
cient Model for the Compilers of an Universal Histo
ry, I submit to thy Oraculous Appointments

In the mean time, I pray the *King Eternal* wh
establishes and dissolves all the Empires in the Work
and has put into the Possession of the *Grand Sig.*
those ample Tracts of the Earth which formerly be
longed to the Successive Monarchies, to extend the Li
mits of the *Mussulman* Empire through the Five Zone

Paris, 1*7th of the 6th Moon,*
   of the Year 16*7*0.

LETTER IV

To Mirmadolin, Santone *of the Vale of*
   Sidon.

IT was a long Time before I could find out
the true Secret of Human Happiness I have so
many Years groped after it in the Dark, and when I
thought I enjoyed a Prospect of it, as clear as of Things
we discern in the Light of a Mid-day Sun, that Sun was
little better than the *Sol mortuorum* of the ancient R
mans, whose Beams served only to give a faint Mock
Glimmering to the Ghosts, that wander on this Side
                                                Charon

Charon's Ferry, and like an *Ignis fatuus* to miſlead them up and down the dark Suburbs of *Elyſium*, the Fens and Marſhes of the *Stygian Lake* So have I ſtraggled all my Life thro' unknown Ways, ſeeking the Road to Heaven, yet finding nothing but the *Paradiſe of Fools*

Sometimes I thought by outward Works of Virtue, to purify myſelf and gain Perfection I was punctual in obſerving every Precept of the Law and performed a few Acts of Supererogation Confiding too much in the Fidelity, and inviolable Faſtneſs of my Wings, the Force of my Religious Paſſions firſt formed by Nature, afterwards improved by pious Tutors, I ſtrove to make Heroick Flights, and ſoar above my Guide But, alas! they were mere borrowed Feathers which bore me up ſo long, dead artificial Wings, cemented to my Soul only by Education, Cuſtom, and the Practice of my Fathers, a Compoſition of Spiritual Wax, or Glew, which could not ſtand the Brunt of hot and fiery Trials, but ſoon diſſolved in my unwarrantable bold Approaches to the Sun So that, in fine, my Wings dropped piece-meal off, and I had the Fate of *Icarus*, to fall a Victim to my own obſtinate Zeal and Raſhneſs

Surely our Souls are like the *Augean* Stable, which no human Power, Art, or Induſtry, can ever cleanſe, did not the Meſſengers and Favourites of God, like *Hercule* teach us the Method of opening a Canal from Heaven and letting in the Torrent of the River of *Purification* from *Paradiſe*

Our *Vices*, *Hydra* like, ſtill ſtart young Infant Heads, as faſt as we cut off the Old Whereas our *Virtues* are like the *Venetian* Treaſure, which being once ſhewed to the *Spaniſh* Ambaſſador in many Coffers of Silver, Gold, and Jewels, the wiſe *Caſtilian* deſiring to ſee the Bottoms of thoſe Wealthy Cheſts turned up, when it was done, made this Remark, *Your Rubies have no Roots, to grow, like thoſe my Maſter poſſeſſeth in the* Indies So are all the boaſted Excellencies acquired by human Diſcipline, more inanimate and dead than the artificial Productions of Minerals, Metals and Stones No traditional Chymiſtry of Men, can ever revive a Soul that is

dead

dead to God   Perhaps, some Theological *Parace..*
Helmont, or *Arabian If qu*, may, from the Ashe
an Original Flower, raise the Fantastick Form of ..
gain, I mean the Colour and Contexture of the Lea.
But none of them is able to bestow the Vital Sap, .
Seminal Juce, the Inward Virtue of the once prosp
ous and flourishing Vegetable   No Mortal can rep
what *Iuam* once destroyed   That *Protoplast* has rui.g
us all

Well then ! Must we despair of Remedy ? Sha'' r
decamp, and sneakingly return to Hell, because we c..
n t take Heaven by Storm, or undermine it, nor ha
recourse to Stratagems to be the Garrison, or m..
a Party among the Co.. Burghers   No, let u.
t er he entrenched with ourselves, till Heaven th
voluntarily open its G.., and sally forth in Love .
invite and lead us in.

Oh ! thrice happy *Santone*, thou hast experie..
what I say My Resolution is to follow thee, by suff
ing myself to be gradually eradicated from the Wo.
and from my own Will. Vouchsafe to instruct me.
the Method, lest Self-love should guide me to my Ruin.

In the mean while, repose thou in the bosom
God, which is the Bed-Chamber of Holy Souls.

Paris, ist of the ○ h *Moon*,
  of the Year 1670

LETTER V.

To the Selictar Aga, *or* Sword-Bearer, *to t*
Sultan

I Shall entertain thee now with a *Medley* of Relation
  some containing News of the freshest Date other
only informing thee of things done many Moons go
yet pleasant enough in the Rehearsal   However I
of thee to accept this as a Testimony of my Devo..
                                         Regard

Regard, in that I have Abundance of Letters to write, many Friends to gratify, and cannot send rhe same Matter to all. I am forced to parcel out my Intelligence, and suit every Letter to the Genius and Station of him whom I address Knowing therefore thy particular Inclinations, I shall present thee with something very agreeable

No doubt but thou art acquainted with the *Christians Carnival* which is a Time of publick Joy, Licentiousness and Sport This Year the King and Queen of *France* observed it with wonderful Magnificence

Among their other Divertisements they were presented with a Play, wherein two Rival Princes by an ingenious Emulation, strove to o tvy each other in regaling a Princess, equally beloved by both The Representation was very fair, and full of Majesty On the right Hand of the Theatre appeared *Apollo* in the Air, returning to his *Heaven*, after he had chased and routed all the *Cyclops*, with the Serpent *Python* On the Left was seen the same God on the Top of *Parnassus*, in the midst of the *Nine Muses*, scattering Flowers on the Arts and Sciences, which were at the Foot of the Mountain. Then a Veil being drawn aside, discovered a Sea, surprizingly natural and fine In the midst of which, the Gods of many famous Rivers appeared seated on Rocks, with *Tritons* and *Cupids* ranged on each Side upon the Backs of *Dolphins* Then from above, amidst the Clouds, King *Æolus* appeared, laying his strict Commands upon the *Winds*, that they immediately retire into their Caverns, excepting only *Zephyr*, who, for his soft and gentle Breezes, was permitted to be present at this Feast After which, came *Neptune* riding in his Cockle Chariot, drawn by Four Sea-horses attended by a Train of *Gods* that dwell within the Deep

Immediately the *Scenes* changed into a Champain, representing the delicious Fields of *Tempe*, where a most excellent and agreeable Comedy was acted to the Satisfaction of all the Court I leave the Dances, Interludes, and other Novelties, to thy Imagination Assuring thee, that all was Astonishing and Magnifick.

But

But not to entertain thee longer with these emp[ty]
Trifles, I shall now acquaint thee with something [of]
Importance, which is a Peace concluded between [the]
King and the State of *Algiers*. On the 2*d* of the [—]
Moon, the Count *de Guiche* brought the Articles of [the]
Treaty to the King, from the Hands of the Marquis
Martel, Lieutenant-General of the *French* Fleet in [the]
Mediterranean.

If thou wouldest know the Particulars of this Agree[e-]
ment, read the inclosed Paper. As for Matter of F[act,]
all the *French* Slaves at *Algiers*, were immediately [re-]
leafed upon the Signing and Sealing the Treaty, [and]
delivered up to the *French* Commander with [the]
French Veffels also which they had feized. And fo [d-]
honourable are their Capitulations, that at the fame
Time they have yielded up a Ship of theirs, which the
French had taken from them, for ever quitting [their]
Claim to it.

In the Beginning of *May*, the King took his Jour[ney]
to *Flanders*, to vifit his new Conquefts there. Th[is put]
his Enemies into a great Confternation, fearing th[at he]
had fome Defign upon them. They began to be [up]
their Guard, and prepare for a fudden Surprize. B[ut]
the King perceiving their Alarm by his Spies, fent them
Affurance on his Royal Word, that he would do [them]
no Violence at this Time.

However, he foon after fent the Marefchal *de Cr*[—]
into *Lorrain*, with a Force confiderable enough to red[uce]
that Prince to Reafon, who had not kept his *Parole* with
him in feveral Inftances. The Effect of this Expedit[ion]
was the reducing *Porta-Moufon*, *Efpiral*, *Clefte*, *L*[on-]
g[—], and all the Principality of *Lorrain* to the *Fre*[nch]
King's Obedience. So that the poor Duke is forced [to]
feek his Refuge in foreign Courts.

Noble *Aga*, this Duke is not to be pitied, being ve[ry]
ungrateful, and a perfect Madman. He owes his L[i-]
berty and Life to the King of *France*, yet could not fo[r-]
bear plotting againft him. Now he is defervedly cha[s-]
ed for his Folly. So may all thofe fuffer, who ab[ufe]
their Benefactors. But upon the Benign and Good, m[ay]

the Favours of Heaven reft till the Splitting of all
Things

Paris 13*th of the* 9*th Moon,*
    of the Year, 1670

LETTER VI

To Iiouf, *his Kinfman, a Merchant at*
Aftracan

I Received thy Letter, and perufed it with much
Complacency, finding thy Sentiments very agreeabl. to Reafon   Yet give me leave to warn thee of an
Excefs which thou art running into. For I have had
experience of its ill Confequence

Thy Loffes have made thee melancholy, and the frau-
dulent Dealing of thy Correfpondents, Factors and fuppofed Friends has taught thee to declaim againft Friendfhip, Men and Bufinefs And not only fo, but it feems
thou haft taken a Refolution to abandon all worldly Affairs, Pleafures and Engagements whatfoever, and turn
Faqu r, Eremit, or *Dervich* at leaft   For thou art dif-
gufted at human Society, and weary of all Things but
Solitude

I muft confefs, *Ifouf,* thefe are very generous Thoughts,
and pious Refolves But they are not eafily put in Practice They are Undertakings fit only for perfect Saints,
Men of unblemifhed Lives, and free from all Sorts of
Vice, Perfons who have a Stock of Temperance, Cha-
fity, Prudence, Juftice, Fortitude, Patience, Humility,
and all the other Virtues, a Fund of Magnanimity,
which can never be exhaufted by any Temptation, Difficulties or Perils, that ufually affault and environ fuch
as enter into fo auftere a Courfe of Life

Wilt thou be able to endure the unrelenting, rigid
Cold of *Winter* in the Defart, where there are no Chim-
neys, Hearths, or Stoves, or any other Method of keep-
                                    ing

ing Fire to warm thee by ? Canst thou sustain the r..
ing Blasts of *Boreas* at that Season, or the killing Te..
pests of *North Eastern* Winds, which blow from far, a..
fill the Air, the Earth and Sea, with baneful M..
Frosts, Ice, Snow, Sleet and other chilling Me...
out of their Eternal Magaz..es within the *Arctick Cir*..
cle, which *Ovid* calls the *Frigid Zone*

There are many other Extremeties to which a M..
exposed in such a solitary State   Nor wilt thou be l..
liable to Inconveniencies and Hardships, if thou should..
ramble as a *Faquir* up and down the World   Mu..
less couldst thou endure the sad Restraints and Mor..
cations of a Convent   Thou wouldst hardly live..
thy *Novitiate* with Patience   It goes against the Gr..
of Nature to obey another's Will, in every trifling M..
ter that he commands   Thou must not eat or drink, b..
thy Superior will set the Place, the Time, and Mann..
of thy Diet; which will be irksome to thy free bor..
Soul   And then thou must forsake thy amorous Ple..
sures for ever, forswearing also the very Thought..
Money, or of being rich. I tell thee, thou must retch..
to become a religious *Drone*, fit for nothing but to mu..
ble over thy Beads, or turn the superstitious Round, t..
thou art giddy, or dance an Hour together to the M..
fick of a thousand *Heu*'s and *Hei*'s hoarsly croaked..
in frantick Tones by thee, and all thy Brethren *Der*..
viches, till ye are sick, and foam at the Mouth   Then you..
Devotions are thought meritorious   Canst thou dige..
these sacred Fooleries ? Or grant this to be a rational
Service of the Divinity, as some will plead, who f..
we ought to employ each Member, and all our Facul..
ties, in praising him that made them, yet canst thou
brook a Confinement all thy Days, to this Religiou..
State ?

I tell thee, *Isouf*, I have been often tempted in th..
Manner, to forsake the *Sultan*'s Service, with all other
Engagements of the World, and throw myself into a
Convent, or spend the Residue of my Days in some ob..
scure and solitary Corner of a Desart, Yet I found..
length, that this was nothing but Delusion, and th..
subtle Sophistry of that malicious Dæmon, who env..

Maa

Man his Happiness It is he that whispers Arguments
of Discontent and Murmuring into our Souls, watching
his Opportunities when any thing gives us exquisite
Pain or Grief, to drive us to Despair

So have I sometimes laboured under an intolerable
Anguish of Mind, besides the fretting Maladies of
Flesh and Blood, with outward Crosses in my Fortune.
Then have I wished myself in some dark Cavern of
the Earth, or on the solitary Top of *Teneriff*, where I
should converse with none but *Spirits* and *Dæmons* dwelling above the Clouds Or else I coveted the melancholy Retirements of the *Lybian* Desart, which affords
no other Society than that of *Lyons*, *Tygers*, *Dragons*, and
other *Beasts* of Prey

When these Wishes have appeared too extravagant
and wild, I then retrenched my Thoughts, and pitched
upon some other manner of Life, equally promising
Comfort, yet less threatning and dangerous I gave myself up wholly to Prayer and Fasting for a while, thinking to hold out thus for ever. So sensible a Pleasure
attends these Exercises, that at certain Moments a Man is
all Rapture, Ecstacy and I know not what. He is apt
to think himself in some new World.   A sacred Pride
invests his Soul.   He seems all Majesty within, an in-
separable Companion of the Immortals, and the darl-
ing Friend of God   Whereas all this results but from
the Ventilation of his Blood by vocal Oraisons, and is
no more than a mere natural Operation, whereby his
Lungs are artificially breathed, and gently forced to
disembogue their over-heated Airs, their thick caligi-
nous Vapours, which fill the Heart, and all the rest of
the Vitals with Seeds of Melancholy, Fear, Suspicion,
Grief, and other doleful Passions

But mark the *Zealot*, when his Prayers are over, his
Fast is done, and all his fervent pious Discipline is accomplished   how like a *Hypocrite* he looks and acts ?
How formal is his Carriage , or at least, how vain and
light ? He either heaves out fulsome hypocondriack
Sighs, with supercilious Looks, and Chaps set like
the

the Furrows of a fowre faced *Hadge*, or elfe he is tickled into a loud ungovernable Laughter, and all his Carriage is ridiculous and wanton. Either his Hunger, Thirst and Faintnefs, the ufual Effect of fuch exceflive Devotion, makes him peevifh, cholerick, and unmortified, or elfe he is as apifh as a Cat.

Human Nature cannot abide long in the fame Humour, and thofe that feem to be always even-tempered People, like the *Cafpain* Sea without Ebb or Flow, are only Counterfeits and Politicians. There is an Art to conceal one's Paffions, but there is none that can annihilate them. We change from one Affection, Apprehenfion and Defire to another. Our Inclinations circulate with our Blood. They are transformed each Minute, Hour and Day, they vary like the Wind and Weather. Therefore never think of taking an eternal Pleafure or Diftafte in any thing here below. Prayer is good in its Turn, I mean the vocal Afpirations. So are Fafting, Abftinence, and other Religious Severities, but if all Men fhould be perpetually at thefe Exercifes, God in a little Time would have but few Adorers on Earth. The Ground muft be left untilled, the Fields would quickly bring forth crops of Briars and Weeds, inftead of Corn. The Gardens then muft turn to Wilderneffes. There would be then no need of Millers, Bakers, and the other Trades, whofe Livelihood depends upon the Hufbandman. And fo for want of proper Suftenance, Mankind muft quickly perifh.

I do not argue againft thofe who feem to be conftellated to a folitary Life, or by fome fpecial Grace of God, are ftrengthened to endure the conftant Hardfhips of an Hermitage. Such as the illuftrious and great Mahammed of *Mount Uriel* in *Arabia*, who is our holy Prophet's Tenant and Succeffor, in the *Cave of Wonder*. Such alfo is *Ileb Rend Hu*, the celebrated *Bramin* of *Cachemire* in *India*, who lives on the Top of an high Mountain, is a hundred and twenty three Years old, foretels Things to come, refolves all Doubts, gives infallible Counfel, heals divers Difeafes, works fome Miracles,

Miracles, and in fine, says and does all Things by a
Spirit worthy of Admiration

The Mountain whereon this Philosopher or Prophet
dwells, seems to be the *Land mark* between *Summer* and
Winter For one Side of it is always covered with
Snow, the other with Bloſſoms, Flowers, Herbage and
Fruits This overlooking a ſpacious Valley, which
they call the *Paradiſe of the East*, that affording a Pro-
ſpect none more agreeable or fair, than what the *Poets*
ſpeak of the *Rablæan Hill*

This *Rend He* has his Habitation in a Cave or Grot,
which paſſes through the Rock, as *Virgil's* does near
Naples in *Italy*, which thou haſt ſeen

In this myſterious Station, he appears like *Æolus*,
Lord of the Weather For it is certain, he commands
the Winds to blow or ceaſe at the leaſt Word, within the
Verge of his accuſtomed Walks If any Perſon dare
profane the Silence of the Place with Words, or other
louder Noiſe they are immediately ſurprized with
dreadful Storms of Thunder, Lightning, Wind, and
Rain, ſuch as ſeem to threaten the Diſſolution of all
Things Which makes all Men in thoſe Parts hold
This *Rend He* in great Veneration He is the only Oracle of the *Indies* They reſort to him from the neighbouring Provinces and Kingdoms, in all their Difficulties The Grandees of *Persia*, *Tibet*, and *Cathay* ſend
to him honourable Preſents, deſiring his Counſel in
Matters of Peace and War Nay, they make devout
Pilgrimages to him from the Kingdoms of *Tunquin* and
China He is the *Apollo* of the *East*

Iouſ it would be ſome Encouragement for thee and
me to embrace a ſolitary Life, if we might ever hope to
attain ſuch wonderful Perfections But, as we have hitherto lived in the World, and ſtained ourſelves with the
common Vices of Mortals, we cannot preſume to merit
theſe extraordinary Favours Our old Habits are rooted in us, and if we have Time and Strength to plant
new ones in their ſtead, yet they will not grow up to
                                        Maturity,

Maturity, but with many Years For, believe me Cousin, no body becomes a *Devil* or a *Saint* all at once

Paris, *6th of the* 11*th Moon, of the Year* 1670.

LETTER VII.

To the Chaiux Baffa.

IT appears, That the King of *France's* Fortune not only procures him conftant Victories and Triumphs in *Europe*, but fuch a Renown and Character in far Countries, as ftimulates the moft remote Princes and puiffant Monarchs of the Earth, to court his Alliance and Friendfhip

Here is at this prefent, an Ambaffador come from the Coafts of *Guinea* in *Africk*, being fent by the king of *Arden*, one of the greateft Sovereigns in thofe Parts, poffeffing an abfolute and uncontroulable Authority over his Subjects, as the *Grandsignior* does over the faithful *Ofmans* But we will not compare the narrow Limits of his Dominion with the vaft and unbounded Extent of the *Muffulm on* Empire, the Inheritance of our fublime *Sultan*, the Lord of the Globe at large Suffice it, that this Black Prince is a wife Man, defcended of a Race of Sages , and, that Policy of State is as natural to him, as common Craft or Cunning to the meaneft of the Vulgar He knows how to make War or Peace abroad, and to keep his Subjects in awe at home

Surely there is a Force and Charm in the Derivation Blood of heroick and wife Anceftors, which fecretly infpires their Off fpring with Maxims and Principle agreeable to tne Inclinations, Aims, and Purpofes of the Fami*y* from whence they defcend And where it is experienced othe erwife, it may be fuppofed that Change of Climate, unhappy Marriages, or fome over ruling Misfortunes in the World, have caufed the Degeneracy

For

, to fome noble Vegetables of *Afia*, and other Quarters of the Earth, lying near the Sun, will not profper,
or e tranfplanted into the cold and barren Soils of
tr ern *Europe* Thus Poverty, Difgrace, and other
 b t Circumftances, chill the greateft Spirits, and
col their Growth Yet there is an inborn Excellency
fome Natures, which with Evennefs fupports the
ftroke of Fortunes, and pufhes through all Difficulties
attain its End

So this great *African* King, informing himfelf not
b by *French* Veffels trading in his Ports, but alfo by
ther Ships of *Chriftendom*, of the Grandeu of the
t King, his Wealth and Puiffance by Sea and
and, with the vaft Intereft and Traffick he has in both
hides, thought it high time to feek his Friendfhip,
beit Enmity would, in all Probability, be very fatal
him For he had heard of his Conquefts far and
de It is no matter, whether by Valour or good
onduct, we make ourfelves happy One is as lauda-
e as the other, in the unequal War we are engaged in
ith *Fate*, *Providence*, and *Chance*, with *angels*,
and *Devils* ; with *Heaven*, *Earth*, and *Hell*

I fpeak this in reference to the celebrated Prowefs,
ignanimity, Riches, and Strength of this *Negro* King,
ho need not yield to the King of *Benin*, his next
eighbour, and the moft potent of all the *South weftern*
aritime Princes of *Africk*, nor to any of his other
eighbours befides, yet could not think himfelf fafe,
be at reft, till he had fent his Embaff. to the King
France, offering his Lands, his Havens, his Seas,
t whatfoever was within his Jurifdiction, to this great
lonarch

The Addrefs which his Ambaffador made to the *French*
ing deferves Remark For after the ufual Obeifances
the Foot of the Throne, he went up Three Steps, and
en proftrating himfelf three times on his Face and
ell, he clapped his Hands in token of Reverence, and
t his Fingers on his Eyes, to fhew that he was not
ble to behold the Luftre of fo much Majefty This is
e *French* Interpretation of his Carriage But I tell
ee, it was rather defigned as a Precedent to the *French*
Ambaffadors

Ambaſſadors, if any ſhould be ſent to *Guin a,* w
it is the Cuſtom of the Country for all Foreign Mi
ſters, to obſerve the ſame Ceremonies to the King
Arder, and other Princes his Neighbours

These *Europeans,* becauſe they firſt found out the
of Navigation, or at leaſt, firſt improved it to the D
covery of many remote Countries, value them
too high, imagining, that all the Nations, forme
unknown, are Fools, and know not themſelve
their own Strength. They thought it was impoſſ
find in *Africk* or *America,* Empires, Kingdom
Commonwealths, as ſtrong and well governed, as th
in the Hermitage of *Japhet* But it is a damned
take. For the moſt High is impartial in the Diſtri
tion of his Gifts and Favours. Thoſe deſpicable *Bla*
whom all the Princes and Nobles of *Europe* and
buy as Slaves, being born of the *Vulgar,* are never
leſs come out of Regions, where Power, Riches,
Wiſdom, are as much in their *Zenith,* as in theſe
tern Countries

They are all outwardly Fleſh and Blood, as we a
notwithſtanding the Contrariety of our Colours
as for their Souls, they are even juſt as capab
Knowledge and Ignorance, Reaſon and Folly, Vice
Virtue, Piety and Prophaneneſs, Superſtition and
theiſm, as we are, who pretend to be Lords of
World, and all Things

May thou and I practice Moderation, and not
temn any of human Race, though they be the Ca
of *Moſambique* But let us always Remember the
Turkiſh Proverb, *That it is not good or ſafe to p*
Mockery behind the Grand Signior's *Back* Adieu

Paris, *3d of the 12th Moon,*
    of the Year 1670.

LETTER VIII

To Mahommed, *the Illuſtrious* Solitary *of* Mount Uriel *in* Arabia.

THE grand Root of the common Injuſtice which Men are guilty of, in reference to the Beaſts, and of the Intemperance with which they corrupt themſelves, I perceive is a falſe Principle which they have eſtabliſhed, denying the Capacity and Uſe of Reaſon to all Living Creatures but themſelves

His Error was firſt publickly maintained by the Peripateticks, Stoicks, and Epicurians, and afterwards by Cleuthus of Naples, out of a particular Averſion they had for the Doctrines of Pythagoras and Empedo-cles two famous Patrons of Abſtinence

Heraclitus Ponticus undertook to explain the Sentiments of the former Sects, and Herma us thoſe of the latter But both of them ſeem to confide more in the little Tricks and Arts of Sophiſtry, than to uſe true Reaſon For at the firſt Eſſay of their Skill, they ſtrive to caſt a Miſt in the Reader's Eyes, by dividing the Generations of Living Creatures, into ſuch as want it Whereas thou knoweſt it is an indubitable Maxim in the Eaſtern Philoſophy, that every Thing which partakes of Senſe, has alſo Reaſon For it is the Mind alone which ſees, hears, &c. the Body of itſelf being deaf, blind, and void of Senſe It is evident therefore, that ſince the Beaſts do ſee, hear and perform all other Actions of Senſe, they have alſo what the Greeks call νουν, or the Mind, in them, which is the very Seminary, or native Seat of Reaſon

It is true, indeed, we cannot affirm, that they poſſeſs a Reaſon ſo perfect as ours, ſince that Perfection is acquired by Diſcipline, which the Generality of the Beaſts want They have no Colleges or Schools, where the Arts and Sciences are profeſſed and taught by

Rules   Nature is their only School-Miftrefs, and th
learn her Inftructions with abundance of Prompt
and Sagacity   They are educated in the open Ele
ments, as in an Academy, or Univerfity founded
the Creator of all Things, where every Thing th
encounter, ferves as a Book to teach them all th
Knowledge which is neceffary to their Well being
Earth   And they need no more

It is manifeft alfo, that fome *Species* and *Individ*
are more capable of learning what is taught them th
others   Even as we difcern the fame Difference amo
the various Nations, Families, and Perfons of M
But we do not ufe to fay of inanimate Things, th
Piece of Wood is more apt to learn than another
a Dog is more tractable and docile than a Hog
of immoveable Things, that This is flower
That   Nor of Things which want Senfe, that a St
is duller of Apprehenfion than a Piece of Iron
could we not probably affirm of Animals, tha
is more crafty and fagacious than another, nor p
vident, chafte, temperate, cleanly, and the like ep
thets, if they were not by Nature capable of kno
ledge and Virtue   And yet we duly fee all
true, in comparing one *Species* of Living Cre
with another, nay, and one *Individual* of the
Kind with fome of its Fellows

When *Antipater* accufed Affes and Hogs of N
nefs, he did not confider how accurately nice and
ous the Lynxes and Cats are, which with fo much
ligence and Care hide their Excrements, that th
never be feen or fmelt again   So the Swallows te
their Young to mute over the Brims of the Neft
which are Arguments of their Prudence and D
tion   Doubtlefs, every Animal has its peculiar G
and Excellence   One is more quick fighted than
other, this has better Ears than that, a Third
paffes in the Goodnefs of his Smell, or the Swif n
his Feet   Let not vain Man therefore boaft and
as if he were the fole Engroffer of all Wifdom and
tue, fince the Beafts of the Field, the Birds of
Air, the Fifh of the Sea, with all the Generation
                                                    Rer

Reptiles, Insects, and whatsoever is endued with Life and Sense, possess their Shares as well as he

It is manifest also, that there are various Principles of Folly, Injustice, and all manner of Ignorance, Error, and Vice in human Nature, equal to what we can possibly find in the rest of the Animals, whom we so much despise And it is a Question, Whether even the very Sea Horse, who murders his Father, and for that Reason was by the antient *Egyptians* made the *Hierogly-*
p of Impiety , may not justly exchange his Character with some of human Race, who made their Parents the continual Martyrs to their Ambition, Pride, Envy, Avarice, and other Vices

I would fain know, Whether any Man would not take it ill, to be told he is Blind and Deaf, because he cannot See and hear so quick as some of the Beasts ? Or, that he is a Cripple, because he cannot out run a Hart Certainly, a strong Man deserves that Character, tho' he cannot pretend to match the Strength of a Camel, or an Elephant And shall we then say, that the Beasts have no Reason or Virtue, because they cannot discover those Qualities so artificial, as Men ?

Besides, do not all Privations suppose some Habits ? And is not Madness a Privation of the Habits of Reason and Prudence ? If therefore Dogs, Bulls, Foxes, and other Animals, are known to be sometimes mad, shall we think it less fit to say of them, that they are out of their Minds, or Wits, than to affirm the same of Men ? And if *Compos*, or *Non Compos Mentis*, are proper Expressions of any Beasts, when it is sober, or mad , who, that is not deprived of *Reason* himself, can deny, that they have the Possession of that *Faculty* by Nature as well as he ?

As oft as I trouble thee with Letters on this Subject, thou mayest conclude, I am newly awakened to a Sense of my Error in not religiously observing the *Sacred Institution* of *Abstinence* , which ought to be the Natural Consequence of these Thoughts For, in a word, if it be lawful to kill the Animals for the sake of Food, I think we may as well turn *Cannibals*, and eat the Flesh

H 2   of

of our purchased Slaves, or of our Captive Enemy over whom we have, by the Law of Nations, an equal Right as to their Life and Death, as over our Beast

Abstemious Sage, I leave thee to the Divine Instructions of the *Genius*, which possesses that *Holy Cave* leave thee to the sacred Whispers of Winds from *L* and to the Sweets of an innocent Solitude, which admits no other Society than that of Angels, or Beast

Paris, *26th of the 2d Moon,*
of the Year 1671

LETTER IX

To Zeidi Alamanzi, *a Merchant at* Venice

I Received thy last Dispatch which informs me thou art commanded to remove from *Venice* with Speed possible, and to visit *Naples, Genoa, Rome, Padua, Milan, Florence,* with the other chief *Cities* Italy In fine, that thou art not to make a long Residence, or take up thy Abode any where, but after Manner of a Traveller to be always in a moving Posture from Place to Place, from one *Province* and *Principality* to another, that thou mayest take a just Estimate of the Strength and Riches of each State through which thou shalt pass That thou mayest discover their Counsels, observe their Motions, watch their Designs, and transmit thy Remarks to the *Ministers of* August Divan, the *Mysterious Cabinet* of the Lord Great *Sovereign*

There may be less of Profit in such a Peregrination for the present, than in thy constant Residence where thou art established in a settled Way Merchandize But thou wilt find abundance more Pleasure And if thou acquittest thy self successfully Grand *Signior* will reward thy Merit Besides, mayest meet with a thousand Opportunities of Tr

..k, even in thy Travels   An active and diligent Spy
..cannot fail of Means to advance its own Interest in
..any Part of the World, and thou dost not want a Stock
..of Money to support thy honest Undertakings.

Thou wilt meet with a new Sort of *Italian*, where-
..e thou shalt set thy Foot   That People being
..largely mixed, and descending from several Nations
..every City has a different *Genius*, which is so re-
..markable and conspicuous, that they have all got pe-
..culiar *Epithets*   As *Rome* the *Holy*, *Naples* the *Genteel*,
..*Florence* the *Fair*, *Bologna* the *Fat*, *Milan* the *Large*,
..*Venice* the *Grad*, *Bergamo* the *Subtil*, *Genoa* the *Proud*,
..*Padua* the *Strong*, *Siena* the *Studious*, *Mantua* the
..*Proper*, *Lucca* the *Industrious*, *Reggio* the *Wild*, *Co-
..mo* the *Amorous*, *Urbin* the *Loyal*, *Verona* the *Worthy*,
..*Ravenna* the *Fortrese*, *Friuli* the *Wanton*, *Rimini* the
..*Civil*, and so of the rest

Beware of contracting Friendship with any *Italian*
And if thou dost engage, be cautious how thou givest
..just Offence   Thou can'st not be too tender in this
..Point   For, as the *Italians* are very constant where
..they have once pitched their Affection, so are they in-
..exorable in their Revenge, where they apprehend their
..Love abused, and they are the most jealous People in
..the World   If thou hast made two false Steps, never
..hope to repair thy Faults by After-submissions, but
..For thou hast wounded his *Soul*, and he will ne-
..ver pardon thee, or let thee live to be guilty of another
..Affair   They have a common *Maxim* in this Case,
*If he that wrongs me Twice, it is his Fault, but if I
let him injure me the third Time, the Blame is* **my**
own

The wisest Course is to be civil and modestly re-
..served, not to be too frank and open in Discourse, or
..loose in Carriage   For this lays a Man naked, and
..exposes him to the Contempt and Censure of such as
..are more composed and recollected, and this is the
..peculiar Character of the *Italians*, ' That they think
..more than they speak, and are many Times dis-
..gusted at the Person on whom they smile.

When thou art on the Roads in *Apulia* and *Campa*
nia, when thou beholdeſt the Beauties of that luxuriant
Soil, and thy Smell is raviſhed with the fragrant O-
dours of the Hedges, adjoining Groves, think on *Eli-*
zium, *Paradiſe*, or whatſoever Place *Nature* has made
delightful, and ſay, I muſt be in this *Country*, or in
ſome *Region* very like it

As thou ſojourneſt at *Naples*, remember with what
Pleaſure *Virgil* paſſed away his Time there   It was
in that happy Air, that *Horace* penned his admirable
Poems   There *Livy* wrote the *Roman Hiſtory*, and
Seneca his *Morals*   From thence we have the *Works*
of *Statius*, *Claudian*, *Laurentius Valla*, and many other
Learned Writers

Forget not when thou art at *Genoa*, the former Glory of that *Commonwealth*, how once ſhe did poſſeſs *Sar-*
dinia, *Cyprus*, *Lesbos*, *Chaos*, and did extend her Conqueſts
to *Pera* near *Conſtantinople*   How ſhe entered the *Black*
Sea, planted a *Colony* of *Genoeſe* at *Caffa*, and ſtretched
her Dominion to the River *Tanais*

Thou wilt find Matter of Contemplation in *Pavia*,
Milan, *Padua*, it would be a kind of Sacrilege not to
caſt back thy Eyes, and view her antient Glory, when
ſhe was the Miſtreſs of the World, when ſhe had three
Millions of Men within her Walls, and a hundred
and fifty Millions of Gold in yearly Revenue   When
ſhe kept in conſtant Pay, at home and abroad, two
hundred five and forty thouſand Men   Her Foreign
Conqueſts may be numbered by her Domeſtick Triumphs, which from *Romulus* her Founder, to *Auguſtus*
Cæſar, were not leſs than three hundred   *Julius Cæ-*
far augmented the *Publick Treaſury* with forty Millions
of *Gold*   In the *Reign* of *Aurelianus*, this City was fifty
Miles in Compaſs, and the Number of her Inhabitants
increaſed to four Millions   And they were prodigi-
ouſly enriched with the Spoils of their Enemies   *Se-*
neca, when he died, left ſeven Millions and five hundred thouſand Crowns behind him   *Claudius Iſidorus,*
though much exhauſted by the *Civil Wars*, yet left
Four thouſand one hundred and ſeventeen Slaves,
three

the thousand and sixty Yoke of Oxen , and of other Cattle two hundred and fifty seven thousand   There were commonly kept in *Rome* five hundred *Gladiators* , a thousand *Bears* , and a hundred *Lions*   There were also five hundred Men employed in looking after the *Aquaducts* , and *Baths* of *Rome*

When *Cineas* the *Ambassador* of *Pyrrhus* , had viewed the City round, and was asked what he thought of *Rome* , He answered, *I think all* Rome *is but One Temple* , (and there were above four hundred in the City) *Her* — *an Assembly of Kings, Since the Beauty of* — *Earth The Houses of Men and dwell within* — *Walls*

Zeidi, This was the State, this the Grandeur and Magnificence of *Pagan Rome*   But since the Incursions of the *Goths* and *Vandals*, the *Lombards*, *Huns*, and other *Barbarous Nations* of the *North*, *Rome's* Glory is eclipsed, her Honour laid in the Dust Whereas before, she lifted up her stately Crest, on seven high Hills, now she is fain to stoop, being humbly seated in the Plain of *Campus Martius* being not by a fifth Part so large as formerly, nor yet so populous

All over *Italy*, thou wilt meet with Reliques of the *Antient Roman* Majesty and Greatness   And, in some Places, thou mayest encounter Persons of great Extraction, but very poor, who may not unfitly be called the Ruins of *Antient Nobility*   Such as the Marquisses of *Cotta*, the *Earls* of *Piacenza*, and the *Knights* of *Bologna*, who are become the *Proverb* of Illustrious Poverty   Such also were the *Counts* of *Lusignani*, Three of whom were once seen upon a Fig-Tree, eating the Figs to keep them from starving   And many *Italian Lords* get their Livelihoods by selling of *Ptisans*, *Lemonade* , *Essences*, *Powders*, and other Refreshments to the Gentry   Yet they are proud, and when any one addresses to them, he must entitle them, *Most Excellent, Most Illustrious*, or else they will frown, and be affronted

Zeidi, if ever it be thy Fortune to be made a *Lord* I pray Heaven give thee an Estate answerable to the

H 4   Title

Title For a *Lord* without *Riches*, is like a *Soldier* without *Arms*, very ridiculous

Paris, 15th *of the* 4th *Moon,*
     of the Year 1671

LETTER X.

To Dgnet Oglou.

THIS Day something has happened to me very prodigious, and I know not what to make of it. About the Hour of *Sheb demah*, I was suddenly taken with strange Fits of Vomiting. My Stomach was in a Prodigal, or rather a Philosophical Humour, resolving to cast off all the Superfluities, and only retain what was necessary to its Ease and Welfare in this Life. I laboured under a Thousand Horrid Agonies, which made me fear, that either an *Imposthume* was the Cause of such violent *Convulsions*, or at least, that they would end in opening the inward Sluices of my Blood by too much forcing of the *Pectoral* Veins.

Whilst I was buried thus with sad Presages of a sudden Death (for I dread to be so unawares thrust out of the World,) I longed and passionately languished for an *Arabian Orange.*

It happened at the same Time, my Mother *Oubro michie, Daria* and *Eliachim* the *Jew,* were with me in my Chamber, and had been there an Hour. They all stood at the Window to see a Procession that was going by. But when they heard the straining Noise I made, immediately they ran to my Bed side, as *Human Nature, Curiosity,* or *Passion,* uses to prompt in such like Cases.

With a faint broken Voice, I told them what I wished for, *Eliachim* forthwith gives Order to his Boy, that waited in an *Anti-Chamber,* to run with speed, and buy the best *Arabian Oranges* he could find.

The

The arch young Lad was gone full Thirteen Minutes by my Watch, and then returned with half a Dozen Oranges of *Spain* (for he could get no other) But *Heaven*, as I have reafon to think, fupplied his Negligence, and unfuccefsful *Mercoting* For long before he came with that fowre crabled *Fruit*, *Daria* fpied an Orange of *Arabia* on the Table

No Body knew from whence it came, or what kind hand had laid it there They were all equal Witneffes, that there were no fuch Thing upon the Table when they came to the Bed-fide, nor a confiderable Time afterward And when it was fuggefted that fome of the Company had privately conveyed it hither, whilft the reft were looking another way, *Eliachim* with folemn Vows and Imprecations cleared himfelf, fo did *Daria*, and my Mother As for myfelf they were all fenfible, it was impoffible for me to do it, as I lay in my Bed A general Aftonifhment poffeffed us all, and the Women would needs have it to be a *Miracle*, whilft I greedily eat the *Delicious Fruit*, not troubling my Thoughts with making endlefs *Scrutinies*, or fo much as caring which way it came there, fo long as I had the Enjoyment of it

Yet I ceafed to be thus indifferent, when I perceived my *Malady* on a fudden removed by eating of this wondrous *Orange* And whereas I had lain for fix whole Days and Nights in a continual Faint and languifhing Condition, not able to get down a Morfel of Bread, now my Spirits grew brifk and frefh, I feemed like one transformed, or in another World My Stomach revived, my almoft diffipated Vigor rallied, and I rofe chearfully to eat a hearty *Supper* Thefe Things I muft confefs, put me, as well as the reft of the Company upon thinking

I tell thee, upon the ftricteft Examination poffible, I am very well fatisfied, that there could be no Defign or Trick in the Cafe For if there were, no Body would be guilty of fo many repeated horrid Perjuries in denying it But every one rather would have been forward to own themfelves the Inftruments of thus happily

pily and unexpectedly refcuing a poor fick Man from the very Jaws of Death. For I was juft then ready to expire

Whether there be a *Magick* in the Strength of a Mans Fancy at fuch Times, and that through the Intenfe Agitation of his exalted Spirits, he moves the *Soul* of the *Univerfe* by *Sympathy*, to exert fome of its hidden and uncommon Faculties, and gratify his neceffary Defires Or whether there be an Order of Officious *Beings Invifible* about us, who have the Charge of *Mortals* committed to them, and are bound by the Laws of their concealed *Kingdoms* to affift us in Extremities, even to the Height of a feeming *Miracle*, where it cannot be done without, I know not But it is certain, any obferving Man may take Notice of fome extraordinary Paffages in the Courfe of his Life, of which he can give no Rational Account, but muft be forced to put them on the Score of *Praeternatural Caufes* Such is our Ignorance of the *Secret* Operations of *Nature*

All the Company were ready to lift me among the *Prophets*, or in the Catalogue of *Saints*, for this ftupendous Occurrence But I had other Thoughts of my felf For comparing this with fome former Occurrences of my Life, I prefently concluded, it was the Fore runner of fome grand, but fhort Affliction And I fo told them all

I believe, my *Dgnet*, that *God* will hedge me in with divers Kinds of Adverfe Circumftances He will rufh upon me on a fudden, like a Troop of *Tartar* Horfe, who fwiftly fpread themfelves all round the affrighted Country, and take Poffeffion of the Roads and Paffes They hunt the confcious *Infidels* from Dens and Caves, and other lurking Places in the *Woods* and *Mountains* None can efcape their Chaftifement and Revenge So my prefaging *Soul* foretels fome fad furprizing Inroad from the *Omnipotent*

That which I have to do in this Cafe is to make fpeedy Expiations for my paft Security and Prefumption, to repair the ruined Faftneffes of Virtue and build new ones where they are wanting, to keep ftrong Guards, and laftly, to retire my felf into a moft profound

found Humility, and Compliance with the Will of God, which is the strongest Fortress in Time of a *Divine Invasion*

Paris 23*d* of the 6*th Moon*,
   of the Year 1671

LETTER XI.

To Sephat Abercromil, Vanni Effendi,
   Preacher *to the* Sultan.

THE Character and Fame of thy Exemplary Life, and profound Doctrine, though studiously concealed and suppressed by thy self, have yet made a forcible Eruption and filled the *Mussulman* Kingdoms with the fragrant Odour of thy incomparable Piety and Virtue Even these remote and *Infidel* Regions of the *West*, are edified by thy sacred Rules and Institutions of a spiritual Life The *Nazarene Priests* and *Doctors* begin to harbour Emulations of thy *Sanctity*, since they have seen no fairer Draught of true acceptable *Religion*, than what the *Chaplains* to the *French Ambassadors* at the Port have copied from thy Principles, and recommend to their Friends among the *Clergy of France* Insomuch as *Francis Malevella*, a blind *Ecclesiastick*, but a light in the *Sciences*, has publickly espoused thy Theorems and Practices, having in Print now lately undertaken the Patronage of a contemplative Life, so much insisted on by thee to which the *College of Sorbonne* have also given their Approbation

That Excellent Man, though he has lost the Use of his Corporeal Eyes, yet has a Soul transform'd all over to Light, by which he clearly can survey the vast luminous Horizon of the Invisible World, and penetrate the most recluse and hidden Secrets of Eternity The Age is ravished with the Book he published He has Ten Thousand Proselytes among the Roman *Priests*

                      and

and *Derviches* None but the *Jesuits* and *Dominicans*
oppose him.

The former of these *Orders* is grown odious through
out *Christendom*, for the Impious *Doctrines* they main
tain, and the Enormous Crimes they have committed
Being notorious Boutefeu's, Traitors, Hypocrites, and
Secret Libertines Their *Colleges* are esteemed the
Shops and Forges of Sedition, Faction, Publick Ani
mosities, Broils and Wars, with all the Mischief that is
done in *Europe* The latter are not loved in *France* be
cause they are generally chosen Officers of the *In*
quisition Which inhuman *Judicature* was first projected
by St *Dominick* their *Founder*, in order to exterminate
the *Moors* from *Spain* There is a Natural and Ir
reconcileable Antipathy between the *French* and *Spa*
niards They mutually abhor each others Custom,
Laws, and Humours But above all, the *French*
can never be reconciled to that *Infernal Court*
which tyrannizes over the Souls of Men, and punish
them for Thoughts It is an equal Crime to speak, or
to be silent, to pray or not, to go to Church, or stay
at Home, provided you are rich It is Wealth the
Inquisitors aim at, not the pretended Safety and Deli
verance of the *Church* from Enemies and Rebels

Therefore the *Dominicans* and *Jesuits* being looked
upon as Favourites and Patrons of the *Inquisition*, and
for that Reason hated by the *French*, in vain they ar
gued against *Maxella's* new reformed Model of Inte
rior *Religion*, which is but a Translation of the Origi
Dogmata laid down by thee Thy refined Sentiment
are Prolifick, as the solar Beams, which by ineffable
Increases, propagated themselves without diminishing
the Illustrious Fountain Each bright and fertil Atom,
by a miraculous Emanation begets another, they mul
tiply by admirable Progressive Issue and Expansion
from every Point of the refulgent Center, till every
splendid Particle becomes a Ray of equal Length, and
all together produce an entire *Orb* of Light Thus the
serene *Ideas* of *Religion* dilate themselves through the
dark Side of the World, as fast as they illuminate the
the *Mussulman Hemisphere*. The honester Sort of *H*
Frank

Franks are already, b, a *Demi Metamorphosis*, grown half *Mahometans*, capitulating with their Prepossessions, Prejudices, and the Force of Education for the rest

They go to *Church*, but not to babble over a Thousand vain *Tautologies*, which are taught them by their *Priests*, and to ensure their Memory are printed in their Pocket Manuals, or Books of Prayer Nor do they number a long Series of the same repeated *Orations* on Beads, or use any other exterior Form of blind and lame Devotion But with inward Recollection, Silence, Peace, and fervent Application of the Spirit, they address themselves to *God*, or rather by a certain gradual Passiveness, Oblivion of outward Things, and dying to themselves, they prepare and fit their *Souls* for the Desire Approaches Thus having barricadoed up their Senses, and made Retrenchments round the Centre of the Mind, to secure it from the last Invasion and Assault of Mundane Objects, thither they retire, desiring Death, rather than to take Quarter by a faint Cowardice or timorous Apostacy and surrender to the World.

These People undergo at certain Times, strange Dryness, Desertions, and Sterilities of Spirit, which are the Torments that compose the most severe and painful Martyrdoms A common Death, or any violent Dissolution of the Body, is but the Recreation, Sport, or Play of Nature, when compared with these tremendous, tragical and dark Annihilations of the *Soul* A Man at such a Season seems to be reduced to an Eternal *Catastrophe* His Spirit descends, and is engulphed in the Abyss of *Hell*, or *Hell* comes up to him, and yawning with its horrid Dragon's Jaws, murders the *Soul* with Baneful and Infernal Breath Yet this they find to be the only near directed Way to *Heaven* This is the Mystick Fence, the Ditch, Bastion and Counterscarp of *Paradise* He that would scale the Wall, or enter by the Gates of *Eden*, must first pass through these terrible Outworks This is the streight and narrow Bridge over which each Soul must pass, that would attain Immortal Life *Moses*, *Jesus*, *Mahomet*, and all the *Messengers* of *God*, have pointed at this as the only Way to our

Supreme

supreme Felicity. Neither was it unknown to the Ancient *Poets* and *Philosophers* among the *Gentiles*. Orpheus and *Hesiod* recommended it in their Mysterious Verse. *Empedocles, Theophrastus, Plato, Plotinus, Porphyry, Jamblichus,* with many others, improved the Sacred Revalation, adding new Lights in to the blest Discovery. And if we take the History in the best Sense, unless I am deceived, *Socrates* died a *Martyr* to this important Truth. Many of the Learned *Hebrew Rabbis* have asserted it. The *Persian* and *Arabian* Doctors, before and since the *Holy Flight,* have been its Advocates. And let not Envy refuse to give some of the *Christian Priests* their due Acknowledgement, who preached this Doctrine in the primitive Assemblies, taught it in the Publick Schools, and entered it to Posterity in Learned Manuscripts. Such were *Origen* and *Ammonius, Clemens* of *Alexandria, Simplicius, Chrysostom, Tertullian, Augustin.* And in more modern Times, *Thomas of Aquin, his filius Ficinus, Bonadventure,* with many others.

And it is esteemed the Height of *Indian Religion* to this Day, the *Bramins* delivering it as an Hereditary *Article of Faith,* and Point of Practice, from Immemorable Ages. Since therefore all Regions in the World agree in this, notwithstanding their other Ceremonial and Speculative Differences. Doubtless it is the Voice and Will of God, not the Contrivance or Innovation of Man.

Reverend *Effendi,* it is a common Proverb among the *Christians,* That wheresoever GOD has a Temple, the Devil has a Chapel. That cunning Spirit, like a Serpent, winds himself into outward Forms and Ceremonies of Devotion. But he that builds a *Mosque* in the Centre of his Soul, may bid Defiance to *Tagot;* for that is the Throne of God, near which the *Daemon* cannot approach.

May thou and I, live always skreened behind ourselves, for in that dark Recess from visible Things the *Eternal* lives to manifest his otherwise invisible Light. Adieu.

Paris, 17*th of the 6th Moon, of the Year* 1670.

LETTER XII.

To Cara Hali, Phyſician *to the* Grand Signior.

After all my Scepticiſms, I at this Hour believe, there is ſomething of us remains immortal and incorruptible, when our groſſer Bodies are diſſolved (call it what you will, an Aſtral Body, a Ghoſt, a Spirit, or any thing elſe   I am ſenſible ſome Part of us will never die   What ſignifies the vain Diſpute of Words, the dark Reſolves of *Plato's Cave?* Let it be Subſtance or *Accident, Matter* or *Form,* or a Reſult of all, There is ſtill a certain Portion of our Nature, againſt which the Strokes of Death, and of ten hundred thouſand Deaths, can never prevail   We may be changed indeed, and Maſquerade it up and down, perhaps thro' infinite Worlds, in ſo many different Diſguiſes, But we can never be annihilated, or made nothing   We cannot be excluded from the eternal Liſt of Atoms   The Loſs or Abſence of the leaſt Particle from the Univerſe, would either cauſe the loudeſt never-ending Thunders and Lightnings, or an everlaſting Silence, Sullenneſs and Darkneſs   This mighty aggregate and ſtupendious Heap of Beings would fall to Ruin, if there were the leaſt *Vacuum,* or the ſmalleſt *Mite* miſſing   Steal but the moſt indiviſible Atom from the reſt, and down comes all the Fabrick, For one ſupports another by an irſeparable Adheſion, reciprocal Congruity, and mathematical Fitneſs   They are ſo cunningly hitched and knit together, ſo cloſely faſtened and indented each with other, by the original Art, or Chance which formed the World, that all the Motions of this grand Machine would at an Inſtant ſtop, in ſuch a Caſe   as does a Watch, when the leaſt Tooth is miſſing from a-ny one of the contiguous Wheels   Every thing in Nature is full and pregnant   Neither can there be any other Emptineſs ſave what we think we ſee n Bottles, or other hollow Veſſels, which, when they are void of
Water,

Water, Wine, or other Liquor, it is but to be cram'd
brim-full of Air, which Element infinuates an
crowds itself into each diminutive Cranny, Chink, an
Pore of groffer Subftances, So if the airy Atoms have
any Hollowneffes in them, the fmalleft Vacancy pof
ble is ftill fupplied with its full Meafure of the pur
Æther, and that again with fome Matter more refined,
if fuch there be, or elfe it drinks full Draughts of im
material Effences And by fuch a fubordinate Grada
tion, human Souls, though in themfelves, perhaps, pure
incorporeal Spirits, are yet faftened, and cemented to our
Bodies Thus is one *Being* fucceffively, and eternally,
either a Syringe, or Sponge to another The Elements
inebriate one another by Turns An univerfal *Epo*
tifm and Drunkennefs reigns

So the hot Stomach of the Earth, parched with in
ward mineral Fires, greedily guzzles down the very
Salt unpalatable Lees of the Sea, rather than be a dry
With a thousand thoufand gaping Throats, it gulphs
the Beverage which *Neptune's* deep and mighty Curr
runs withal It pants, and fucks eternally, the thick
ropy Settlements of the *Ocean's* Bottom Thefe are di
ftilled again in hidden Limbecks, Cylinders, and other
chymical Veffels below, that fo the gaping Channels on
the Superficies, may be conftantly fupplied with more
refined Liquor, through the Springs and Fountain
and yet the Globe not having quenched its Thirft with
this perpetual Draught, continually fips up the Rain, a
Liquor more fublime and pure than all the reft But
this is only on certain Holy days of Late, when the Ce
leftial Powers, the Planets, Stars, and Conftellations, or
der a *Dunalma* for the vegetable Race below, to refren
the Herbs, the Corn, and Trees, with Banquets from
the Clouds Then the big-bellied Tuns above are roll
ed out of their hidden Store-houfes, and broached the
Conduits of the upper Region fpout and run with plenti
ful Showers and Cataracts of Nature's feminal Juice th
radical all-cheering Nectar of Heaven The greedy Soi
imbibes the facred ftrong *Cafcade*, each joyful Turf is
frolickfome, and fwallows down large Bumpers of the
elemofinary Wine, Whilft the leaft dry and crumbling

•

　　　　　　　　　　　　　　　　　Lump

...mp of the late fainting *Glebe*, has Drops and *Super-*
... enough to revel on, till party-coloured *Iris,*
... *D* ... of these yearly *Festivals*, perceiving the
... Seeds and Roots are well-nigh fuddled with what
... hand they have exhausted from the over la-
... Ground, makes her Appearance in the Clouds, in-
... the Guests to a splendid Collation of warm
... and Rays, with which the *Sun* is minded to re-
...them

... grateful, soft and chearful Noise was heard through-
... the Room before The Earth and Air were in a
... Humour Well pleased with the Debauch, they
... have sat till Morning at it, being loth to leave the
... behind them or change it for dry Meat But at
... of *his*, every one changed Countenance, an
... *Hum* ... ran throughout the *Hall*, they were
... thus to be baulked in the midst of their Mirth
... softly *Zephyrs* come with their soft Compliments,
... them, it is necessary for their Lafe and Health
Then are the Tuns and Bottles removed, with all the
... Tackle The Table soon is spread, and covered
... rich Course of glittering Charges sent from *Phoebus.*
... That sponging *Planet* only lives by bantering and
... dle The illustrious Figure he makes in the
World is always borowed He never wore a fashiona-
... in his Life, but what he took up by Tally
... the first Source of Lights For which he is bound
... pay so vast an Interest, that he would necessarily be-
... a bankrupt, did he not repair his broken Fortune,
... playing Tricks upon the Earth Thus whilst he
... this sublunary World with his pretended Treats,
... makes it pay for all with costly Exhalations He
... the Elements, picks the Pockets of the Earth,
... robs the Treasures of the Sea Nor can he forbear
... something from the Air, and when he has stolen
enough, he slinks away in the Dark, and flies to the o-
... side of the Globe, there to commence new Shams
... Cheats upon the *Antipodes* And all the while, the
Stars are full as bad as he For, like a brave Highway-
... that Luminary frequents the publick Way of
Heaven by Day, he robs in open Sight of all the World,
and

and leaves a generous *Viaticum* wherever he borrow
ny thing But the *Stars*, those little Bullies of the Sky,
are perfect *Night Pads*, *Shop-lifts* and *Sharpers*, they
sku k about in the Dark, through all the private *ways*
of the *Firmament*, and commit a thousand Murders,
Rapes, and other Violences Some of their *Aspects* are
as venemous as the fatal Eyes of *Basilisks*, they carry di
vers kinds of mortal Poisons in their Looks, which they
disperse at Random in this lower World They fra
the Earth with *Henbole*, *Aconites*, and other *bane*
Weeds They also scatter up and down the more con
tagious Seeds of Envy, Avarice, and a thousand Un
nternal Vices, which take Root in human Souls
our Nativities, and growing up with us, in time br
forth the fatal Fruits of Death The ugly Race of Dra
gons, *Serpents*, *Crocodiles*, and all the *reptile* Generations,
with every thing that is hideous, cruel and destructive
on the Globe, derive their Natures, Qualities, Forms
and Dispositions from some *malignant Stars* or *Constella-*
tions, if *Astrologers* say true So do the *scaly Monsters* of
the *vast Abyss*, and every *Bird* of *horrible Figure* flying
in the *Air* They are all the Brood, the *Emissaries*,
Spies, and Agents of the Powers above, sent down on
thievish Errands, to prey on other Animals more inno
cent than themselves

There is an *eternal Clause* in *Nature*, whilst every
thing is either on the Hunt or Flight Thus *Heaven* pur
loins from Earth, and that from *Heaven* again When
we are first conceived, our wandring *Souls* are catched,
as in a well baited Trap And when we die, it is but
the *Soul's* Escape from one Snare to be soon trepanned
into another Perhaps a *human Body* may be our Prison
again, or we may be a tracted by some more agreea
ble *Embryo* This magnetick Star may draw us up to
Heaven, or the wide Jaws of all-devouring *Orcus* may
swallow us down into the hungry *Paunch* of *Hell*,
which God avert

Learned *Haly*, let not thou and I be too sollicitou a
bout these things For all our timerous Forecasts are in
vain But, considering the secret Magnetisms dispersed
throughout the Universe, and that every thing attracts

i, Like, let us take care to qualify ourfelves with celeftial Habits and Difpofitions, and then we cannot
fail of being drawn up to *Paradife*

Paris, *2d of the 9th Moon,*
    of the Year, 1671.

LETTER XIII.

To the Mufti.

IN Obedience to thy Commands, I fhall now proceed
in relating the moft memorable Tranfactions of
former Ages during the four Great Monarchies, obferving thy Inftructions, not to be prolix, or over-curious
in tracing down the particular Succeffions of Kings and
Princes, but rather to relate the Actions of famous
Men, the wife Sayings of the Antients, with fuch other
Remarks, as may be at once delightful and inftructive.
It will be no Breach of this Rule, to begin where I
left off in my former Letter, with the Death of *Darius,*
and Succeffor of *Xerxes,* his younger Son, there being
fomething of Nicety in the Plea between him and his
elder Brother *Artabazenes* for the Crown, For this laid
Claim to it on the Account of his Primogeniture But
in regard he was born before *Darius* was made King,
the Succeffion was determined in Favour of *Xerxes,* who
had a double Advantage, in being begot by a crowned
King, and born of *Atofh,* the Daughter of *Cyrus,* who
firft eftablifhed this Monarchy

As foon as *Xerxes* was fettled in the Throne, he led
an Army into *Egypt,* and fuppreffed the Infurrections in
that Country Then he fitted out a Fleet of 4200 Ships,
on board of which were above five hundred thoufand
Men He had a Land Army alfo confifting of Two
millions and five hundred thoufand Soldiers, of feveral
Nations With this vaft Multitude he marched againft
the Grecians, and to facilitate the Voyage of his Fleet,
                                                    he

he caufed one Part of his Army to dig a Paffage thro
Mount *Atho*, whereby the Sea was let in, and the Ships
might fail two a-breaft, whilft another Part of the Sol
diers were employed in building a Bridge of Boats over
the *Hellefpont* No fooner was this done, but there a
rofe a vehement Tempeft, which fo difcompofed thofe
narrow Seas, that between the Winds and Waves, the
Boats which made this Bridge were all difperfed bro
ken, and caft away

This fo incenfed *Xerxes*, that he commanded the Sea
to be fcourged with Whips, and a Chain to be thro n
into it, as a Mark of its future Subjection He alfo be
headed thofe who built the Bridge, and caufed other to
make a new one

Here one of *Xerxes's* Eunuchs, and a particular Fa
vourite of the King, fent for a *Grecian* of the ifle of
Chios, who had formerly deprived him of the Evidence
of his *Virility* And the old Man coming with his Sons,
to wait on this great Courtier, the Eunuch caufed him
firft to caftrate his own Sons, and afterwards forced
them to do the fame by their Father, in Revenge of his
own Lofs and Difgrace

From hence *Xerxes* marched with his Army by the
Place were once ftood the famous Town of *Troy*, went
in Pilgrimage to the Tomb of King *Priamus*, where
he facrificed ten Hecatombs of Oxen to the Ghoft
the antient Heroes, and to the Divinity of the River
Scammander, which his Soldiers drank dry, and yet he
of them had not quenched their Thirft

After this, he came to the *Hellefpont*, where taking a
Survey of all his Land and Sea Forces, which covered
the *Hellefpont*, and all the neighbouring Shores, and
contemplating the Shortnefs of Man's Life, and that
of fo innumerable a Multitude, not one fhould be alive
at an hundred Years End, he wept bitterly

Then having facrificed to the Sun, for the good Suc
cefs of his Expedition, he caufed all his Army to pafs
over the *Hellefpont* by his Bridge of Boats, after which,
they drank their Way through another River, which
had not Water enough to fatisfy half his Men and Cat

it. For his Army increased all the Way, by the Ac-
cessions of Soldiers out of every Nation through which
he passed. Yet *Leonidas*, King of *Sparta*, with a small
Body of 4000 *Lacedemonians*, gave Battel to the whole
Army of *Xerxes*. And in a Sea-Fight at *Salamis*, the
Persians lost 500 Ships, with a considerable Part of their
Army, which with other Disasters, or Sickness, Famine,
&c. so terrified this great Monarch, that he posted back
again as fast as he could, by the Way of the *Hellespont*,
which he crossed in a poor Fisher Boat all alone, leaving
Mardonius to pursue the Wars in *Greece*. But an ill Fate
attended their Arms, for at *Plataea* the *Grecians* set upon
them under *Pausanias* their General, and routed the
whole Army, killing above two hundred thousand of
them upon the Spot, and burning their Camp and Navy.

Xerxes hearing these ill Tidings, fled towards his own
Country, and by the Way set Fire to the Temples of
the Gods of *Babylon*, and other Parts of *Asia*, sparing
none but that magnificent Fane at *Ephesus*, which was
renowned throughout the whole World.

About this time died *Pagepates* the faithful Eunuch
of *Darius*, who had passed seven whole Years Mourning at the Tomb of his Master.

I must not omit the Treachery of *Pausanias*, the
Lacedemonian General, who held a private Correspon-
dence with *Xerxes*. And having been twice accused of
Treason, and as often acquitted, was the third Time
discovered by a Boy, whom he kept as his Minion, and
by the Sentence of the *Ephori*, was starved to Death.

Thou hast forbidden me to augment the Bulk of these
historical Letters, with Glosses, or Remarks of my own,
or else it were a proper Occasion to put thy Holiness in
mind, how great a Value ought to be set on a faithful
Man, and let Nature itself plead my Excuse for en-
croaching on thy Orders, whilst I vindicate myself from
the Calumnies of the Envious, and beg of thee to
rest assured, That no Man on Earth can be truer to his
Trust, than the *Arabian* Slave *Mahmut*.

But to return to *Xerxes*. He was unfaithfully dealt
with by the Captain of his Guard, why by the Assist-
tance

tance of *Spamitres* the King's Chamberlain, and seve
other Conspirators, killed him in his Bed with his eld
est Son *Darius*, and crowned *Artaxerxes* in his stead

To him fled *Themistocles* the *Athenian*, who was su
pected a Partner in the Treason of *Pausanias* The K
received him in his Favour and made him Governor of
a Province, adding the Gift of five great Cities, to
nish him with Money for the Expences of his Table an
Wardrobe　And this the King did, not as a Rewar
or Encouragement of Treason, (from which he kne
Themistocles was free, being falsly accused by the
man,) but he heaped those Honours on him, as a Deb
to the Merits of that once illustrious Enemy, now be
come a Friend, and seeking Shelter in the *Pers* King
dom, from the barbarous Ingratitude of his own Cou
trymen, who for all his eminent Services to G
could think of no better Acknowledgement, than t
put to death as a Traytor, the bravest and wisest Ca
tain of that Age

Not long after this, the *Persians* lost two hun
Ships in a Sea-Fight with the *Grecians*, and were rout
at Land by a Stratagem of *Cimon*, the *Grecian* Gene
who after the Naval Victory, but his Men on Board
Persian Vessels which he had taken, and apparell
them in the Garments of the *Persian* Captives, lan
them near the Enemies Camp in *Pamphilia*, who tak
them for Friends, suffered them to enter their Trench
without Jealousy, and so were all slaughtered, exce
a few, who escaped by the Swiftness of their Hors

About this time, *Pericles* was made Prince of
of whom I made mention in my former Letters
Themistocles being made General of the *Persian* Arm
and sent against the *Grecians*, rather than fight again
his Country, or betray the Cause of his new Master
became a voluntary Victim to his own Integrity and
Honour　For, sacrificing a Bull in his March, he dran
off a Bowl of the Blood, and fell down dead a
Foot of the Altar

The next War the *Persians* were engaged in, wa
with *Egypt*, where, in a Battel near *Memphis*, they lo

an hundred thousand Men But sending fresh Recruits, they dried up the River *Nile*, where the *Athenian* Fleet, confederate with the *Egyptians*, lay at Anchor Which so amazed the *Egyptians*, that they made their Peace with them And the *Athenians* set their own Ships on fire, in number 200, and returned home with Disgrace, when they had been six Years in *Egypt* And after this, a Peace was concluded between the *Persians*, and those of *Greece* And in the first Year of the 8th *Olympiad*, which soon followed, there was an universal Peace throughout the World, which continued till the first Year of the 8-th *Olympiad*, at what time began the *Peloponnesian War*

In the 4th Year of the 88th *Olympiad*, *Artaxerxes* died, and his Son *Xerxes* was invested with the Crown But at a Year's End, being overcome with Wine, and falling asleep in a Place where no Guard was kept, his Brother *Secundianus*, with the Help of an *Eunuch* murdered him, and took the Government on himself He also was soon after dispatched by his Brother *Darius*

I ever run whole *Olympiads*, without mentioning any thing save the Transactions which made most Noise in the Times But I am unwilling to slip the Reign of a King, though I speak but two Words of it, that so thou mayest have a perfect Idea of their Succession

During the whole Series of *Darius's* Reign, History reports nothing remarkable, but is taken up in relating the little Quarrels and Reconciliations of several Provinces in *Greece*, some private Treaties between the *Persian* Governors of *Lesser Asia* and those of *Peloponnesus*, or the Overtures of Peace between the *Lacedemonians* and the *Persian*, the End of the *Peloponnesian War*, with such other Passages, as would be too tedious for a Letter

I will only rehearse a memorable Saying of *Darius*, on his Death-bed, to his eldest Son *Artaxerxes*, who was to succeed him in the Throne The Prince being assured by the Royal Physicians, that his Father's End drew near, thus addressed *Darius* ' My Father, since it is
' the Will of the Gods to take you from Earth, into
' their own blessed Society, and that you have been
                                   ' pleased

' pleafed, with the Confent of the Nobles, to decla

' me your Succeffor in the Kingdom, tell me, I befee

' you, by what Methods of Policy you have gove n

' this Empire ' To whom the King replied, ' W

' Son be affured, That if my Reign has been bleffed

' with greater Succefs and Peace than thofe of my Pre

' deceffors, it is becaufe in all Things I have hono

' ed the immortal Gods, and done Juftice to every M

As foon as *Artaxerxes* was poffeffed of the Crown

fent for his Brother *Cyrus*, and put him in Mana

Gold, with defign to make him privately away, b

at the Interceffion of his Mother, he releafed him a

gain, and reftored him to his Government of *Iy*

About this Time, *Plato* the Philofopher being very

young, gave an early *Specimen* of a ripe Wit, in c

forting *Antimachus* the Poet, who loft the Girland i

Conteft with *Niceratus*, at the *Lyfandrean Fef*

when he beheld the Poet extremely vexed at the Ig

rance and Partiality of *Lyfander*, who knew not how

diftinguifh between his lofty Meafures, and the

Rhimes of his Antagonift, *Plato* bid him be of

Courage For, faid he, *Ignorance no more Ig*

thy Knowledge, than a blind Man's miftaking the way

ther, would deprive thee of thy Sight

When *Cyrus* was returned to his Government he plo

ted to depofe his Brother, and to win *Lyfander* to

Party, he prefented him with a Ship built all of Go

and Ivory *Alcibiades*, the famous *Athenian* Cap

peceiving this, defigned to give *Artaxerxes* notice

his Brother's Treafon But by the Way he wa smo

thered himfelf by fome Soldiers, hired for that Pu

by *Lyfander*, who yet durft not fet upon him i

Day time, when he was armed in his own Defence, t

in the Night fet his Houfe on Fire, and as he wa

caping through the Flames and Smoak, they lying

Ambufh, fhot him dead with Arrows

However, *Artaxerxes* quickly became fenfible of

Brother's Defigns, and raifing an Army of Nine h

dred thoufand Men, gave him Battel not far from *b*

In the Fight he was wounded by *Cyrus*, but after a hot Dispute, *Cyrus* was killed, and *Artaxerxes* got the Victory

Parisatis, the Mother of *Cyrus*, to revenge the Death of her Son, caused those that wounded him to be killed with lingring Torments, and inviting Queen *Statyra* the Wife of *Artaxerxes* to a Feast, she divided the Bird *Rhindaces* asunder with a Knife poisoned on one Side, and gave the venomed Part to *Statyra*, eating the other herself   Upon which the Queen died in horrible Anguish and Torture

The famous Deeds of many Heroes are also recorded, during the Reign of this *Artaxerxes*, as of *Agesilaus*, king of the *Spartans*, *Iphicrates*, *Pharnabazus*, *Tissaphernes*, and *Tiribazus*, *Persians*, with *Conon* the *Athenian* But fearing to entrench on thy Patience, I content myself with only mentioning their Names, and so finish my Letter with the Conclusion of *Artaxerxes* his Life, who died of Grief, for the Death of his Son *Arsames*, whom *Ochus* his Brother had caused to be murthered out of Envy and Jealousy, because his Father doated on him

If I have not answered thy Expectation in this Letter blame not me, but the Historians, from whom I have collected these Passages, or accuse the Men of that Age, that they did not perform *Greater Action*, However, in the next thou shalt hear of the Birth and Life of a great *Prophet*, even *Alexander*, the Conqueror of all *Asia* In the mean time, I plunge myself in the Den of the Dust thou treadest on, and shrinking into an Abstract of Humility, I bid thee adieu

Paris, *2d of the 9th Moon,*
  of the Year 1671

The End of the Third Book

LETTERS

Writ by a

SPY at *PARIS.*

VOL. VII.

BOOK IV.

LETTER I

To Pesteli Hali, *his Brother,* Master *of the* Customs, *and* Superintendent *of the Ar se*nal *at* Constantinople.

I Know not well, whether it is my Part to be for or glad, when I hear thy Son is wild and prou that he is amorous, and very much addicted to t lick with *Women, Wine,* and *Musick,* that he freque the *Baths* and *Play-Houses,* on purpose to make t Interest for his *Love,* that he may sometimes get a S of beautiful Ladies, and have the Pleasure of being mitted into their Company, that he haunts the Sho of *Foreign Merchants,* the Houses of *Christian Ambassa* dors, and insinuates himself into the Acquaintance Familiarity of all Travellers who make any Figure the *Imperial* City.

In

I proteft, it feems difficult in my Opinion to determine, Whether thou thyfelf hast Reafon to be grieved
at all this, or not rather to rejoice, as at a Prefage of his
future good Fortune, fince it is a manifeft Argument of
the Greatnefs of his *Soul* And let that alone to work
out its own Way to Happinefs Never check a *Generous* Spirit For fuch are full of the *Divinity* They
are the *Eagles*, the *Lions*, the *Kings* and *Princes* of the
Earth Their Veins flow with *Sacred BLOOD*
Their Nerves ftrut with the Milk of *Paradife* A thoufand Excellencies poffefs their Hearts, and ten thoufand Perfections take Root in their Brains Whatever
of precious is fcattered up and down in the *Elements*,
meets in their accomplifhed Nature, as in an *Epitome*,
or rich *Compendium* of the brighteft *Effences*, an Extract of all that is valuable, good, and lovely in the
Univerfe.

Be not difcouraged to fee thy Son amorous of Women It is a Sign of good Nature And he is looked upon as a Monfter, or degenerate Perfon, who feels no
Warmths or Paffions for that lovely Sex *Women* are fent
into the World on purpofe to blow up thofe gentle
Flames within our Breafts, which fublimate our groffer
Mould, and make us more refined *Love* is a facred
Frenzy of the Soul, a Divine Madnefs elevating a Man
up to the Pitch of a *Saturne*, and rendring him the
Care of the benigner *Dæmon.* He is every where fafe,
having the Favour of *Gods* and *Men*, as the *Roman Poet*
expreffes it

Quifquis amore tenetur, eat tutufque facerque

And had it not been for thy own Experience of this
Noble Paffion, thou hadft not had a Son to complain of
Perhaps it makes him expenfive and coftly in his
Manner of Living He would, no Doubt, appear gay
and polite in the Eyes of his *Miftreffes* He would be
generous and magnificent in his Entertainments, liberal
to his Friends and Acquaintance, charitable to all Perfons in Diftrefs. And canft thou really blame him for
putting in Practice fo many amiable Virtues ? Is not
this better than to fee him of a fneaking, fordid Tem-

per, addicted to Avarice, and other *Ignoble* Vices? Remember thy own *Genius*, when thou wert young, what a paffionate Delight thou tookeft in *Travelling* Yet, this could not be maintained without great Charges Confider therefore, that it is thy own Blood, running in the Veins of thy *Son*, which prompts him to a noble Way of Living And do not thou imitate thofe Fathers, who by their Severity, teach their Children to degenerate, inftead of making them better, or more reformed They frighten them from the Paths of innate Virtue, for the Lucre of their Gold, take abundance of Pain to inftruct them in the Methods of Covetoufnefs, as if that alone were the *Zenith* of Wifdom and Virtue, whereas it is in Truth the very *Sink* and Seminary of all Vice

I will relate to thee a Story which I have heard in *Paris*, which has fomething in it very fingular and remarkable, concerning the Affection and Care of a Father toward his *Extravagant* and *Prodigal Son* This old Gentleman had a fair Seat, about ten Leagues from the City, which had belonged to his Family for the Space of Five hundred Years His yearly Revenue was very confiderable, and having only one *Son*, he gave him the Liberty of managing half his Eftate, when he came to the Age of One and twenty Years

This young Spark being of high Spirit, was fo far from harbouring any Thoughts of Frugality, that he could hardly brook the Neceffity of living within the Compafs of his Allowance He addicted himfelf to *Gaming*, *Drinking*, and other Lewd Courfe, which in a fhort Time confumed his Means, and reduced him to great Streights

About the fame Time his Father died, and left him the Remainder of his Eftate giving him all the Inftructions that are ufual in fuch Cafes, and among the reft of his fage Counfels he charged him, if it fhould be his Misfortune to become a *Bankrupt* again, fo as to be forced to fell his Eftate, that he would at leaft not part with that Houfe which had been fo long in the Poffeffion of their Family Efpecially he conjured him to referve one particular Chamber for himfelf as long as he lived,

bred, which was the same where he then lay a dying, *For this*, said he, *will be a Sanctuary for you, when you have no other Place of Refuge in the World*

After the old Man's Decease, his Son fell to his former Course of Life, and to make short of it, in a few Years spent all his Patrimony, even that very House itself which he was forced to sell at last for an Underprice, to supply his present Necessities However, he obeyed his Father's last Injunction, and in the Sale of the House, made *Articles* for the perpetual Claim and Use of that *Chamber* to himself

It was not long before he had consumed the Money which he had received for the House So that now his last support was gone He tried to borrow of some of his Friends and Acquaintance And in Charity they supplied him at first with small Sums But when he often pressed them they grew weary of him, and denyed to part with any more

The disconsolate Gentleman, over whelmed with Grief and Melancholy, returns to his Chamber, hoping to find some Ease in that private Recess, where he might at least have the Privilege of venting his Sorrow in sighs and Tears.

He passed away some time in this dejected Condition, when at length he cast his Eyes on an old *Trunk* which stood in a Corner of the Chamber, and which he had scarce ever regarded before An odd Curiosity prompted him to rise and look into this Trunk, perhaps not so much in Hopes of finding any Relief there, as to divert himself and pass away the tedious Minutes *And yet it is natural for People in great Calamities and Misfortunes, to flatter, themselves with the Imagination of unexpected Reliefs, and to catch at every the least Glimpse or Shadow, that seems to presage any Good* Be it how it will, he fell to rifling the *Trunk*, but found nothing, save a Parcel of old Rags and Papers, with other Remnants, and Fragments of Silk, Linen, and Velvet, the Reliques and Spoils of his Father's Wardrobe. This was no Booty for him However, he ceased not his Scrutiny, till he had quite emptied the *Trunk* When to his no 'mall Aftonifhment he found thefe Words on the Bot tom *Ah Preaigel! haft thou fpent All, and fold thy Houfe? Now go and heng thyfelf There is a Rope ready provided for thee in the Beam of the Chamber*

The young Gentleman looking to the Cieling, and feeing a Halter hang there being faftened to an Iron Ring, was ftruck with fuch a Damp, that concluding i was the *Will* of *Fate*, that he fhould fulfil the Words he found on the Bottom of the *Trunk*, immediately took a Chair, or Stool, and placing it juft under the Rope, got up and raifed himfelf upon it, that fo he might the better reach the defigned Inftrument of his Death

He ftood not long mufing For Life appeared now in fupportable to him Wherefore putting the Halter a bout his Neck, in the Height of Defpair he kicked the Stool away When behold, inftead of hanging there, he fell to the Ground, the weighty Swing of his Body having pulled out a Piece of fquare Timber from the Beam, being that part to which the Ring was faftened Immediately he was like to be overwhelmed, and buried alive in a great Heap of Gold, which came fhowering down upon him out of the hollow Place, which his Fa ther had contrived on Purpofe in the Beam, to put this kind *Sarcafm* on his Son, now fufficiently mortified by fo many Sorrows

In a word, this made fo deep an Impreffion on him, that he grew reformed, buying all his Eftate back again with Part of the Money, and employing the reft in Merchandizing, grew to be a richer Man than his Fa ther, or any of his Progenitors

Dear *Pefteli*, thy Son is Generous and Witty It is thy Part to reclaim him by Methods agreeable to his Nature For Ruggednefs and Aufterity will make him but the worfe.

Paris, 5th of the 11th Moon, of the Year 1671.

LET

LETTER II.

To Codorafrad Cheick, *a Man of the* Law.

HERE has happened an Accident of late which testifies the Zeal of the *French* for their *Religion,* well as it discovers the Rash and Unwarrantable Fury of a bigotted *Desperado* This Person was one of that Sect they call *Hugonots,* of whom there are great Multitudes in *France,* and they are diametrically opposite to those of the *Roman* Faith in their Principles, and the Manner of worshipping *God*, yet are tolerated by the State to prevent the Inconveniencies of a *Civil War,* and the Effusion of Human Blood The King chusing rather by Clemency to win him to his Party, than by a severe Execution of the Laws in Force against them, to compel their Consciences in Matters relating to *God*

Yet many Men are of Opinion That this *Royal* Condescension will not have its desired Effect, upon a stubborn and Ungrateful Sort of People, who instead of being obliged to Fidelity and Obedience by such Indulgent Favours, are apt to interpret them as Arguments of the *King's* Impotence and Disability to punish those that resist his Authority, and to harden themselves the more in their Factious Insolence As it will appear by what I am going to relate of a certain Religious *Furioso,* a *Hugonot* by Profession This Fellow coming one Day into the great *Temple* in *Paris,* which they call *Nostre Dame,* makes up directly toward the *Priest* who was celebrating the *Mass,* and waiting a convenient Season to execute his Purpose just as the *Priest* was elevating that which they esteem the *Sacramental Body of Jesus* the *Messias,* above his Head, according to Custom, that it might be adored by all the Congregation, this Ruffian step to him, and stricking the Wafer out of his Hand, trampled it under Foot, and then assassinated the Priest with his Dagger

I 4

Th

The whole Affembly were aftonifhed at fuch an un
exampled Attempt. They ftood ftill like Statues for a
while, and fuffered the Villain to pafs through the
Throng, till he came to the very Gate of the Temple.
When beginning to rouze out of their Stupefaction,
fome run after him, and fo he was feized, and carried
before the next *Cadi* or *Judge* of *Criminal Caufes*, who
condemned him to have his Right Hand firft cut off be
fore the Gate of the fame Temple where he had been
guilty of this Affaffine and Prophanation, and his Body
prefently afterwards to be burnt alive. Which was ac
cordingly executed.

But not thinking this a fufficient Expiation of the
Difhonour done to God, the Archbifhop of *Paris* com
manded Prayers to be made, which they call the *Ora
jens* of Forty Hours. He appointed alfo a folemn Pro
ceffion of all the *Clergy* to the Temple of *Noftre Dame*,
to cleanfe it from the Defilement (which according to
their Belief) it had contracted by this impious Action.
The fovereign Companies of the City likewife attended
thefe Ceremonies in their Robes of Honour, to teftify
their Devotion.

Thou wilt not conclude me an *Infidel*, or fay that I
undertake the Patronage of the *Roman Religion*, if I
condemn this Fellow as a Martyr to his own Prefump
tion and Arrogance. The *Romans* and *Hugonots* are all a
like to me, fo long as they are equally Enemies to the
Meffenger of God. But it is not decent or wife, neither
good Manners nor Policy, to affront the eftablifhed *Re
ligion* of the Country where a Man lives. It was fuffici
ent that this Ruffian and all his Brethren had the Li
berty of ferving *God* after their own Way. It was an
unpardonable Immorality to difturb the lawful *Prieft*
of the Nation, efpecially in fo barbarous a Manner, in
the very Height of their Myfteries, the midft of their
daily Sacrifice, at the *Altar* of their *God*, where they
profefs to immolate after a tranfcendent Manner no lefs
than the *Body* and *Blood* of the Meffias.

Doubtlefs, all *Nations* are zealous for their *Religion*,
and we *Mufulmans* fhould not fcruple to put to Death a
head

her *strong G after*, who would presume but to pollute our Sacred *Mosques* by his Uncircumcised Presence, much less should we spare him, if he attempted to offer any Violence to *a True Believer*, as he was adoring the *Eternal Unity* after the Way observed by our *Fathers*, and commanded by the *Prophet* And though these *Nazarenes* are Worshippers of Images and Pictures, tho' they adore that which to all outward Appearance is but a Piece of Bread, yet the Precept of *Moses* ought to be regarded, which says, *Ye shall not blaspheme the Gods of the Nations whither ye go to dwell*

Venerable Successor of *Moses* and the *Prophets*, vouchsafe to pray for *Mahmut*, that whilst he dwells among these *Infidels*, he may neither make Shipwreck of his Faith by embracing their Vanities, nor yet forfeit his Discretion by any Rude, Unseemly, or Violent Carriage against them

Paris, *23d of the* 12*th Moon,*
of the Year 1671

LETTER III.

To Dgnet Oglou.

THERE are a Sort of Men among the *Nazarene Ecclesiasticks*, whom they call *Casuists*. These are profoundly versed in the Learning of the *Schools*, which (if thou rememberest) Honest Father *Antonio*, the Old *Sicilian Priest*, our Friend, used to term *The Science of Husk* A dry, chaffy sort of Knowledge, consisting only of empty, vapid Motions, windy *Ideas*, Distinctions made in Sand, which may be effaced, altered, or formed at Pleasure. The very Contemplation of these Metaphysical Trifles, is enough to put one in a Fever, so subtile is the Poison they contain A spiritual Venom, which darts like Lightning thro' one's Thoughts, and soon ferments the Soul, boiling our Reason up, to

scum

fcum and froth itfelf away in Divine Jargon and *Rel-gious* Nonfenfe.

Thefe Men will fplit a Hair in Divinity to make a Scruple, or to difannul it They raife a Duft in the Fyes of thofe that give heed to them, and play faft and loofe with Human Reafon, as it ferves a Turn They will make a Hog of a Cufhion, and turn an Elephant into a Coffee-Difh, with their enchanting *Hæcceities*, *Identit*, *Quaten us*'s, and the reft of their Learned *Legerdeme*, the perfeît *Hocus-Pocus* of the *Sarborne* , by which they juggle Men out of their Senfes, and frame *Chimara's* far more monftrous than thofe in the Fiîtions of *O-a*, or the more early and myfterious *Poems* of *Mufæus*, *Orpheus*, and *Hefiod* They teach Men to ftumble at a Feather in the way of a Religious Life, yet not to boggle at a Milftone or a Mountain, where Intereft calls for Refolution and Speed They ftart more Difficulties than themfelves can anfwer in the Cafes of the Poor But where Plenty of Gold appears, every Thing is made eafy and plain Mere Higglers in Religion , Quack and Empiricks in Matters of Confcience , murdering a Thoufand diftempered Souls, for one they cure Pretending to be Guides to *Paradife*, they lead Men through uncouth Paths and intricate Windings, till they are loft in Labyrinths of Error, bordering on the Confines of Hell And then they leave them to themfelves where, if they make one falfe Step, they go out of their Bounds, trefpafs on the *Devil's* Frontiers, and fo are either in Danger of a Precipice, or at leaft of being taken Captives by the outlying Scouts of the *Infernal Kingam*, from whom it is difficult to efcape

There were fuch as thefe alfo among the *Jews* and *Gentiles* of old, and fo there are at this Day in all Religions, Men who are fevere in *Punctilio's*, and negleît the more Important *Precepts* of the *Law* Nor can the *Muffulmans* themfelves be free from this Embarraffmen of the Faith and Truth brought down from Heaven

If thou obfervest the grave and fupercilious Looks of our *Imaum's*, *Mollah's*, *Cadi's*, &c thou wilt take them for the jufteft Men, the holieft Saints on Earth Mark

b

but their Difcourse, it is an Abridgment of the *Alcoran*
They are feen each Morning at the firft Hour of *Pub-
l Prayer*, walking before the *Mofques*, or fitting in the
Royal Cemeteries, under fome melancholy Cyprefs, reading the Book of *Afforaik*, or fome other fpiritual Trea-
tife With Eyes caft up to Heaven, or humbly fixed
upon the Ground, and mimick Poftures of their Hands,
they act Devotion to the Life Yet, in their Hearts,
perhaps, are ftudying how to circumvent their Neighbours.

Go to thefe Perfons for Inftruction in any doubtful
Cafe, they will hamper thee with far fetched Terms
and crabbed Problems, with formal Afpects, and tedious Circumlocutions, ftroaking their Beards, and figh-
ing from deceitful Breafts, they will induftrioufly amufe
my Soul with dark *Ænigma's*, and trepan thy Senfe in
Snares of infignificant and unintelligible Words, ftriv-
ing to make thee believe, they are the *Picklocks* of the
Firros Cabinet, if not the *Privy Corncellors* of *Heaven*
Whereas the way of Piety is plain, and circumfcribed
with certain noted Boundaries It is hard indeed for a
bewildered Traveller to find the narrow Gate, and firft
Avenue of this facred Path, amongft fo many gorgeous
glittering Porches ever ftanding open and inviting Men
into the fpacious Fields of Vice But when he has once
entered the obfcure Pafs, he has nothing elfe to do, but
go directly on, without turning to the right Hand, or
the Left, only regarding the fixed Land marks of eternal Truth, invariable Reafon, and found Morality To
fpeak plainly, a Man's Duty is comprehended in a few
eafy Rules, and he that goes to render them difficult, by
knotty, thorny Glofles, throws Stumbling blocks before
the Feet of *True Believers*, and interrupts their Pilgrimage to Heaven

My Friend, if any pious Scruple trouble thee or me,
let us henceforth be our own *Cafuifts*, and not by blind
implicite Faith, enflave our *Souls* to Men perhaps more
ignorant than ourfelves The *Law* is plain and pofi-
tive, in neceffary Matters. What need we feek to en-
tangle ourfelves more?

If we perform our *Oraisons* at the appointed Hours, what matter is it, whether we observe the six *Traditionary* Postures, or no? We that are illuminated, I only speak of such. As for the Phlegmatick, dull Multitude, it is fit they should be curbed with Discipline, and made to observe the nice *Punctilio*s of Obedience. What signifies the old versatile Turn of the Head, from one Side to the other, as if we thought to catch the *Prophet* peeping over our Shoulders? Or, where is the Sense of the profounder Mystery of poring on our Fingers with extended Palms, as if we were at *School*, and learning our *Alphabet*, or imitated the clownish Rusticks of *Armenia*, who as they work in the Fields and Vineyards, will make a Dial of their Hand, a *Gnomon* of a Straw, and lose an Hour in stedfast gazing on their dirty Fists, to know what time of Day it is? Then the mysterious resting of our Hands upon our Knees, with other formal Ceremonies. What are they all, but an eternal Discipline, confirmed by ancient Custom, and observed for Order's sake? This need not trouble thee or me, whenever we have occasion to retrench such indifferent Niceties.

Nay, to go farther, if we should neglect the stated Periods of solemn Adoration, compelled thereto by Sickness, Travelling, or any other Necessity, Be not disconsolate, as if thou hadest been guilty of a mortal Sin. Some supererogating Work of Charity, will cancel ten such Faults as that. Or at least, thou mayest look boldly in the Face of GOD, when at another Season, on thy Knees, thou makest ample Compensation, or by sacred Abstinence and Fasting, dispersest all the Mists and Clouds of Guilt, that sat so heavy on thy Soul. The Times are all alike to him that is Eternal. There is no Distinction of Day or Night, with that immortal Essence, who made the Sun and Stars, and is Himself the unchangeable Source of Light.

So, if we should address ourselves to Heaven, without the usual Forms of Prayer, or any Words at all, we have no reason to be sad, as if our Oraisons were ineffectual and unheard. In the Eternal, High Recess, our silent Vows, and softest Whispers of the Soul, eccho as

loud

loud as the most bold, and noisy Clamour of the Tongue   There is a Rank of Spirits among the rest above, on purpose made to waft the secret Thoughts of mortal Men to Heaven   We cannot fail of Audience here, whenever we send the least Ejaculation up, with firm Credentials from the Heart

In a word, believe my Dguet, That the *Supremly Intelligent* and *Wise* chiefly regards the Intention and Fervor of our Minds, the habitual Bent of our Souls, with the innocent and pious Actions of our Lives.   He is not to be moved (unless to Indignation) by the vain Tautologies of our verbal Orations, the nauseating Crambe of devoutest Words, common to Hypocrites and Persons of Sincerity, to the most incorrigible Sinners and the greatest Saints   The humble Silence of a Heart resigned to Destiny, is a pacifick Sacrifice, atoning for the greatest Sins, attracting choicest Favours, Smiles and Benedictions from the Eternal   This is the Discipline of sacred Love, the Rule of perfect Life, the secret Chart of the Elect, whereby they steer their Course to *Paradise*

Which of the Prophets was a formal *Beadsman*, to number out his Orations at Finger's-End, and offer up to God a short and vain Retail of Words, in recompence of infinite Bounties past, and in hopes of more to come ?

When *Mahomet* was pursued by cruel Infidels and forced to make the Wilderness his Sanctuary, and hide himself within the Hollow of an aged Oak, he did not seek to amuse the *Eternal* with studied Forms of Speech, and human Eloquence, or tire the immortal Ears with a religious long Harangue , as if he thought to ensnare the general Mercy of the *Holy One*, in Trains of artificial and elaborate Language, or catch his more particular Indulgence, in a Trap of subtle Rhetorick   The harmless Saint, with Heart and Face composed with self denying Thoughts and Looks, stood like a Statue in the blessed *Asylum*   Whilst gentle Rivulets of compassionate Tears trilled down his Cheeks, his Soul was pierced with sacred Pity to his Enemies   He sighed and wished, in short, whatever blameless Piety could
suggest

suggest for him and them　Angels immediately carried
the Prophetick Vows to Heaven　His silent passionate
Prayer was heard　The cruel Persecutors blinded with
impious Fury, rushed into the Desart, they spread
themselves abroad and rode at large　One Traytor
spurred his Horse through thickest Webs of low en
tangled Thorns and Underwoods, greedy of the Royal
and Majestick Prey, whilst others took the open Paths,
hoping to overtake the *Prophet* on the Flight　They
seemed to swim, or fly rather than ride, such was the
Swiftness of their Course, fierce was the Cry, re-eccho
ed from the Hollows of the Rocks and Valley
(*Mecca, for the Head of Mahomet*)　Some stumbled on
the out-creeping Roots of Trees, and broke a Leg or an
Arm, by a precipitate Fall from off their Beasts, while
others had their Eyes struck blind by interfering
Twigs.　One had his Turbant rudely brushed off, and
Scalp severely shaved, by broken Stumps of Bough,
and Rows of knotty Branches, placed and bent down
by Fate, on purpose to avenge the Apostle's Cause
on such a miscreant as this　Another could not
curb his Horse from jumping down into a deep Quarry,
digged in the midst of the Wood, where the poor
Heretick dashed his Skull and Brains upon the Mar
ble Pavement at the Bottom　So sensible and vindica
tive are inanimate Creatures, when a good Man
a Saint, a Friend of God is wronged　The very
Stocks and Stones, and all the Elements are touched
with sacred Sympathies at such a Time　The Frame
of Nature feels strange tender Passions, Fits and Quams
of amorous Regard.　And God himself, if I may so
express my self, is rouzed as from a Trance and snatch
ing up the Power and Wrath, runs like a Champion to
defend the Cause of injured Innocence

　　But I forget that I am writing a Letter, and there
fore ought to be brief　Besides, what I have said is
sufficient to convince thee, that I have an Idea of Re
ligion, far different from that which the Casuists, whe
ther *Mussulmans* or *Christians*, would imprint in Mens
Minds.

If thou canst not think as I do, I condemn thee not
Use thy native Freedom , but remember, that though
Mens Reasons and Opinions vary as do their Faces ;
ye Truth is *homogeneous*, uniform, and ever of the same
Complexion, in all Ages and Nations

Paris, *1st of the 2d Moon,*
of the Year 1672

LETTER IV.

To the Kiamacham

THE King of *France* has lately made a League
with the King of *England* Whereupon the
People, by way of Proverb, say, that *Mars* and *Jupiter*
are now in *Conjunction* Reflecting thereby, on the different Temper of these two Princes The one debon-
air and jovial, excessively addicted to Women and
Wine, yet not forgetting or declining martial Affairs,
when his Honour or Interest invites him to take up
Arms The other seeming wholly taken up with the
Thoughts of Conquest, and enlarging his Dominions ,
yet sparing some time for the Enjoyment of himself,
and Prosecution of his Amours

However, both of them now have proclaimed open
War against the *Hollanders*, by Sea and Land The
king of *Sweden*, who was before an *Ally* of the *Dutch*,
has of late declared himself a Neuter And the Bishop
of *Munster*, who is one of the Electors of the German
Empire, is engaged in the *French* Interest

Thus are some of the Princes and States in *Europe*
divided already , and GOD knows how far the Breach
may extend in time

It is not altogether unworthy of Remark, what different Factions there were of late amongst the *Hollanders* themselves, though a *Republick*, pretending to
a greater and faster Union of Interests than what can
be found in any Monarchy. Yet this Common wealth

was rent into three several Parties Whereof one was headed by the Prince of *Orange*, the other of *John de Wit*, and the third was composed of the *Commons*, without any *Chief* of note

I will not trouble thee with a Character of the Prince of *Orange* He is already known by Fame at the Sublime *Porte* As to *John de Wit*, I can give no other Account at present, but that he was a Person, whom Fortune had raised to such an Eminence in the *Commonwealth*, as made him the Prince of *Orange*'s Rival, and Competitor for the Supremacy Therefore he sought to exclude him from all Employments and Offices of Trust, that he might establish himself in his Place

The third Party, whom we may call *Republicans*, were of Opinion, That it was not for the Honour of the *Commonwealth* to acknowledge any *Head*, judging that the Establishment or Exclusion, the Rise or Fall of the Prince, or *De Wit*, ought to be a thing indifferent to the *States* In regard the *Commonwealth* appeared in their Sight sufficient to flourish, under the Protection of her own Arms and Riches, without having any need of either the Prince of *Orange*'s Assistance, or *De Wit's*

However, notwithstanding these Animosities of the *Hollanders* among themselves, as soon as they found themselves engaged in a War with two such potent Monarchs, they all unanimously chose the Prince of *Orange* as General of their *Army* Remembring the famous Actions of his Fathers, the Princes of the House of *Naffau*, by whose Valour and Conduct they had gained and conserved their Liberties On the other Side, *De Wit* having rendered himself odious to the Vulgar, was by them torn in Pieces, Such a Destiny oft happening to those who aspire to raise themselves by unlawful Methods, and who are ambitious to be the Ringleaders of a Faction

The *French* call the Prince of *Orange* a General without an Army, in regard the *Hollanders* being as yet only upon the Defensive, and their Towns wanting strong Garrisons, their Soldiers are all disposed

of

of this way, so that there is little or no Appearance of
a Field Army.

This is certain, the King of *France* is the most gallant Prince in *Europe*. He passes from Divertisements
to the Toils of the War, and from the Campaign returns to his Pleasures again. Thus it is difficult to distinguish between his Labours and Recreations, his
Pleasures and his Business. They seem to be so near of
kin, that he takes equal Pleasure in both.

It was but a little before the first Appearances of
the War, that he and his Queen were revelling in the
Gardens of *Chantilly*, where a *Royal* Entertainment was
prepared for them by Night. The *Court* attended
them thither, and there the *Roman* Luxury was seen in
Royal Miniature. As soon as the Gates were opened,
there appeared an artificial Day, so light was the Place
made with Flambeaus and Lamps. Which being well
placed among the Trees with other refined Illuminations, adorned with Chaplets of Flowers, which presented the Eye with a pleasing Medley of Colours interspersed with Oranges, Citrons, and other agreeable
Fruits, transported the Company with exquisite Delights. All together pretty well resembled a Forest
in a Chamber. For the Walls not being far from the
Place where the King sat, were hung with Arras,
with a Multitude of Lights burning near the Hangings. And there was a Spring of Water in the Middle
of the Garden, raising itself after a wonderful Manner
into the Form of a high Pyramid, and falling again
into three Basons of Marble successively, from one to
the other, made a pleasant Spectacle to the Courtiers.

Then a most magnificent Collation was served up
with vocal and instrumental Musick, so soft and fine,
with a sudden Dew cooling the Air, which had a
Smell like Sweet-Bryars, as rendered the Place a perfect *Paradise*. After which followed the King's Supper, far surpassing the other Banquet in all manner of
Delicacy and Politeness, as well as the stupendous
Abundance of Dishes. When Supper was ended,
they were entertained with a Show of something admirable and new in Fire-works. But though it be
so

fo to them I will not trouble thee with a De
fcription of it, fince you haft feen a far finer and
more coftly at *Conftantinople*, or where ever the great
Sultan kept his Refidence at the Time of a *Divalma*

After this, the King went to fee the New Fortifica
tions of *Dunkirk*, which he had ordered not long be
fore And in a little time followed this *Declaration of
War* againft *Holland*

So things go in a Circle from *War* to *Peace*, from
Peace to *War* again However, thou wilt the better
know by what I have faid how to comport thy felf,
in cafe of any Difference between the *Englyfh*, *French*,
and *Guardens* at the *Sublime Porte* God infpire thee
with a Chiracie iral Wifdom, to adjuft all Difficulties
in their ftated Periods.

Paris, *26th of the 3d Moon,
of the Year* 1672.

LETTER V.

To Cara Halı, *Phyfician to the* Grand Signior.

THOU haft borne with a thoufand Impertinencies
in my Letters, and I know not whether what I
am going to write, will deferve a better Character
However, I feel a Spirit within me, checking my ftu
pid Mind, in that I was not before fenfible of my Error, but muft make fo late a Recantation It is im
poffible for me to reflect on the vain and trifling Sub
jects I have all along entertained thee with, and not
blufh at fo grand an Over-fight, fince I then feemed
not fo much as to regard thy Knowledge and Practice
in *Medicines*, which has exalted thee to the Honour of
being placed in the Front of thofe who take care of
the *Grand Segnior*'s Health Much lefs did I prefent
thee with Matters fuitable to thy more interior Know
ledge

ledge, and that hidden Wisdom, which deservedly rank thee among the most perfect and accomplished Morals

In ancient Time, *Theology* and *Physick* were counted to be of such a near Relation and mutual Dependance, that one could not subsist without the other By *Physick* they meant the general *Science* of *Nature*, otherwise termed *Magick* Which comprehended under it an Knowledge of the *Heavens*, the *Elements*, and every Thing within their vast Circumference The Motions of Sun, Moon, and Stars, their various *Aspects*, *Influences* and *Directions* in this lower World The Nature of all kinds and *Meteors*, with their Effects, the Virtues of all *Plants*, and living *Creatures*, as also of insensible Thing, the *Metals*, *Minerals*, and other Substances found both on the Surface of the Earth, within its Concave, and in the Sea

Such as those of old, were *Appolonius Thyanæus*, with the *Magi* of *Persia* and *Chaldæa* Such as *Hierarchas* among the *Brachmans*, *Tespion* the *Gymnosophist*, *Budda* the *Babylonian*, *Numa Pompilius* at *Rome*, *Zamolxis* of *Thrace*, *Abbaris* the *Hyperborean*, *Hermes Trismegistus* of *Egypt*, *Zoroaster* the Son of *Oromases*, King of *Bactria*, *Evartes* an *Arabian* King, *Zacharias*, a *Babylonian*, *Joseph*, a *Hebrew* With many others of different Nations, as *Zenotenus*, *Kiranmides*, *Almadal*, *Israel*, *Alchind*, *Abel*, *Ptolemy*, *Geber*, *Zabel*, *Nazabarab*, *Thabith*, *Solomon*, *Astrophon*, *Hipparchus*, *Alcmeon*, &c. And of later Date, *Albertus*, surnamed *the Great*, *Arnoldus de Villa Nova*, *Cardan*, *Raymund Lullius* With a few more not worth the Naming

These contemplated the secret Force and Virtue of celestial and sublunary Things, the hidden Sympathy between them and the mysterious Powers of Nature. Then having by a curious and painful Scrutiny traced out the true Genealogies of Things, cast their Nativities, and discovered all their Kindred, Allies, Friends and Enemies, knew by applying in due Season *Actives* to proper *Passives*, how to produce Effects appearing stupendous Prodigies to the Vulgar, and no less than

Miracles

Miracles Whereas, all this is but a pure Result of Nature, helped by human Art So Watches, Dials, Clocks, and Mirrors, appeared at first to the ignorant World, the Effects of Magick Especially the simple Natives of *America,* shewed little more Wit than Apes or Cats, which look behind the Glass, to find the active Figures of themselves, that they saw in it

And now I am got a nongst those poor *Barbarians,* I cannot forget a Passage of a poor *Peruvian* Slave who being sent by his *Spanish* Master with a Basket of choice Fruit, and a Letter to his Friend , the silly Ignoramus being faint, by reason of the excessive Heat , his Journey being also tedious, from the Town of *Lima* to a Village near the Mountains of *Ptof,* eat up the Fruit by the Way, to allay his hungry Thirst However, not having so good a Stomach to the Letter, he delivered it safe to the Person to whom it was addressed, never once dreaming that an insensible Piece of Paper could tell Tales But that discovering his Crime, when he came home, his Master ordered him to the *Bastina*, to make him sensible of it Then he was sent again on the same Errand with Oranges and a Letter, and meeting with the same Temptation, he knew not what to do At last, he hid the Letter under a Heap of Sand wisely concluding, That if it saw him not it could not betray his Fact However, to secure it from all means of Peeping, he spread his Mantle over the Place, and then fell roundly to his Banquet , thinking he should have no Accuser In fine, he eat up all the Oranges, and was worse banged for his Pains than the Time before.

Generous *Hah,* thou feest I am fallen into the same Error for which I made Apology at the Beginning of this Letter But thou canst easily forgive such Crimes as these Suffer me only to relapse thus far, That I may mention the Mathematical Magicians , such as *Archytas,* who made a *Wooden Pigeon* to fly , and *Albert the Great,* who taught a *Brazen Head* to speak Not forgetting him unknown by Name, who gave to the Statues of *Mercury, Voluble Tongues,* and *Eloquent Languages,* by whose Mechanick *Art a Brazen Serpent*
learned

learned to hiſs   and Birds of the ſame Metal with other Helps, out-vied the Nightingales and Thruſhes in their Melody

I will not omit the execrable Practices of *Necromancers* or ſuch as invocate the Dead, and with nefandous Ceremonies, Rites and Sacrifices, call to aid Infernal Spirits, bind them in Cryſtals, or ſome other Vehicle, and then adore them as the ancient *Romans* did their *Lares* and *Penates*   Theſe are the Oracles which they conſult in all Emergencies, and by their Help, work wonders in the World, foretel Things future, and reveal the moſt remote and hidden Secrets, whether paſt, or preſent   Nor is this a Fable, or an Old Wife's Tale, for unleſs the experienced Nations of the Earth had found ſome real Evils from Wizards, Magicians and Witches, they would not have made ſo ſevere Laws againſt them, as to aim at their Extermination from the Earth

Neither need we admire, that Women are as much addicted to theſe curſed Vanities as Men, ſince they are naturally more inquiſitive into Secrets, and leſs cautious of being impoſed upon   They are prone to Superſtition, and from their Infancy, bred up to obſerve their Dreams, their Moles, and other Marks upon their Bodies   They covet all the Depth of Palmiſtry and Phyſiognomy, beſides a thouſand other little Follies

If they meet a Man in the Street at firſt going out, they are encouraged, and take it for a Sign of their good Fortune   But if one of their own Sex encounters them, they curſe the undeſigning Female, and return home again   They obſerve fatal Days and Nights, and certain critical Hours, wherein they try Experiments to know their future Huſbands   They brew enchanting Philters for their Lovers, and intoxicate them with Liquors, wherein young human *Cupids* have been boiled with Herbs, as powerful to effect their Wiſh, as thoſe that *Circe* or *Medaea* knew   In ſhort there is no Species of *Sortilegy*, or Divination, which vain and young Maidens are not practiſed in   Which has a fair Diſpoſition, or Introduction, to the blackeſt Kind of Magick.

But

But bleſſed are they, O Pious and moſt Learned *Hali,* who being profoundly ſkilled, and daily converſant in the Science of Nature, have never tainted themſelves by any unlawful Commerce with Spirits Unclean, Infernal, and Enemies to God. They are Divine Magicians, having Celeſtial Characters, the hidden Name of God imprinted on their Souls, whereby they are able to attract the Angels, and make the higheſt Spirits obey him.

Hali, God grant that thou mayeſt be one of this Venerable and Happy Number. Farewel.

Paris 5*th of the* 4*th Moon,*
of the Year, 1672.

LETTER VI

To Orchan Cabet, Student *of the* Sciences, *and* Pensioner *to the* Grand Signior

IT has been a long Time ſince the Chriſtians have openly publiſhed Libels agaiſt our *H ly* Law-giver, and the Book which he received from the Hands of *Gabriel,* one of the chief Princes of Heaven. They affirm for an undoubted Truth, that *Mahomet* himſelf compoſed that Volume of Light, by the Help of *Sergtorius* a Chriſtian *Monk,* and *Abdalla* a *Jew.* And that it is but an Artificial *Medley,* a Hotch-potch, or a ſtrange manifry of *Pagan,* *Jewiſh* and *Chriſtian* Principles, cunningly ſuited and blended together, in order to gain Proſelytes of all Religions.

I proteſt by the Veneration I owe to the Eternal God of Heaven, that I really believe the *Alcoran* to be of Divine Original. Such is the inimitable Elegance of the Stile, the Brightneſs and Force of its Reaſons and Arguments, the wonderful and charming Contexture of Things *Hiſtorical,* *Moral* and *Divine,* that all the Writings in the World beſide, ſeem to be flat and inſipid, compared with this Sacred and Stupendous Pile

4

&c. of Wisdom   Yet I must confess. I know not how to answer the Accusation of the *Nazareens*, because I have never read any *Mussulman* Treatise, that undertook to refute these Calumnies   Which makes me apt to think, there is none such extant   For I have made diligent Enquiry, discoursed with several learned Doctors of our Law but can gain no Satisfaction in that Point

Perhaps, our Fathers in former Ages, were ignorant how the Messenger of God had been traduced by the Christians, or if they knew it, yet they disdained to answer such malicious Lies   And as for these modern Times, the Zeal of Religion is grown too cool among the true *Believers*   Every one is carried away with Self Love, whilst no Man will be at the Pains to defend the Truth, or manifest the Errors of our Enemies   Besides, it is now impossible to disprove what they say concerning *Nestorius* and *Abdalla*, unless we could produce Authors of unquestionable Authority, who lived in *Mahomet's* Time, and so could give a more exact Account of his Life, than those that came after them

However, if we consult common Reason, we shall find it very improbable, That three Men of such contrary Principles, as a *Jew*, a *Christian*, and a *Pagan*, should all voluntarily agree and jump in one Design of brewing their several *Religions* together, and drawing such an Extract from them as could suit with neither of their Parties singly, and was like to have all of them together for its Enemies and Persecutors   There was no Ground for them to expect the Conversion of any *Jews*, so long as the *Alcoran* asserts *Jesus, the Son of Mary*, to be *the True Messias, the Word and Breath of God, Worker of Miracles, Healer of Diseases, Preacher of Heavenly Doctrine, and Exemplary Pattern of a perfect Life*, denying that he was *Crucified*, but affirming that he *Ascended into Paradise*   Whereas the *Jews* call him an *Execrable Impostor, Magician, Seducer of the Nations*, and finally, by way of extreme Derision, they term him *the Man that was hanged on a Tree*

Neither

Neither was the *Alcoran* like to find any better Entertainment among the *Christians*, for this last Reason, in that it denies the Crucifixion of the *Messias*, which is the Basis whereon all the Superstructure of their Religion is built It is the Angular Stone of *Christianity* Besides, they could never be reconciled to Polygamy, Circumcision, abolishing of Images and Pictures, nor to a great many other Things which the *Mussulman*-Law enjoins Especially they could never brook the Denial of the *Trinity*

And for the same Reason, this supposed, patched Form of Religion would have been as little welcome to the *Gentiles*, in that it took from them the Multitude of their Gods, and asserted the Unity of the Divine Essence So that all Circumstances being weighed, it appears that the *Alcoran*, since it has such Success in the World, could not be forged by those Three, nor composed by any human Pen, but is of divine Original Besides, had there been such a Triumvirate known in the Case, the *Coræi's* of *Mecca*, and other Mortal Enemies of *Mahomet* and his Doctrine, would not have spared to upbraid him with it   And if they were not known to the *Arabians* who were conversant with him, how came the *Christians* to be informed of this private *Cabal*, who were altogether Strangers to *Mahomet* at that time

Consider well these Things, and thou wilt have no reason to give credit to the Calumnies and Imputations cast on the *Apostle of God*, by Unbelievers, but being more and more confirmed in the Undefiled Faith, wilt glorify God, who has guided thee in the right Way, and not into the Way of *Infidels*, and those with whom he is displeased

Orchan, as thou art endued with great Learning, I counsel thee to employ it in defending the Cause of the Prophet, who could neither write nor read.

Paris, 15th of the 6th Moon,
of the Year 1672.

LET.

LETTER VII

To Hamet, Reis Effendi, Principal Secretary
of the Ottoman Empire

HERE has been hot Work this Summer in the
West. The King of *France* has made such swift
and large Conquests on the *Hollanders*, that they have
hardly had Time to consider their Losses, and the
Number of their Towns fallen into their Enemies
Hands.

It always falls out so, when this Monarch goes in
Person to the Campaign, as he did this Year. In a very
little Time he took *Burick, Orsay, Rimberg, Vezel,*
P..., Emmerick, and many other Places. Yet this Success was allayed with the Death of the Duke of *Longue-*
ville, who fell a Victim, either to his Dullness or Te-
merity, in not hearing or not receiving the Cries of
the Enemy, who demanded Quarter as the *French* were
passing the *Rhine.* He was shot with a Musket-bullet;
and the Duke of *Enguien,* his Cousin, very narrowly
escaped, for they were both jointly engaged in the
same Action.

The Death of this Prince is much lamented, not only
by those of his Family, but by the whole Court and
City, as being in the Flower of his Time, having signalized his Valour at the Siege of *Candi,* the Conquest
of the *Franche-Compte,* and other warlike Expeditions.
And they discourse, as if he had been designed to stand
Candidate for the *Polish* Crown.

I am the more particular in this Relation, because
the Enterprize of the *French* King in passing the *Rhine,*
is looked upon as one of the most hardy and bold, that
ever was taken in Hand. In all the Histories of these
Parts, there is not one Example of so surprizing an
Expedition. And the Success answered their Expectation. For the *Hollanders* were extremely daunted and
disheartned by the News of these Exploits. In a little Time *Arnheim, Nimeguen,* were reduced to the King's

Obedience, with the Fort of *Skn*, and Towns of
D Oefburg, Bomel, Zutplen, Deventer the *Metropoli* of
a *Province*, with *Wetfet, Torgi*, *Mafick, Dortewo*,
Elbourg, Woorden, chnlem, another Capital City, with
many more Places, too tedious to be rehearsed.

In a word, such are his expeditious Marches, his
sage Counsels, his never failing Success, that the People
think it no Flattery to call him a second *Alexander* the
Great, Tamerlane, Scanderberg, Scipio, Hannibal, and all
the great heroick Names in the World.

To speak the Truth, the King of *France* hath all
along made an illustrious Figure in the World. And
their famous Exploits in War, with their heroic
Actions in Time of Peace, afford sufficient Matter for
the highest Panegyricks, without an Occasion of *Hyperboles*. Which made one of the *Roman Muftis* in a Letter to the King of *France*, thus express himself ' By
' how much the Royal Dignity transcends the State of
' other Men, so far is the Monarchy of *France* exalted
' above all the Kingdoms in the World.' Pope L IV
said, That the King of *France* was as the *Polar
Star* in the *Firmament* of *Princes*, brighter than all
other Kings, a perfect *God* on Earth. It is afferted by
another Author, That by the King of *France*'s Shadow the whole World is ruled. And such was the
Esteem which Pope *Clement* had for this Monarch,
that he granted a hundred Days Indulgence to every
one that prayed for the King of *France*, to which Pope
Innocent IV added Ten Days more.

It is a Maxim in the *Salique* Law, That the King
of *France* never dies. But this indeed is altogether so
true in *Spain, Great Britain*, and other *Hereditary* Kingdoms, till the Succession fails. For then it degenerates
to an Elective Monarchy, or otherwise into Aristocracy, or last of all into Democracy, or a Republick.

But *France* is yet free from these painted Forms of
Slavery. Her Kings are masculine and vigorous,
her Queens chaste and fruitful. There never wants an
Heir apparent to the Crown. And this secures the
Nation from a thousand Calamities, which attend French
Iffue

lative Monarchies, and more popular Forms of Government

What Injuftices, Cruelties Maffacres and all manner of publick Grievances were complained of in *Rome*,
after *Claudius Cæfar* had bought the Empire of his Soldiers ? What Bickerings between the Senate, the People and the Armies Each Party would have an Emperor of their own chufing, one Province was emulous
of another So that fometimes there have been twenty
or thirty Emperors together, all claiming the Sove-
reignty And when there were but two, fuch was
the obftinate and Proud Difpute between them, that
they have been forced to fhare the Empire equally,
the only Means to prevent its utter Diffolation
Hence fprung the firft Inftitution of Colleagues in the
Empire And this was the Root of thofe Factions and
Divifions, which increafing and growing up with
Time, branched forth into fmaller Sciffions, till at
length by Ambition of fome, the Misfortune or Care-
leffnefs of others, or at leaft their want of Power and
Courage, that the mighty Empire was cantonized,
cut in Pieces, and dwindled into that narrow Dominion which it now poffeffes under the Tutelage of the
Houfe of *Auftria* And there appear no Hopes of its
ever being reftored again to its priftine *Grandeur*, until the *Bourbons*, with their growing Fortune, fhall
crown the *Eagle* with a Chaplet of *Flower-de-Lys*, and
change the Seat of the *Weftern Monarchy*, from imperious *Vienna* to all conquering *Paris*

In a word *Henry* IV began the Defign, *Lewis*
XIII carried it on, and this prefent King has fo far
improved it by his matchlefs Fortune and Courage,
that in all probability, this or the next Age will fee it
brought to Perfection

Accomplifhed Minifter, I bow my felf with abundance of interior Veneration, to the Duft of thy Feet I
affectionately kifs the Border of thy Robe, and bid
thee a devout Adieu

Paris, 14*th of the* 8*th Moon,
of the Year* 1672

LETTER VIII.

To William Vofpel, *a Recluse of Auftria.*

THY Letters make me very reftlefs and inquifi tive, they awaken new Doubts and Scruples in my Breaft, inftead of removing or fatisfying the old ones Frefh Queries ftart in my Mind, and the more thou labourcft to faften me in thy narrow Superftition and bigotted Zeal for the Infallibility of the Pope and the *Roman* Church, the loofer I grow My Soul is like a wild Colt in the Wildernefs, that tofles up his Head fnuffs the Air in Indignation, and fcorning the bride of Servitude, neighs for Joy at his native Liberty, fcampering at large through the folitary Wafte, nor can he be wheedled by human Craft, to lofe his beloved Freedom, or change it for a tame Captivity

I have revolved in my Mind the Ages that are paft, and the Years of untraceable Origin I have examined the Times and Seafons of the World, recorded in *Hiftory*, from *Adam* to *Mofes*, from *Mofes* to *Jefu*, and from *Jefus* to the prefent Days wherein we live After all, I find that the *Memoirs* of former Tranfactions are covered with great Darknefs, yet there are not wanting fome Glimmerings of Light, to direct a diligent Mind, and impartial Lover of Truth

Jefus the Son of *Mary*, was of the Stock of *Abraham*, and *Jacob* He was educated in the Law of *Mofes*, which he obferved in all Things to a Tittle And in his Life-time he faid, *Think not that I came to deftroy the Law but to perfect it* His Apoftles obferved the fame Rule, and in all Things were ftrict Obfervers of the ftated Precepts So were the Primitive Chriftians, even to the keeping of the *Jewifh Sabbath*, befides the firft Day of the Week appointed for the publick Celebration of their own *Myfteries* They abftained from Blood, and from Things ftrangled, and from all unclean Meats, and fuch as were facrificed to Idols. They had no *Images* or *Pictures* in their Churches

Church Chapels, or Oratories In fine, they observed all the necessary Purifications, and adored *One* God
with Purity of Heart, and lively Faith and good Work
Whereas thou seest, the present *Roman Church* follows
quite contrary Maxim   They give the Lye to our
Lord's own Declaration, and positively say that he
came on purpose to abolish the *Law*, and introduce an
Universal Liberty, that we may now as freely banquet on the Blood of slain Beast, as on the Milk of
the Living, and eat of Swines Flesh, and other abominable Food, with as little Detriment to our Souls, as
on the Flesh of Lambs, or other clean Creatures allowed by the Law of God   How can this hang together or be credited by any Rational Man ?   It is no
wonder there are so many *Libertines* and *Atheists* in the
World, when they find *Christianity* to be a meer Heap
of ridiculous Contradictions

To this thou wilt answer, according to the common
Rules of *Divines*, that during the *Primitive Times*, the
Apostles, and all other *Christians*, observed the *Law*
of *Moses*, for fear of giving Scandal to the *Jews*, of
whom great Numbers were converted to the *Christian*
Faith, when they saw that the Followers of *Jesus* did
not deviate from the Institutions of the *Seniors*, the Sta-
of the *House* of *Jacob*   But that afterwards, when
the *Gospel* was preached far and wide on the Face of
the Earth, and that many of the *Gentile* Nations were
brought over to the Church, it was no longer necessary for the Sake of so contemptible a People as the
Jews, to scandalize all the rest of the World, and im-
pose on them a Yoke which they were not accustomed
to bear, and which would tempt them to shake off
Christianity it self, rather than submit to so intolerable
a Burthen   Therefore the Church, to facilitate as
much as in her lay, the Conversion of the *Roman* Empire, which then extended it self over the greatest Part
of the Earth, accomodated her Injunctions, Precepts,
Manners and Ceremonies of Religion, to the present
Humour and Mode of those Times   And whereas
the Apostles eat of all Meats indifferent, so they were
taught, that this was agreeable to the Will of our Lord

Jesus

...., who came to rescue Men from the Slavery and Bondage of *Mosaick* Superstitions

By the very same Rule they introduced the Usage of Images and Pictures in their Churches And the Vestments of the Priests, the Ornaments of the Altar, the ... Lamp, Incense, Flower pots and other Religious Gaieties, were fashioned according to the Patterns they received from the Priests of *Jupiter*, *Apollo*, *Venus*, *Diana*, and the rest of the .... Deities He ... Festivals of the G... and C... were turned to Holy-Days of Saints And Temples before consecrated to the *Sun*, *Moon*, and *Stars*, were afresh dedicated the *Apostles* and *Martyrs* Thus the very P... ... itself is *Pane*, or *..... of all the God* , in Pickets of *Iron*, by an Ecclesiastical Dexterity, was converted to the Church of *All Saints* In a Word, ... in all Things seemed no other than *Gentilism* in Disguise And it must be thought a *Pious Fraud*, thus to wheedle so many Millions of Sinners into the Bottom of the Church, whether they would or no

O! Father *William*, dost not thou blush at these ... vial Excuses, for the manifest Violation of the Laws of *God* Can Man be wiser than the Omnipotent? Or will he presume to correct the Ways of him that is perfect in Knowledge? Is the *True Religion* to be propagated by imitating the *Idolatrous Rites of Infidels*? Or by prostituting the Sacred Injunctions of Heaven to the Caprices of human Policy? Did ever any wise Lawgiver condescend to alter and new model his Laws, to humour a peevish captious Subject? Would he add or diminish any Thing for the sake of gaining a Factor or Part? And can we think, that God either designed, or can be pleased to have his Divine Institutions jumbled and mixt with prophane Indulgences, Dispensations, and Amendments of *Mortals*? As if he had been ignorant what he did, when he divulged his Statutes, and wanted the Counsel of his Creatures to help him out at a dead Lift

Was that Tenderness to be only shewed to the *?*

... Time : And were they for ever afterwards to be
... In vain does the Church daily pray for
the Conversion of that People, whilst by her Doctrines
and daily Practices, she hardens them more in their In-
... The Ethiopian Church is a standing Witness
against her to this Day, where the Christians from all
Antiquity, even from the Times of the Apostles, have
... that Part of the Law of Moses, which relates to
Cleanness and Uncleanness, and prescribes the Choice
we are to make of Meats allowed to be eaten, forbid-
ing those that are Execrable, and an Abomination
Hence it is, that there are more Jews converted to the
Christian Belief in that Country, than in any other Part
of the World besides

It was, in my Opinion, to begin at the wrong End,
and to neglect the Salvation of the Jews, our elder
Brethren, from whom we received the Oracles of God,
and run to proselyte the Gentiles by such preposterous
Methods, as rendered us in a manner as much their
Converts, as them ours. Since we shuffled our Religions together at random, and made a Lottery of divine and human Institutions, exchanging one Species
of Superstition and Idolatry for another; bartering *Jupiter* for *Peter*, and *Mars* for *Paul*, *Venus* and her *Cu-
pid*, for the *Virgin Mary* and her Child *Jesus*. A God
for an *Apostle*, and a Demy God for a Martyr. Whilst
the Law it self, which is the Foundation and main Prop
of *Jew Religion*, lies neglected and trampled under Foot

The Christians of the East seem more excusable than
we. For, tho' they are not so punctual in observing all
the Niceties of Cleanness and Uncleanness, Meats, and
Drinks, &c. as those of Ethiopia. Yet they will not taste
of Blood, or any Thing strangled. And their Ecclesiasticks abstain from all manner of Flesh, during the
whole Course of their Lives. They observe also many
Institutions, and wholesome Rules of Life. Whereas
we of the *Latin* Church wallow in all manner of
Uncleanness like Swine, and bless our selves, as if
we were the only True *Catholicks*, the Elect of God,
in the high Road to Heaven. I am at a Loss
what to think of these Things, neither can I ever
hope

hope to fee the *Jews* converted, till thefe Offences are removed

There is a Rumour fpread up and down, of the *Wandring Jew* I fuppofe thou haft heard of fuch a Man He is now at *Aftracan*, and preaches every where, that there will be a *Reformation of Chriftianity*, after the Year 1700 That the *Jews* fhall be converted, and all this to be performed by the admirable Gifts of an *Englifhman*, who fhall reftore *Truth* to its Primitive Luftre and Integrity They fay, he will caufe the *Images* and *Pictures* to be utterly deftroyed, and the *Law of Mofes* to be kept, fo far as relates to Cleannefs and Uncleannefs, *&c* That in his Days the Temple of *Solmon* fhall be rebuilt, and the World fhall put on a new Face

Father *William*, I would not have thee defpife thefe Things, fince they have been long foretold by *Joachim* the *Abbot*, by St *Methodius*, by *Noftrodamus*, the *French Prophet*, and many other eminent Perfons, whofe Writings are extant, and many of their Predictions are already come to pafs The *Roman* Church manifeftly ftands in need of a Reformation And fince the Governors of it cannot be prevailed on to fet their Hands to fo pious a Work, we know not but God may effect it by the Means of a Stranger, fome obfcure Perfon at prefent, but whofe Light may fhine hereafter through all Generations.

Father *William*, thou wilt pardon the Liberty I take in difcourfing about thefe Things, and remember, that it is a Work of Charity to bear with Impertinencies of others However, I thank God I am out of the *Parleu* of the *Spanifh Inquifition*.

Paris, 1ft *of the* 10th *Moon*,
    of the Year 1672.

LETTER IX.

To Codabafiad Cheick, *a Man of the* Law.

I Have a Kinfman by Blood, refiding at *Aftracan*, in the Parts of *Mofcovy* His Name is *Iſouf*, a Man of an ardent Spirit, and active Wit, a great Traveller, and one who makes good that Character, by the folid Remarks he has made on the moſt important Things in his way, through *Aſia*, *Africk*, and *Europe* For he is not in the Number of thofe who come home from Foreign Countries, only laden with Vanities and Trifles.

From him I receive frequent Difpatches, fince his being fettled at *Aftracan*, in Quality of a Merchant, where he improves his Eftate to great Advantage, enjoys the innocent Pleafures of human Life, without fuffering himfelf to be tainted with the Vices which are unprofitable, troublefome, and bring Scandal to a Man's Reputation For fome Vices, thou knoweft, pafs into the Predicaments of Virtues, when Intereſt or Neceffity gives an Indulgence

There is a mutual Intercourfe between my Coufin and me And among other Letters which he fends, I received one lately, wherein he informs me, that he whom they call the *Wandring Jew*, of whom I have made mention formerly in one of my Difpatches to the Sublime Port is now at *Aftracan*, that he preaches openly in the Markets, and at the *Bouſe* or *Exchange* ; not refufing private Converfation with any that defire it

There is a great Confux of People from all Nations, and of all Religions to that City He carries himfelf with an equal Indifference to every various Sect, and they all feem mightily taken with his Doctrines The chief Thing he aims at in all his Difcourfes is, that there will e're long be an univerfal Change of *Religion* over all the Earth, and that every

Nation on the Globe shall worship One God, obey the Law of *Jesus* the Son of *Mary*, and embrace One Faith When he insists on this, he seems to be void of all Doubts and Hesitations, speaks magisterially, like a Prophet, who has received a sure and certain Revelation of the Thing he foretels But when any dispute with him, not in Spirit of Captiousness, but to find the Truth, he freely condescends to answer all their Objections with solid Reasons, and to convince them by their own Principles, that it must be so

He says, That about the Year 1700 of the *Christian Hegira*, the invincible *Otmans* shall break down the Fences of *Europe*, and shall overflow all *Christendom* like a mighty Torrent that has over topped its Banks In those Days there shall be great Desolation in *Hungary, Poland, Germany, France*, and other Regions of the *West* Only *Denmark, Sweden, Muscovy*, and other Countries of the *North* shall remain untouched but above all other Nations, he says, *Italy* will be made a perfect Wilderness, her Cities laid in Ashes, her immense Wealth plundered and carried away by the greedy *Tartars, Arabians*, and *Turks*, who will spare neither Age nor Sex, putting all to the Sword, especially the *Ecclesiasticks*, none of which shall escape the publick Vengeance, save three Cardinals, sincere and holy Persons, who shall fly into *England* for Sanctuary by the Way of the Sea

That Island, he says shall become the Refuge of all such who can escape the Calamities involving the adjacent Countries Thither they shall flock with their Wives and Children, and all their Wealth, when they shall hear of the approaching Terrors, the present Devastations of *Italy* and the universal Conquests of the *Otmans* The King of the Country shall receive those afflicted Fugitives with open Arms, and shall assign them certain Portions of Land, where they may build Houses and Habitations for themselves and their Families, there being abundance of waste Ground in that Island, which they may manure and improve to their own and the publick Advantage

After

After this, says he, shall arise a certain Man in *England* from his obscure Center, a Person filled with all
manner of Divine Knowledge and Wisdom, endued
with the *Spirit* of *Prophecy*, of a graceful Aspect, and
elegant Speech, of a composed Gravity, and calm
Address, a Man mild, innocent, temperate, chaste,
and merciful above the rest of human Race. People
shall let their Eyes fall on the Ground, when they meet
him in the Streets, even before they know what he is,
overcome by the Lustre of Modesty, Grace and Virtue
which shines in his Countenance. A Person highly
beloved of God and Man.

This Man shall meet the three fugitive Cardinals in
an Hour of Destiny. Then that which lay long smothering, shall suddenly burst forth into a Flame. The
Light of God shall be diffused through his Soul, his
Heart shall be like a Lamp, and his Tongue shall utter marvellous Things. When he opens his Mouth in
divulging the Mysteries of God, his Words shall be
like the Sparks of an eternal Fire, kindling Flames of
Love in the Breasts of the Hearers. The Cardinals
shall rise from their Places, and run to embrace him.
A Council of the chief Bishops and Priests of the Land
shall be assembled by the King's Order, where the
three Cardinals also shall be present, and after mature
Deliberation, with unanimous Consent, they shall call
for the Holy Oil of Consecration, and shall anoint him.
They shall proclaim him the great Father, and Patriarch of the Faithful, the Director of such as would
go to *Paradise*.

He shall shew them a new Pattern of the Law of *Jesus* the Son of *Man*; or rather the old and true One,
free from the Corruptions and Errors which have been
superinduced for many Years. Their Hearts shall yield
as to an Oracle, and the King of the Country shall approve of their Counsel. So shall all those of the Noble and Vulgar, whose good Fate is written in their
Foreheads. As for the rest, they shall remain in their
Incredulity.

The holy Person shall reform the Errors of all the
Churches utterly abolishing the Use of Images
and

and Pictures, convince the *Jews* of their Infidelity, and chace away the Darkness of Superstition from the Earth He shall argue with Reasons so forcible and cogent, so clear and demonstrative, that none but the wilfully obstinate will resist the Truth which he divulges, or oppose his authentick Mission Thousands shall be converted by the Dint of his Words, and ten thousands by his Exemplary Life For he shall go up and down preaching and doing good Works throughout *Great-Britain*, till the Number of his Proselytes is compleat Then he shall send Apostles and Messengers into *Swedeland, Denmark, Muscovy*, and other Parts of *Europe*, who shall also convert an innumerable Multitude to his *Law* Foreign Princes shall send their Ambassadors to the King of *Great Britain*, and to him, for he shall be at the King's Right Hand They shall enter into Leagues and Convents, and all the Christian Princes shall be at Unity Mighty Armies shall be raised in the *North*, who shall come down and give new Courage to the oppressed *Nazarenes* of the *West* They shall all take up Arms, and chace the *Osmans* back again to their own Country, recovering the Wealth which they had taken from them

After this, by an universal Agreement of the Christians, this holy Person shall be proclaimed the Great Pastor of the *Church* A prodigious Army shall be gathered together out of all the Christian Nations to conduct him to the *Holy Land*, and to crown him in *Jerusalem* They shall vanquish and exterminate the *Osmans* out of *Palestine*, and all the adjacent Regions Then shall *Jerusalem* be rebuilt gloriously, and the *Temple of Solomon* with *Saphires* and *Emeralds* That City shall be the Seat of the *Christian Mufti's*, this new Patriarch and his Successors, to the Day of Doom Then shall the Eyes of the *Jews* be opened They shall acknowledge *Jesus* the Son of *Mary*, to be the true *Messias*, whom they have so frequently cursed In a Word, he says, both *Jews* and *Gentiles*, People of all Nations, shall resort to *Jerusalem*, or send thither their Gifts and Presents. It shall become the Mistress of the whole Earth

Sage

Sage *Cheick*, this is the Substance of what my Cousin *Ibuf* acquaints me with concerning the *Wandring Jew*, and his new Doctrines   The Censure of which I leave to thee, who hast a discerning Spirit, and art able to distinguish Truth from an Imposture   GOD only knows what is hid in the Womb of Futurity   Every Age is pregnant, and brings forth strange Events   Yet when it is over, all founds like a Dream   The World itself is no better, and I that write this, am but, methinks, the Shadow of a Vision or Trance   I hardly know whether I am asleep or awake whilst my Pen feems to move   Therefore, it being very late, I lay it aside, and bid thee adieu   Praying that thou and I may have the Happiness, even in this Life, to taste the sweet Slumbers of *Paradise*

Paris, *7th of the 12th Moon,*
of the Year 1672

LETTER XIII

To Hamet, Reis Effendi, *Principal Secretary of the* Ottoman Empire.

I Think all the sensible World are inquisitive into the Life of *Cardinal Richlieu*   He was the Pole-Star of Statesmen, whilst living   And now he is dead, his *Memoirs* and *Maxims* serve as a Chart and Compass, by which the Politicians steer their Course to avoid the Rocks and Shelves which threaten a Kingdom, or Common-wealth, both in the Tempests of War, and the ferene Calms of Peace

Thou hast formerly received some Remarks from me, on the Life of this great Minister, yet I am not surprized at the Contents of thy last Dispatch, which require a farther Account of him   No body can know too much of a Man who was the Miracle of his Time, and not only startled the wifest of Contemporaries, by his
pro-

prodigious Actions, but has puzzled all that survive him, to trace his Footsteps

Undoubtedly, *France* owes to his Conduct all her present Grandeur, with the Hopes she has of increasing it To him she is indebted for her Conquests in *Flanders*, *Sicily*, *Catalonia*, *Piedmont*, and the *German* Frontiers It was he first taught her the compleat Way to humble her insolent Neighbours, and to suppress her rebellious Domesticks He much abated the troublesome Weight of a Crown, and made it sit lighter on the Head of *Lewis* XIII Whilst *Cardinal Mazarin*, his Successor in the *Prime Ministry*, acting by the same Principles, rendered it as soft and easy to the present King, as the *Grand Signior's* Turbant In a word, through the Efficacy of *Richlieu's* Politicks, *Lewis* XIV is become the most absolute Monarch in *Christendom* For he either undermines or over reaches his Enemies, by specious Treaties of Peace, where he is sure to have the better on it, or he runs them down with the Force of War To conclude, he has a long Head, and a long Sword, which all will confess that have to do with him And this is the pure Result of *Richlieu's* Memoirs

Yet after all that Minister had his blind Side too as well as other Mortals Publick Virtues, and private Vices, state Perfections, and Personal Frailties He served his Master with Zeal and Fidelity, with a Wisdom and Courage, difficult to be matched, but he served himself after the common Manner of Men He indulged his favourite Passions, which were Love, Jealousy, and Revenge

There is a Letter of mine registered in the Archives of the *Sacred Porte*, wherein I mentioned a particular Amour of this great *Prelat* Besides that, he had several Intrigues with the Dutchess of *Elbœuf*, the Countess of *Soissons* and other Ladies of Prime Quality No, there are some that ng such as confidently report, that he had two Children by one of his own Nieces and I could say more about on that Subject

As for that *Jesuit of the Queen o* Women, the whether d

or Interest   He would never suffer any Man to live, ,
who n he once suspected to be in a Capacity, and to
make the smallest Advantage to thwart his Designs.

For this Reason, he gave the most considerable military Offices, bo h by Sea and Land, to Ecclesiasticks,
who depended on him, which occasioned a certain
waggish Poet to pass this Jest on the Publick Adminis-
tration

> *Un Archeveque est Admiral*
> *Un Gros Eveque est Corporal.*
> *Un Prelât President aux Frontiere ,*
> *Un Avtre à des Troupes guerrieres*
> *Un Capuchin pense au Cumbat,*
> *Un Cardinal à des Soldat,*
> *Un autre est General issime ,*
> *France je croy qu icy bas*
> *Ton Eglise si Magnanime,*
> *Milite & ne triomphe pas.*

Reflecting hereby on the Archbishop of *Bourdeaux*, the
Bishop of *Chartres*, the Bishop of *Nantes*, the Bishop
of *Mande*, Father *Joseph* a Friar, Cardinal *de Valette*,
and Cardinal *Richlieu* , these being the chief Comman-
ders of the Land and Sea Forces

It will make thee smile, perh. ps, to read an Epitaph
that was made on that Father *Joseph* above-named,
who being esteemed a very infamous Man, and lying
interred in the same Tomb with another Friar named
Father *Angel*, provoked some satyrical Wit to put this
Sarcasm on him

> *Passant, n'est ce past close et ange.*
> *Devan Diable auprès d un Ange?*

I believe Father *Joseph* was the worse beloved for being Cardinal *Richlieu's* Confessor   It was observed that
he died suddenly without confessing himself, which occasioned another Epitaph to be made   r .

Soufe ce Tombeau gin un bon Pere,
Qui cut tant de Difcretion
Que pour etre bon Seciétaire
Il mourut fans Confeffion

Every body fufpects the Cardinal had a Hand in his precipitate Death, to prevent his telling of Tales For he knew all his Secrets, and the Cardinal was known to be with him when he died It was during the Siege of *Brifac*, a City on the *Rhine*, which was then upon the Point of furrendring to the *French* And the News coming to the Cardinal, juft as Father *Jofeph* was in his laft Agonies, he came to his Bed fide, and laying his Mouth clofe to the poor Friar's Far, cried as loud as he could, *Courage, Courage, mon Pere, Nous avous pris, Brifac.* A ftrange Cordial for a dying Man; and fome body made thefe Verfes on it

Ite Cucullet, vobis fi Purpura ridet,
Fungitur Iferis Munere Pontificis

There is another Inftance of this Cardinal's Revengeful Temper and his Cruelty One Day the Duke of *Orleans*, who hated him mortally, went to his Palace, under pretence of giving him a Vifit, but really with a Defign to ftab him However, as foon as he came into the Cardinal's Prefence his Nofe fell a bleeding, Which appearing to him as an ominous Prefage of what he was going about, he was ftruck with fome Remorfe, and frankly confeffing his Defign to the Cardinal, begged his Pardon That cunning Minifter diffembling his Refentments, knowing the Duke was not a Man of Refolution enough to undertake fo bold an Action, unlefs he had been extremely animated by fomebody near him, he prefently reflected on Monfieur *Puylaurent*, the Duke's chief Favourite Immediately he decreed his Ruin, and to effect it with more Eafe, he pretended an extraordinary Friendfhip to him, offering him one of his Nieces in Marriage. Monfieur *Puylaurent*, who fufpected

pected not the Train which was laid for him, embrac-
ed the Proposal with much Joy, as hoping thereby to
raise and establish his Fortune under the Protection of
his potent Uncle In fine, he married the Cardinal's
Niece, but lived not to enjoy her, for on the very
Nuptial Day, the Cardinal caused him to be arrested
and sent Prisoner to the *Bastile*, where he was poisoned
by a Fryar, in a Glass of Wine As soon as he had
swallowed the fatal Potion, the Fryar told him, *It was
necessary for him to confess his Sins that very Moment, in
regard he had but a few Minutes to live* Monsieur *Puylaurent* threw the Glass at the Fryar's Head, giving him
two or three swinging Curses, and then fell on his
Knees to Confession, which being performed, he expired.

Sometimes the Cardinal was very singular and ingenious in the Execution of his Revenge, as if he endea-
voured to persuade the World, that he fulfilled the Law
of the *Talio*, which requires an Eye for an Eye, and punishes by an exact kind of Proportion As it happened
in the Case of the Dukes of *Guise*, *Montmorancy*, and
Monsieur *de Bassompierre*. These were the Heads of a
Faction, which diametrically opposed the Cardinal and
his Party He was the grand Eye-sore, the chief Ob-
stacle of their Designed Prevalence at the Court.
Wherefore, if they could but once remove him out of
the Way, they thought themselves sure of the King's
Ear in all Things To effect this, they consulted together how to dispose of him The Duke of *Guise* was of
Opinion, he should not be killed, in regard he was a
Prince of the holy Church, but that he should be sent
to *Rome*, there to attend the proper Affairs of the *Ecclesiastical* Function, among the rest of his purpled Brethren. The Duke of *Montmorency* was clearly for taking off his Head But Monsieur *de Bassompierre* was a-
gainst both these Methods *For*, said he, *if he be sent to
Rome, he will be always plotting of Mischief against us
And it would be an eternal Blemish to France, if the Pur-
ple of the Holy Church should be stained with Blood Let us
send him close Prisoner to the* Bastile, *where he may spend
the Remainder of his Days in writing learned Books.*

The Cardinal, who had his Agents busy about in all Parts, soon was informed of this Consult. And he retaliated every Man's Sentence upon its own Author. For he banished the Duke of *Guise*, confining him to *Rure*; he beheaded the Duke of *Montmorency*; and imprisoned Monsieur de *Bassompierre* in the *Bastile*, where he lay till the Cardinal's Death.

I could insert a great many more Remarks concerning Cardinal *Richelieu*. But I am afraid of offending by Tediousness. If thou commandest me, another Letter shall present thee with more *Varieties*.

In the mean time, with humblest Obeisance and Respect, I desist, and take my *Conge*, wishing thee a long Life on Earth, full of Honour, and a Fame without Blemish when thou art translated to Heaven.

Paris, 15*th of the* 1*st Moon,*
　of the Year, 1673.

LETTER XIV.

To Musu Abu'l, Yahyan, *Professor of* Philosophy *at* Fez.

THOU hast laid a grand Obligation on me by thy last Dispatch, whose learned Contents have opened my Eyes, or rather drawn back the Veil which covered the Interiors of *Africk*, from the View of Strangers. Now I stand as it were on the Top of a high Mountain, from whence I take a clear Prospect of those fair Regions, inhabited by *Blacks*. I survey the *Paradises* of the *Torrid Zone*, a most fertile and populous Climate, though blind Antiquity could not discern a Blade of Grass growing there, nor any of human Race fetching their Breath.

My Mind revels in perfect Voluptuousness, and all the Faculties of my Soul banquet on the Contemplation of that most delectable Precinct of the World. On *frail!* Thou mayest be called the *Bauer*, or *Nurse*, where

where Nature exhibits all her choicest Wonders Thy
Mountains are higher than the Clouds, their Tops are
inacceffible   They approach the Borders of *Paradife*
On them fall the Rivers of *Eden* in mighty Cataracts
The Noife of the precipitate Waters is heard afar off
like the Sound of Remote Thunders   It deafens the
Ears, and aftonishes the Minds of Mortals The ambi-
tous under growing Rocks are proud of the glorious
Cafcade, and envy thofe that fhoot up above them
which receive the facred Flood at the firft Hand, from
the very Wings of *Gabriel*.

Happy are the Valleys which lie beneath, and are
yearly impregnated by the heavenly Deluge The grateful Fields and Plains in humble Acknowledgement,
make the Returns of Corn and Fruits in due Seafon
The Marfhes of *Egypt* are as the Gardens of *Afia*, and
the Banks of the *Nile* as the fecond eminencies of *Babylon*, fragrant and abounding in all Sorts of vegetable
Delicacies.

My Heart is ravifhed with the Speculations of thefe
Things   I am full as the Moon, and cannot utter my
Sentiments in order   Vifions of *Æthiophia, Morocco,
Fez*, and the Land of *Archers* invade my Eyes   I behold the beautiful Provinces of the *South* in a Trance, I
ftand gazing in Ecftafy on the fhady Groves of *Benin*
and *Arder*, the Haunts of lovely *Dæmons*, the *Genii* of
the upper Element, who daily defcend to thefe refrefhing Solitudes, and converfe with their younger Brethren,
incarnate mortal *Dæmons*, the Sons of Men

I confider with Admiration the Monfters of *Africk*,
the Creatures of the Sun and Slime   With contemplative Horror, I draw near the Dens of Dragons, the
Purlieu of Crocodiles, and other amphibious Animals,
which lurk among the Reeds of *Nile* and *Niger*, to trepan with feigned Cries the unwary Traveller

In fine, I am moved with fuperlative Devotion and
Joy, when I purfue this accurate Defcription of the principal *Mofque* at *Fez* Methinks I fee the ftupendous Fabrick making its lofty Advance towards Heaven My
Eyes revere the holy and magnificent Structure, on the
outfide

outside adorned with stately Towers and Minerats, and covering fifty hundred Paces in its Circuit But when my Fancy enters in by any of the one and thirty Gates by Night, I am dazzled with the insupportable Splendor of so many thousand Lamps, as burn within hat most illustrious *Temple* I admire with proportionate Veneration, the Character thou givest of all the other Magnificences in that ancient and noble City, with whatsoever else thou sayest of the whole Kingdom, and the adjacent Regions

In answer to thy Request, I will in another Letter send thee a short Pourtraiture and History of *Constanti nople*, but now I am interrupted by Company Besides, my Letter would be too long

I beseech thee to cherish that Friendship which thou hast hitherto shewed me And let me have the Honour of thy frequent Conversation by Letters For though I live in a populous City, yet my Life seems like that of an Owl or a Pelican of the Desart, extremely solitary and dejected.

Paris, 19*th of the 3d Moon,*
of the Year 1673.

LETTER XV

To the Same.

SUCH is the Zeal I have to demonstrate how highly I value thy Friendship, that I would not suffer this *Post* to escape without gratifying thy Expectations I just now dismissed my Company, and having time enough, will entertain thee with an Abstract of what I know to be most remarkable in the State of *Constantinople*, both at present and in ancient Times

In the first Place, it will be convenient for thee to know, That this City was formerly called *Byzantia*, from one *Byzas*, Admiral of the *Spartan* Fleet, under

Pau

Paufanias the King of *Sparta*, who laid the firft Foundations of it   The Story 's this

In old Time the *Grecians* having a mind to build a new City in fome Part of *Thrace*, and being at odds about the Choice of a Spot of Ground fuitable to fo great and impor ant an Undertaking, they at laft agreed to confult the Oracle of *Apollo* They did fo, and were anfwered, *That they fhould lay the Foundations of the City right over againft the blind Men* , For fo the Inhabitants of *Chalcedon* were called, becaufe when they were upon the fame Defign of founding a new City, they could not difcern between the Fertility of the Soil on that Side the *Proportis* where *Conftantinople* now ftands, and the Barrennefs and Defart State of the Ground where they built, on the other Side

Paufanias therefore bufying his Mind about thefe things, and pitching right upon the Senfe of the Oracle, caufed the Foundations of the City to be laid exactly over againft *Chalcedon*, And when it was finifhed it was called *Byzantium*, as I have faid from *Byzas*, who had the Overfight of the Work

It retained this Name many Years and Ages, flourifhing in a high Degree among the other Cities of *Greece* and *Thrace*, being efteemed the Gate of *Europe* and *Afia*, by which the mutual Commerce of both thofe Quarters of the Earth was interchangeably held up

But after the Days of the *Meffia*, there arofe an Emperor of *Rome*, whofe Name was *Conftantine* This Prince as it is recorded in *Roman Hiftories* faw a Vifion in the Air, when he was at the Head of his Army, marching againft *Licinius*, and preparing to give Battel He and all his Soldiers beheld the Figure of a Crofs, with thefe Words plainly engraven in the Firmament *In hoc Signo vincers* *Conftantine* took this for a good Omen, and caufed a Standard of Silver to be made exactly after the fame Form To which he appointed fifty Standard Bearers, to carry it by Turns, and to guard it for it was exceeding rich, being emboffed all over with Rubies, Diamonds, Pearls, and other precious Jewels of the *Orient* He built a Pavilion alfo for the

glorious

glorious Idol, and being instructed in the *Christian Law*
by *Eusebius Pomphilus*, and other learned *Mollahs*, he
was at last baptized by *Sylvester* the *Pope*.

This great Monarch, as the Story goes, being very
pious, and having conceived a profound Veneration for
Pope *Sylvester*, left him the Dominion of *Rome*, and a
great Part of *Italy*, whilst he removed the Imperial
Court to the *East*, and took up his Residence at *Byzantium*, which he augmented with innumerable stately
Edifices, striving if possible, to equal it with the Majesty and Grandeur of *Rome*. He collected whatsoever
was precious and beautiful in all the *East*, to adorn the
City withal. Witness the Places of superb Architecture,
the admirable Heighth and Form of divers Obelisks and
Pillars all made of Marble, Porphyry, or Jasper. No
to insist on the prodigious Strength and Firmness of the
Walls, the costly Aqueducts, with other serviceable
Things. At last, that he might consecrate himself to
immortal Renown, he called the City by his own
Name, *Constantinople*, or the City of *Constantine*. By
which Name it is known even to this Day. It was also
so called *New Rome*, after it once became the Seat of
the *Christian Emperors*. In whose Possession it remained,
till it was taken by *Mahomet* II. invincible *Emperor* of
the *Ottomans*, the Year 1453, according to the Æra
of the *Nazarenes*, on the third Day of the Week which
they call *Pentecost*.

It had been a grand Neglect and Oversight in any
Prince so potent and politick as *Mahomet* was, to suffer
such an Opportunity to escape as Fortune offered him,
of taking the most opulent and glorious City in the
World. For there was an irreconcilable Schism broke
forth between the Churches of the *East* and *West*. There
were two or three Popes at the same time, quarrelling in
Rome for the Supremacy, there was a War of fifty Years
standing between the *French* and the *English*, which un-
hinged all the Courts in *Europe*. The *Christians* had
long before, (by dear-bought Experience the loss of
many hundred thousand Men, and infinite Sums of Money, consumed in those vain and rash Expeditions which

they

they sanctified with the specious Title of the *Holy War*,) found, that it was not easy to wrest one Town of strength out of the Hands of the tenacious *Mussulmans*, much less to defend it long, or save their most important Cities from the Fury of a *Turkish* Reprizal They were sick and surfeited with the visionary Stuff of *Peter the hermit* and all Illuminatos like him, grew out of Fashion Every Prince and State in *Western Christendom*, began to mind their own Interest, no more enthusiastick Tales of that Kind would go down The great ones had opened their Eyes

Besides, he that was then Emperor of *Greece*, Constantine *Palaeolgas*, was looked upon by the *Christians* as a Tyrant, the Off spring of Tyrants and Usurpers. The *Grecians* still retained the black Memoirs of those horrid and nefandous Tragedies, acted by *Michael* and *the rest*, *John* and *Manuel*, the Predecessors and Ancestors of this *Constantine* And they had such a particular Aversion for his Government, that tho' there were infinite Treasures of Gold and Silver in the Hands of the rich Citizens of *Constantinople*, when the City was besieged by *Mahomet* II yet no Man would part with the least Sum of Money to support the *Publick Cause* But chose rather in a Kind of revengeful and desperate Sullenness, to fall into the Hands of the victorious *Officers*, than to afford their hated *Sovereign* any Relief

Thus fell the Queen of Cities, the Glory of all the *East*, under the Power of our puissant Emperor, in whose Possession it remains to this Day, and may it so remain till the Moon shall be in her last Wane, and the Sun shall cease to shine on the World

In the mean time I will entertain thee *en passant*, as the *French* call it, with a short View of the chief Magnificences in *Constantinople*

That which first draws the Admiration of Travellers is the glorious Structure of *Santa Sophia*, a Temple consecrated to the Eternal Wisdom by which the Worlds were made Built by the Emperor *Justinian* with inimitable Magnificence, tho' afterwards spoiled and plundered of its chiefest Ornaments, by the greedy Soldiers

diers of *Mahomet* II whom I have so often mentioned,
and six Parts of it entirely subverted by succeeding Emperors.

Pity it was, if furious and ill-grounded Superstition
was the Cause of such deplorable Ruins. What can be
said of those who demolished the *Sub-Fano* of the third
Temple, celebrated in the Universal History of the
World? That of *Diana* at *Ephesus*, it is true, was the
Pattern; yet it was not much beyond *Solomon*'s boasted
Fane at *Jerusalem*, without Iron, Pins or Nails or o-
ther Work of the Hammer, excelled but a little in the
Article and Symmetry. Indeed, the Lustre of *Sion*
Mosque was more radiant and glorious in Workmanship
of Gold, the Walls and Floor being over laid with that
Metal, and the Roof on the Outside was, as it were,
studded with Spikes of beaten Gold so thick, that there
was not Room for a Bird to perch between them. And
this was done to prevent the Prophanation of the Temple by their Muting on it.

When the Sun shone in its full Strength, the covering
of the Temple thus adorned looked like a Firmament
glittering with innumerable Stars.

But to return to the *Mosque* of *Sancta Sophia* let us
consider it in its primitive State, and we shall find some
excellent Curiosities. Among the rest there was a Can-
dlestick or Sconce of beaten Gold, so admirably contrived, that it spontaneously fed the Bowls of ten
Branches, with a constant Stream of Oil which in e-
qual Measures flowed into them from the Hollow of the
Shaft. So that if the Flame but of one single one had
wanted Aliment, all the rest must have been extinguish-
ed at the same Time.

The Walls of this glorious *Mosque*, within and without, present the Eye with nothing but white Marble,
Porphyry, and other precious Stones. The Roof is of
a prodigious Height, covered with Lead without but
proudly ostentous of its inward Cieling, which is divided
into Vaults and Arches richly adorned with GoldenFret-
work, and supported by Pillars of *Cyprian* Jasper, purest
white Marble and Porphyry. There is a Marble Stone

in the *Mofque* had in great Reverence by the True Faithful, becaufe the *Tradition* goes, *That on it* Mary, *the Mother of* Jefus, *wafhed the Infant Prophet's Linen.*

There are alfo under the *Mofque*, innumerable Vaults or *Oratories*, full of Altars and Sepulchres But there is no Accefs to them, in regard the Doors are walled up.

In a Place not far from thefe, you find ten huge Veffels full of Oil, referved there ever fince the Days of *Conftantine the Great*, yet remains uncorrupted being of Colour white like Milk It is an inexpiable Crime for any but the *Grand Signior*'s Phyficians and Surgeons to ufe or touch it And they compound certain Medicaments with it, for the Service of him and his *Serail*

Now I remember what I have read in a very Authentick *Hiftorian*, concerning an Oil made by certain Holy Perfons who only had the Secret of it As the Story goes, it was extracted from the Leaves and Chips of Wood which are found floating in the Rivers that defcend out of *Paradife* This Oil they compounded with our Ingredients, and performed Cures therewith, which were efteemed miraculous It was fent from one Prince to another, as a Sacred and Invaluable Treafure Till at laft it came into the Hands of the *Eaftern Patriarchs*, who prefided over the *Chriftians* of the *Greek*, *Armenian*, and *Egyptian Churches*, who pretend to the only True Myftery and Power of making it at this very Day And that though the ancient *Popes of Rome*, were formerly prefented with a yearly Portion of it, fo long as they remained in Communion with the *Patriarchs* of the *Eaft*, yet after *Victor* had once made the Fatal *Schifm*, which never could be healed fince, the Holy Favour was denied to his Succeffors Who inftead of the Original Genuine Oil, were forced to counterfeit it, ufing a fpurious Unguent, to preferve the Authority of their Religious Sacraments. And hence they fay, it comes to pafs, that few or none are ever healed by the *Extreme Unction* of the *Latin Church*

God knows, whether this be Truth or no But I am apt to think, that the ten Jars of Oil before mentioned, which lie under the *Mofque* of *Aja-Sophian*, are Relicks

licks of the Ancient *Patriarchs* of *Constantinople*, who had the Secret of compounding the Mysterious Extract.

From the Place where these Vessels are kept, you descend into the *Dormitories* of Royal *Ottoman* Carcases, the Sons of our renowned Emperors. From thence you pass into two Caverns, one leading directly to the *Seraglio*, the other extending it self under the Buildings of the City, by a vast long Tract of Ground. I know no Use there is at present of the former Cave. But the latter serves for a Work-room to certain poor Silk-Spinsters.

This Letter would be too tedious, if I should describe all the other *Mosques* and Buildings of Note in *Constantinople*. Wherefore not to tire thee, I will reserve what remains to be said of that glorious City for other *Dispatches*.

In the mean Time, with an affectionate *Conge* of my Soul, I bid thee Adieu. Praying *God* to let thee crop the choicest Flowers of Human Happiness.

Paris, 14*th of the* 5*th Moon,*
   of the Year 1673.

LETTER XVI.

To Hamet, Reis Effendi, *Principal Secretary of the* Ottoman Empire.

NOW I will perform the Promise I made thee long ago, which was, to present thee with an Idea of the different Strength and *Policies* of these Nazarene *Kingdoms* and *States*, wherein, I will begin with *Germany*, which is, as it were, the last Retrenchment of the declining *Roman Empire*.

The *Annals* affirm, that in the Reign of *Char.* V. when the *Mussulmans* invaded *Austria* with innumerable Forces, that Emperor opposed him with an Army of 90000 Foot, and 30000 Horse. *Maximilian* II. went

beyond

beyond him, and raifed 100000 Foot, and 35000
Horfe. Neither was Corn dear in fo vaft an Army.
It is certain, that the *German* Emperor can, upon Occafion, fend into the Field 200000 expert Soldiers   It
is moreover obferved, that from the Year 1560 of the
Chriftian' Hegira, even to thefe prefent Times, there
has been no War between *France*, *Spain*, and the *Ne-
therlands*, wherein many Thoufands of *Germans* have
not ferved

Their beft *Infantry* is gathered out of *Bavaria*, *Auftria*, and *Weftphalia* And their choiceft *Cavalry* come
out of *Brunfwick*, *Juliers* and *Frankerdal* Both Foot
and Horfe fight better, or more fuccefsfully in an open
Plain or Field, than in narrow Covert Places, fuch as
Lanes and Woods, &c For they are not good at
taking Advantages of Ground, or at Politick Skir-
mifhes, and cunning Ambufcades   They have not
Patience to lie long waiting the Enemies Motions, neither care they to divide their main Body into Fragments, or Detachments, but they love to wedge themfelves altogether in Form of a Triangle, and fo march
with grave and flow Pace, that fo they may break
through their Enemies and confound their Order,
which they efteem a certain Step to Victory   They
fight better alfo under a foreign Commander than a
General of their own Nation They cannot endure the
Hardfhips and Afflictions of a long Siege, but when
once they begin to fmart for Want of Provifions, they
foon capitulate, and furrender Neither have they
more Patience in a Camp, to bear the Injuries of Weather, but they make Hafte to fet upon the Enemy,
and decide the Quarrel in a pitched Combat Wherein, if their Onfet fail, they feem like Men ftupified,
aftonifhed, or in a Trance; not knowing whether they
beft renew the Affault, or to fly   And if they once
fly, there is no rallying them again Yet thefe Armies are not raifed without a vaft Expence nor maintained without a greater, being cumber'd with a Train
of Women, Children, and Servants, who confume the
Provifions of the Soldiers, fo that many Times they
ftarve for Want of common Ammunition Bread

The r

Their Horses may be called rather strong than sprightly and bold, being for the most Part taken from the Plough, or other Rural Drudgeries In a Word, they are like their Riders, Phlegmatick and Dull, having this also peculiar in their Constitution, that at the Sight of Blood they shrink, and are ready to faint Whereas the *Spanish* Horse gather fresh Courage from this Spectacle.

The *Germans* also have considerable Forces by Sea, but they seldom make use of them, unless it be against the *Danes* and *Swedes* Besides all this, their Auxiliary Armies are not to be forgot, which they receive from *Italian* Princes, from the Dukes of *Savoy* and *Loiar*, and from the trusty *Suisse*

But there are two Things chiefly wanting in this *Empire*, amidst all its numerous Forces One is Unity and Concord among the Subjects, another is, a fixed Resolution and Readiness to enterprize any Thing of Moment Their *Hans-Towns* are always jealous of the Neighbouring Princes. And these again give them Occasion to suspect their Power, and hate their Interest, which they so often employ against them, by incroaching on their Privileges Then the *Catholicks* and *Protestants* are always quarrelling And one Sect of *Protestants* perpetually persecuting another Hence it falls out, that the Princes go so unwillingly and rarely to the *Diets* And when they come there, they spin out so much Time in adjusting their private Pretensions, Claims and Privileges, in performing of State Ceremonies, and in deliberating concerning the publick Good, whilst every one contradicts his Neighbour, and labours with all his Might to establish his own Opinion, and get it passed into a Decree by the Sanction of the *Diet*, that before they come to any Resolves, an expeditious and potent Enemy might rush into the Heart of the Country, and even take all these *Northern* Blockheads Prisoners

The *German* Empire is *Elective*, and the Power of chusing *Cæsar*, is in the Hands of Seven Princes. These are first, the *Archbishop of Mentz, Grand Can* cellor of the Empire, in whose Custody are the Archives and Decrees of the German Diets. The Second is, the Archbishop of Triers, or Treves, Great Chancellor of the Empire for France The Third is, the Archbishop of Colen, Great Chancellor of the Empire for Italy The Fourth is, the King of Bohemia, Cup-Bearer to the Emperor The Fifth is, the Count Palatine of the Rhine, Master of the Imperial Palace The Sixth is the Duke of Saxony, Marshal or Sword-Bearer to the Empire The Seventh and last is, the Marquess of Brandenburg, Great Chamberlain, or Treasurer of the Empire

There are reckoned 25 Politick Princes or Dukes of the Empire, 6 Marquesses, 5 Lantgraves, 9 Archbishops, and Bishops 47, Abbots who enjoy the Title and Dignity of Princes 12, Abbots of a lower Degree 52. With innumerable others too tedious to be named They reckon also 82 Counts of Principal Note, besides many of a meaner Figure They number 49 Barons and Free Lords, 90 Hans-Towns, and 10 Circles of the Empire.

In the German Diets, this Order is observed When the Emperor is placed in the Throne, the Archbishop of Triers takes his Place just over against him He of Mentz sits next to the Emperor, on his Right Hand, the Second Place belongs to the King of Bohemia; and the Third to the Count Palatine of the Rhine On the Emperor's Left Hand, the Archbishop of Colen takes the first Place, the Duke of Saxony the next, and the Marquess of Brandenburg the third

The Hans Towns which acknowledge no other Lord but the Emperor, are governed by their own Municipal Laws and Privileges In some of them the Common People bear Rule, in others a Mixture of the Commons and Nobles, and many of them wholly obey the Nobility

No Man salutes by the Title of Emperor him whom the Princes have elected to that Dignity, till he be crowned by the Pope or Mufti of Rome They call him Cæsar, or King of the Romans, or King of Germany:

many, but not *Emperor*, till the Coronation is finished Nor does the *Emperor*, even after he is crowned and established in the Throne, exercise an *Absolute Power* in all Things, Affairs of Importance being generally referred to the *Publick Diets* or *Divans* of the *Empire*, where the *Electoral Princes* deliberate all Things, On whom the very Power of the *Emperor* himself depends

These *Diets* are very confused and tedious, in regard the Princes seldom appear there in their own Persons, but send their *Ambassadors* and *Deputies*, who yet have not full Power to conclude any Thing without particular Orders from their respective Masters So that a prodigious deal of Time is taken up, in sending Couriers to inform the Princes of all emergent Counsels and Transactions, and in waiting for their express Instructions and Answers again

In a Word considering the Diversity of Interests carried on by the *Electoral Princes*, their Mutual Feuds and Dissentions, Domestick Animosities, and Foreign Engagements, both on *Religious* and *Political Accounts*, it is a Miracle that this tottering Empire stands so long, and does not fall o Ruin Especially being environed, and almost continually assaulted by Three potent Enemies, the King of *Sweden*, the King of *France*, and our invincible Monarch   Not to mention the frequent Incursions of the *Muscovites* and *Tartars*, the Revolts of the *Hungarian*, *Transilvanians*, *Bosnians*, *Croats*, and other Nations, which are counted Members of the *German Empire*   But he abounds in Men and Money, with all other Necessaries to support his Wars   There not being a more rich and populous Region on Earth than *Germany*

Sage *Hamet*, when the determined Period is come, *God* will abase the Pride of these *Infidel* by the Hands of the *True Believers*   The Riches of the *West* shall become the Spoil of *Eastern HEROES*, and the *Posterity* of *Shem* shall take Root in the Cities of *Japhet*,

Mayeſt thou live till that Time, to triumph in the Glory of the Houſe of *Iſhmael*, when they ſhall be exalted more than in the Ages that are paſt

Paris, 9th of the 7th Moon,
of the Year 1673

LETTER XVII.

To Cara Hali, *Phyſician to the* Grand Signior.

THY Memory is like the Smell of Incenſe, refreſhing as Wine of *Tereaſ,* in a Goblet of pure Gold. When my Heart is almoſt dead with Melancholy; when I can find no Pleaſure in Company abroad, and the very Elements of which I am made frown upon me; when the Time of Night forces me to come home ſighing as to a Priſon, and the Hangings of my Bed Chamber look dull, and ſeem to be painted with horrid Tragedies. In a word, when every Thing in Nature appears in an angry threatning Fit, then I think of thee, my Friend, and that Thought relieves me. Thy beloved *Idea* is a perfect *Taliſman,* working Wonders in my Soul. It charms or Counter-charms, as my Occaſions do require. No Fears or Griefs, or other Melancholy Paſſions dare abide its Energy. As ſoon as it appears, each baneful Thought is gone; the Troops of ſad *Chimera's* vaniſh like the Morning Miſts before the Sun. Thou art as a ſtrong Tower or Fortreſs, where I can take Sanctuary from my Enemies. An impregnable Citadel, ſeated on the Top of a high Rock, from whence I can look down with Scorn on my Perſecutors beneath, poſſeſſing my ſelf in perfect Security.

I dare not ſo much as vent my Thoughts to another, though a *Muſſulman,* for fear of ſome outward Conſequence. So induſtrious is the Malice of moſt Men, ſo vigilant and ſtudious for an Opportunity of doing Miſchief. And as for theſe *Infidels,* my Converſation is for the moft part *Hiftrorick* I am conftrained to act to the Life a very zealous Chriftian and a *Catholick* When, *God* knows, my Heart keeps not Time with my exterior Actions and Words Not but that there are Scepticks among the *True Believers* But they are generally very private and referved For open Blafphemy, or what is reputed fo here, is certainly punifhed with Death

I fometimes meet with ingenuous and candid Souls, with whom I can difcourfe freely, and like a Man that doubts of many Things, which others currently believe Yet we dare not try each other too far, nor the very Air in which our Words vanifh, after it has helped to form them, left fome fly envious *Dæmon* fhould catch the tranfient Sound, and reverberate the articulated Body of Particles which made it, into fome inquifitive Ear to ruin us For there are certain bufy goffiping *Eccho's* fcattered up and down the Elements, which are always liftening to the Word of Mortals And if the frightful *Elves* can but take hold of any fyllable to do a Man an Injury, they are big till they have vented it Yet they make no Shew or Noife, but whifper out their Tale in fecret, fometimes in Dead of Night, when Men are faft afleep, at other Times when they are deeply mufing on the hidden Things of Nature For it is only to the Wife, the Sage, the Noble, and the Great, that they reveal thefe Paffages, becaufe it is fuch alone that have Ears to hear them They haunt the Bed-Chambers of Kings and Princes, to tell them News in Dreams They are the fwifteft Couriers in the World For they have Wings, and fly from Court to Court, and from one Climate to another in a Moment's Time They are always buzzing in the Ears of *Statefmen* and great *Politicians*, to whom they fhew the dark Intrigues of foreign and domeftick Enemies Thus are Confpiracies and Plots of Rebels oft difcovered, though managed never fo fecretly They vifit now and then the *Clofets* of *Philofophers*, and fuch as love the Sciences Men of abftracted Souls, whofe Thoughts are volatile and pure, their Fancies lively and

vegete.

vegete   To thefe they unfold the covert Myfteries of
Nature, and fhew them Things to come They frame
the Ideas of remote, unknown Events, which they imprint upon the ductile Minds of Prophets and holy Men·
Infpiring them with ftrange and unaccountable Prefages
of what fhall fhortly happen to themfelves or others,
whether it be good or evil   For thefe unfly-bodies are
the Daughters of the World's great Soul , and they inherit an univerfalfenfe and Feeling of whatfoever hap-
pens in the Elements   It is true, fome Knowledge they
acquire by Study and Obfervation, even as we Mortals
do , but at a far fwifter Rate   Their airy Bodies do not
fo opprefs their intellectual Faculties, as our grofs Hulks
of Flefh do ours   We are forced to dig and plough, or
to fow and harrow for fmall Returns of Science   Our
Soil is barren, it muft be manured and cultivated with
Art and Coft, before it yields a tolerable Harveft of
what deferves the Name of folid Knowledge But thefe
defecate Tenants of the Air, have no more to do, but to
be merely paffive, and they ftreight learn every Thing .
For the eternal *Sapience* wanders through the Univerfe,
to feek out fuch as will or can imbibe her free Impreffion She voluntarily flides into receptive Souls, and
fills them with her Rays Thus the fublimer *Genii* of the
Air, bafk in an open Orb of intellectual Light, becaufe
they are embodied in the moft refined and pureft Matter Whereas we Mortals muft be thankful for her Illuminations by Retail She only fhines on us through
Chinks and Crannies of our dungeon Flefh And yet
but feldom fo in direct Beams Few Men can boaft that
Privilege The greateft Part walk only in the uncertain
Twilight of Opinion , or at beft, in the faint languid
Glimmering of human Reafon , which, like the Moon,
conveys the Original Light of Science to us by Reflection, and at a fecond Hand We are fain to learn from
Books, from Converfation, and Experience

   Courteous *Hali*, thou wilt pardon the Confufednefs
and want of Order in this Letter, when thou fhalt confider the Force of Melancholy which firft prompted me
to write it. For, being very fad, and overcaft with
                                                    Clouds

Clouds of dark and gloomy Thoughts, which different Paffions caufed to joftle one againft another in my troubled Mind, I knew not how to efcape the Tempeft better than by writing to thee, my learned Friend, tho' only to exprefs my Circumftances For when I began, I knew not what to fay, but it was an Eafe to write at Random, any Thing to breathe my Heart, and ventilate my Spleen But the fpecifick Remedy of my Grief, confifted in addreffing to thee, my dear Phyfician, whofe very Remembrance is a *Catholicon* Proof, againft all my Maladies

Adieu, thou *Æfculapius* of the *Ottomans,* and live for ever

Paris, 15*th of the 8th Moon,*
    of the Year 1073

LETTER XVIII.

To Mufu Abu'l Yahyan, *Profeffor of* Philofophy *at* Fez.

THOU fhalt fee, that I am a Man of my Word, and will keep my Promife For this Difpatch contains a farther Defcription of *Conftantinople,* which I engaged to prefent thee with in my laft

This famous City is fixteen Miles in Circuit, and contains Nine hundred thoufand Inhabitants It is divided into three Parts, by the Intercourfe of certain Arms of the Sea, and almoft forms the Figure of a Triangle The Walls are of an incredible Height, and encompafs feven Hills within their Extent One is near the *Grand Signior's Serail* Another is in the oppofite Corner of the City, which leads to *Adrianople* Between two others, there lies a Plain, which is called the great Valley In this is to be feen an Aqueduct of admirable Contrivance and Structure, the Work of *Conftantine the Great,* who by this conveyed Water to the City from
                                                       feven

feven Miles Diftance *Solyman* II augmented it, by opening a Current of Waters two Miles beyond the Source of *Conftantinople*, which run through feven hundred and forty Pipes into the City, befides thofe which ferve the *Mofques*, the *Baths*, and Houfes of *Purification*.

At the Extremity of the Town is feen the antique Building of a Fortrefs, which is called the *Caftle of the feven Towers*, a Work of inimitable Architecture There is a Garrifon in it of two hundred and fifty Soldiers, not one of which dares to fet his Foot out of the Caftle Gates, without the Leave of the *Vizir Azem*, unlefs it be on two certain Days in the Year, that is, the firft of *Beiram*, and *Ramezan*

In this Place formerly the *Ottoman* Emperors ufed to lay their Treafures of Gold and Silver, their Arms and Ammunition, their Books, and whatfover they efteemed precious But *Amurat* the Son of *Selymus* II tranflated all thefe Things into the *Serail*, where they have been kept ever fince And this Caftle is turned into a Prifon for *Kings* and *Princes* taken Captives by the *True Faithful*; as alfo for rebellious *Baffa*'s, and other Perfons of Quality Here *Corefqui*, *Vayvod* of *Moldavia*, was fhut up in the Year 1617 of the *Chriftian Æra* And in the Year 1622 of the fame Date, the rebellious *Janizaries* imprifoned their Sovereign Lord, *Sultan Ofman*, whom afterwards they ftrangled in the fame Place

There are above two thoufand *Mofque*, Oratories and Sepulchres, within the Walls of *Conftantinople* I have already defcribed that of *Aija-Sophian*, in my laft It remains now, that I fpeak of four others, built by fome of our former Emperors The firft nnd chiefeft, was built by *Sultan Mahomet* II to exprefs his Gratitude to God for the taking of *Conftantinople* It is a magnificent Structure, raifed according to the *Pattern* of *Sancta Sopha* He caufed a hundred ftately Chambers to be built round about it, both for the Service of the *Imaum's* and *Mollahs* who belong to the *Mofque*, and for the Entertainment of Strangers, let them be of what Nation or Religion foever He raifed alfo fifty other Chambers without thefe, for the Ufe of the Poor And endowed

the

the *Mosque* with sixty thousand Duckets of yearly Revenue

The second *Mosque* was built by *Bajazet* II the Son of this *Mahomet* The third was built by *Selimus* I The fourth, by *Solimon the Magnificent* The three last of these Princes lie buried each in his own *Mosque*, under Monuments of a superb Figure, Innumerable Lamps burning over them and round about them Night and Day, whilst certain *Molla's* pray by turns, without ceasing for the Health of the departed Royal Souls.

But the last of these *Mosques*, which was built, as I have said, by *Sultan Solimon*, far exceeds all the rest, and comes not short of *Sancta Sophia*, in the Richness of Marble, Porphyry, and other excellent Materials

The *Greeks* have forty Churches and Chapels in *Constantinople*, wherein they perform the *Nozarene* Worship The *Armenians* have four Those of the *Latin* Communion have a College annexed to it for a certain Number of *Jesuits* This is seated in *Pera*, which is a kind of Suburb to *Constantinople*

The *Jews* have great Liberty in the Imperial City Their Habitations are contiguous, taking up nine Principal Streets, and they have eight and thirty Synagogues

The Walls of the City remain very entire, and are double towards the Land There are nineteen Gates in them; one of which is called the *Holy Gate*, in respect of a vast Multitude of Christian Saints who lie buried in a Chapel hard by it It was through this Gate that *Mahomet* II made his triumphant Entry into *Constantinople*, on purpose, as it were, to prophane the reputed Sanctity of the Place, and insult over their false Gods, whilst he came to establish the Law and Worship of the only true GOD, Creator of Heaven and Earth

There are abundance of antique Monuments in the City, as Pyramids and Obelisks of admirable Figure and Contrivance In one place, there are three Serpents of Marble, stretching themselves to the Height of two Men, and mutually twisting about each other The Report goes, That these were erected by a Magician at the

time

time when the Citizens were much infested with living Serpents, and that by this Enchantment they were freed.

One of these has a Wound in the Neck, which was given it by *Mahomet* II when he rode into the vanquished City   For, he beholding the horrid *Idol*, and guessing right, that it was the Work of some Magician, was moved with holy Zeal and Indignation   Wherefore, couching his Spear, and giving Spurs to his Horse, he ran full tilt against it, and wounded one of the Serpents in the Neck, which is seen to this Day

In the same Pavement there stands a very elegant Column of rustick Workmanship, as they call it   The Marbles of which it consists, being fastened together without the Intervention of Mortar, Bitumen, or any other Cement   It has within, a winding tar-Case by which one may go up to the top

In this place, which is called the *Hippodrome*, the *Ottoman Grandees* exercise themselves on Horseback, and sometimes the *Grand Signior* himself   Especially on great Festivals.

Round about it, there are above two thousand little Shops of Taylors or Botchers, for the Use of those who would have their Garments mended, scowred and polished at a small Price   And yet out of this so contemptible a Trade, the *Grand Signior* receive a yearly Custom of eleven thousand *Zequins*   By this thou mayest take an Estimate of his other Revenues, which flow into his Coffers from all Parts of so vast an *Empire*

There are above forty thousand Ware houses and Shops of Merchants, Brokers, Pedlars, Huckster, and such like Callings   Each Trade having their proper *Bazar*, or Market, according to the Quality of the Goods they sell   But there is one more eminent than all the rest, which is called *Bayslain*, where are Goldsmiths, Jewellers, and such as deal in any manner of fine costly Things   This Place is environed with very strong Walls, six Foot thick, and is shut up every Night by four double Gates, and at other times as Occasion requires   So that it looks like a little well fortined Town

In

In this wealthy Market, there is a Gallery or *Piazza* neatly arched and supported by twenty-four Pillars Under this, there are abundance of little Shops, six Foot long, and four in Breadth   Here all those precious Commodities are exposed to Sale on Tables or Counters, and with their Lustre dazzle the Eyes of such as pass by

Thou mayest also conjecture at the vast Gains of these Merchants, by the Rates which they pay to the *Grand Signior*, only for their License to sell in this Place.   I have known one Man, that was my particular Acquaintance, give yearly two thousand Franks for this Liberty, and he told me, That no Man could enjoy the Freedom of the Place under that Price, unless he had great Favour shewn him, which is very rare, and even then it would not be much abated

As one passes from this Market one Way, there arises a stately Column of Porphyry begirt in many Places with Iron Hoops   And little distant you see another more lofty than this   It is called the Historical Column, being engraven all over with the Figures of Men In this also, there is a Stair-case to the top, but much broken, and in Danger of falling, if it were not strengthened and held together with vast Hoops of Iron

The next thing worthy to be seen, is the old Palace of *Constantine the Great*   Worthy I say to be seen only for its Antiquity, for it is no very elegant Building, yet it has this Commendation, That it stands in the purest and most wholesome Air of the whole City

There is another Market also walled in, besides that of the Goldsmiths, &c which has a *Piazza* supported by sixteen Pillars   In this are sold all Manner of Silks And a little way off from this, is the *Bazar*, where they sell Slaves. So great are the Gains of this Traffick, that those who use it, pay to the *Grand Signior*, by way of Custom, the Yearly Sum of sixteen Thousand *Zequins*

The Vintners, Victuallers, and Sutlers who sell Wine to the *Christians* and *Jews*, and privately to the *Musulmans*, pay yearly fifty Eight Thousand, Seven Hundred and Eighty Eight *Zequins*   The very Fisher men of *Constantinople*, who live along the *Strand*, pay the yearly Sum of Twenty Nine Thousand There Hundred Ninety four *Zequins* The Corn Market, where all Sorts of Grain, Pulse, Meal, and Flower are sold, pays yearly into the Treasury 14 Purses of Money, each Purse being worth a Thousand, Six Hundred, Thirty and Three *Zequins* The *Egyptian Merchants*, who bring their Goods from *Alcaire*, to sell them at *Constantinople*, pay 24 Purses The Fraught of all Foreign Merchants Ships, make up 180 Purses of Gold I have mentioned the Value of each Purse before. The great *Shambles* without the City, pays 32 Purses There serve in this Place 200 Butchers, over whom there is a *Præfect* or *Master*, without whose Consent no Man can kill any Beast, unless it be in the Case of *Corban* Nay, so great is the Authority of this *Præfect*, that the *Jews* themselves are forced to ask his Leave to kill the Beasts after their own Fashion The Reason why the *Shambles* is without the City is for *Purity* sake, lest the City be polluted with *Blood*

It is impossible to cast up the prodigious *Revenue* which arises to the *Grand Signior* from the Sale of *Hungarian* Sheep and Oxen, in the 10th and 11th *Moons*. But thou mayest comprehend that it is very great, when sometimes in one Day's Time, there are sold 25000 Oxen, and 40000 Sheep

Neither is it more easy to reckon up his Incomes from the Sale of the Houses, Skiffs, Galleys, Saicks, and bigger Vessels Besides, it would be too tedious for one Letter What shall I say of the *Tribute* which the *Jews* and *Christians* pay, amounting Yearly to a prodigious Sum of Money? Time, Paper, Ink, and Human Patience itself would fail in rehearsing so many Particulars.

But thou mayest frame a Regular Judgment of the immense Riches which the *Grand Signior* is possessed of, when thou shalt know that there is a *Mint* in the *Imperial City*, where Four Hundred Men perpetually labour in coining new Money, having a *President* or *Overseer*, who supervises the Work, who must be a *Grecian*, by a special Privilege granted to that *Nation* by our *Munificent*

cent Emperors, becaufe the Mines of Silver and Gold, are within the Limits of the *Grecian Empire* So that none but Greeks are admitted to affift at this curious Artifice

The *Prefident* is obliged every *New-Moon* to fend into the *Serail* Ten Thoufand *Zequins* of Gold, and Twenty Thoufand in Silver For fuch is the Pleafure of the *Grand Sultan*, that the *Royal Palace* fhould always abound with fair new Money

Sage *Mufu*, affure thyfelf, that *Conftantinople* is the Grand *Treafury*, *Exchequer*, or *Bank* of the whole Faith, where all the Riches of the *Eaft*, *Weft*, *North* and *South* and of the *Seven Climates*, are refunded and laid up as in their proper Centre But I have more to fay in another Letter concerning this glorious City Only *Time* juft now gave me a Prick with the End of his Scythe, to put me in Mind of an urgent Affair, not to be neglected this Moment Wherefore, in Hafte, Adieu

Paris, *1ft of the 8th Moon* *of the Year* 1673

The End *of the* Seventh Volume

Lightning Source UK Ltd.
Milton Keynes UK
UKOW07f0934040416

271488UK00010B/463/P